Economic and Policy Developments in East Asia

In this collection, academics and policy-makers from Australia, Japan, New Zealand and Singapore present research results on a variety of topics based around three key themes: macroeconomics and trade, labour and social issues, and taxes and government spending. The chapters are empirically-oriented and include both cross-country studies and individual country studies. They include examinations of key topics, such as the problem of corruption, the relationship between trade liberalisation and growth and the impact of migration on the Asian welfare state, as well as studies of Chinese manufacturing exports and the income volatility of Indonesian banks. The scholarship contained in this collection is a crucial resource to researchers and commentators on the economies in the Asia-Pacific region.

This book was originally published as a special issue of the *Journal of the Asia Pacific Economy*.

Noel Gaston completed his doctorate at Cornell University, USA, and has worked at universities in Australia, the United States, Germany, Canada, South Korea and Japan. His research interests primarily concern the analysis of the effects of globalisation on labour markets. He is the founding Director of the Globalisation and Development Centre (GDC) at Bond University, Australia. In 2012, he was the Principal Adviser Research at the Australian Productivity Commission. In February 2014, he joined Curtin University as Research Professor and is the Director of the new Centre of Asian Business.

Economic and Policy Developments in East Asia

Edited by
Noel Gaston

LONDON AND NEW YORK

First published 2015
by Routledge
2 Park Square, Milton Park, Abingdon, Oxon, OX14 4RN, UK

and by Routledge
711 Third Avenue, New York, NY 10017, USA

Routledge is an imprint of the Taylor & Francis Group, an informa business

© 2015 Taylor & Francis

All rights reserved. No part of this book may be reprinted or reproduced or utilised in any form or by any electronic, mechanical, or other means, now known or hereafter invented, including photocopying and recording, or in any information storage or retrieval system, without permission in writing from the publishers.

Trademark notice: Product or corporate names may be trademarks or registered trademarks, and are used only for identification and explanation without intent to infringe.

British Library Cataloguing in Publication Data
A catalogue record for this book is available from the British Library

ISBN 13: 978-1-138-78856-5

Typeset in Sabon
by Taylor & Francis Books

Publisher's Note
The publisher accepts responsibility for any inconsistencies that may have arisen during the conversion of this book from journal articles to book chapters, namely the possible inclusion of journal terminology.

Disclaimer
Every effort has been made to contact copyright holders for their permission to reprint material in this book. The publishers would be grateful to hear from any copyright holder who is not here acknowledged and will undertake to rectify any errors or omissions in future editions of this book.

Contents

Citation Information	vii
Notes on Contributors	ix

1. Introduction
   Noel Gaston — 1

2. Recent trends in consumption in Japan and the other G7 countries
   Charles Yuji Horioka — 3

3. Government size, fiscal policy and the level and growth of output: a review of recent evidence
   Norman Gemmell and Joey Au — 11

4. Trade liberalisation and growth: a threshold exploration
   Rod Falvey, Neil Foster-McGregor and Ahmed Khalid — 38

5. Trade, finance, specialization and synchronization in the Asia-Pacific
   Shihan Xie, Tianyin Cheng and Wai-Mun Chia — 61

6. International migration and the welfare state: Asian perspectives
   Noel Gaston and Gulasekaran Rajaguru — 79

7. Corruption, democracy and Asia-Pacific countries
   Neil Campbell and Shrabani Saha — 98

8. Trends in income inequality in China: the effects of various sources of income
   Pundarik Mukhopadhaya — 112

9. The export response to exchange rates and product fragmentation: the case of Chinese manufactured exports
   Nobuaki Yamashita and Sisira Jayasuriya — 126

10. Income volatility of Indonesian banks after the Asian Financial Crisis
    Barry Williams — 141

Index — 167

Citation Information

The chapters in this book were originally published in the *Journal of the Asia Pacific Economy*, volume 18, issue 2 (April 2013). When citing this material, please use the original page numbering for each article, as follows:

Chapter 1
Guest editor's introduction
Noel Gaston
Journal of the Asia Pacific Economy, volume 18, issue 2 (April 2013) pp. 193–194

Chapter 2
Recent trends in consumption in Japan and the other G7 countries
Charles Yuji Horioka
Journal of the Asia Pacific Economy, volume 18, issue 2 (April 2013) pp. 195–202

Chapter 3
Government size, fiscal policy and the level and growth of output: a review of recent evidence
Norman Gemmell and Joey Au
Journal of the Asia Pacific Economy, volume 18, issue 2 (April 2013) pp. 203–229

Chapter 4
Trade liberalisation and growth: a threshold exploration
Rod Falvey, Neil Foster-McGregor and Ahmed Khalid
Journal of the Asia Pacific Economy, volume 18, issue 2 (April 2013) pp. 230–252

Chapter 5
Trade, finance, specialization and synchronization in the Asia-Pacific
Shihan Xie, Tianyin Cheng and Wai-Mun Chia
Journal of the Asia Pacific Economy, volume 18, issue 2 (April 2013) pp. 253–270

Chapter 6
International migration and the welfare state: Asian perspectives
Noel Gaston and Gulasekaran Rajaguru
Journal of the Asia Pacific Economy, volume 18, issue 2 (April 2013) pp. 271–289

CITATION INFORMATION

Chapter 7
Corruption, democracy and Asia-Pacific countries
Neil Campbell and Shrabani Saha
Journal of the Asia Pacific Economy, volume 18, issue 2 (April 2013) pp. 290–303

Chapter 8
Trends in income inequality in China: the effects of various sources of income
Pundarik Mukhopadhaya
Journal of the Asia Pacific Economy, volume 18, issue 2 (April 2013) pp. 304–317

Chapter 9
The export response to exchange rates and product fragmentation: the case of Chinese manufactured exports
Nobuaki Yamashita and Sisira Jayasuriya
Journal of the Asia Pacific Economy, volume 18, issue 2 (April 2013) pp. 318–332

Chapter 10
Income volatility of Indonesian banks after the Asian Financial Crisis
Barry Williams
Journal of the Asia Pacific Economy, volume 18, issue 2 (April 2013) pp. 333–358

Please direct any queries you may have about the citations to
clsuk.permissions@cengage.com

Notes on Contributors

Joey Au is an Analyst in the Chief Economist's Unit at the Treasury, New Zealand.

Neil Campbell is an Associate Professor of Economics at Bond University, Australia. His areas of research include the economics of corruption, the economics of innovation and technological transfer, and the economics of trade liberalisation.

Tianyin Cheng is currently an Analyst in Quantitative Research at Daiwa Capital Markets Singapore Limited. She holds an MSc in Econometrics and Mathematical Economics from London School of Economics (LSE), and a BSc in Mathematical Sciences from Nanyang Technological University (NTU), Singapore. She graduated with distinction from LSE, and was awarded the Lee Kuan Yew Gold Medal for excellent academic performance by NTU. She started research in macroeconomics under the supervision of Assistant Professor Wai-Mun Chia in her undergraduate second year. So far, she has accomplished five conference papers, among which three have been accepted for publication.

Wai-Mun Chia obtained her Bachelor's degree in Economics from the University of London, UK, with first-class honors in 1996. In 1998, with the support of the London School of Economics (LSE) Scholarship, she pursued her Master's degree at LSE. In 2006, she graduated with a PhD degree from Nanyang Technological University (NTU), Singapore. She is currently assistant professor at the Division of Economics, NTU. Prior to joining NTU, she was an industry analyst at the Federation of Malaysian Manufacturers. Her current research interests are international macroeconomics and economic integration in East Asia. She is associate editor of the *Singapore Economic Review*.

Rod Falvey is Professor of Economics in the Business School at Bond University, Australia. He has degrees from the University of Canterbury in New Zealand and a PhD from the University of Rochester in the USA. His previous appointments have been at VPI, Tulane University, ANU and the University of Nottingham. His research interests are in international trade theory and policy.

Noel Gaston completed his doctorate at Cornell University, USA, and has worked at universities in Australia, the United States, Germany, Canada, South Korea and Japan. His research interests primarily have to do with the analysis of the effects of globalisation on labour markets. He is the founding Director of the Globalisation and Development Centre (GDC) at Bond University, Australia. In 2012, he was the Principal Adviser Research at the Australian Productivity Commission. In February 2014,

NOTES ON CONTRIBUTORS

he joined Curtin University as Research Professor and is the Director of the new Centre of Asian Business.

Norman Gemmell holds the Chair in Public Finance in the Victoria Business School at Victoria University of Wellington, New Zealand.

Charles Yuji Horioka was born in Boston, USA, in 1956. He received his BA and PhD degrees from Harvard University, USA, and the Seventh Nakahara Prize from the Japanese Economic Association in 2001. His research interests are household saving, consumption, and bequest behavior and parentchild relations in Japan, the United States, and emerging Asia.

Ahmed Khalid is Professor and Head of the Department of Economics and Statistics at Bond University, Australia. His PhD is from Johns Hopkins University, USA, and he worked at the National University of Singapore before joining Bond. He is a Co-Director of the Globalisation and Development Centre at Bond University. His research interests include applied macroeconomics, monetary economics, applied econometrics, financial crisis and financial sector reforms.

Sisira Jayasuriya is Professor of Economics in the Department of Economics at Monash University, Melbourne, Australia.

Neil Foster-McGregor is a Senior Economist at the Vienna Institute for International Economic Studies (wiiw) and External Lecturer at the University of Vienna, Austria. He obtained his Masters degree and PhD from the University of Nottingham, UK. His primary research interests are in international trade, economic development and applied econometrics.

Pundarik Mukhopadhaya's research interests are in the income distribution analysis, welfare economics, poverty, gender, severance pay, trade relations and economics of law. He also has applied interests in labour economics and the economics of education. His publications include one book, 10 chapters in books, more than 30 academic papers in internationally refereed journals on theoretical and empirical economics, such as *Researches on Economic Inequality, Applied Economics, Journal on Income Distribution, Journal of Asian Economics, Asian Economics Journal, Economic Record, Journal of Contemporary Asia, Developing Economics, Netherlands Journal of Law, International Journal of Educational Development*. His consultancy clienteles include UNESCO, the World Bank and WHO.

Gulasekaran Rajaguru is an Associate Professor of Economics and the Co-Director of the Globalisation and Development Centre (GDC) at Bond University, Australia. He obtained his PhD in Economics from the National University of Singapore. His ongoing research is in Time Series Econometrics and examines aggregation issues in economic relationships. He specialises in the areas of panel data analysis and applied time series econometrics.

Shrabani Saha is a Lecturer in Economics at Edith Cowan University, Australia. Her research areas include political economy, economic growth, development economics and international trade issues. Her major research focus has been on the causes and effects of corruption across countries and corruption's relationship with democracy and economic freedom.

NOTES ON CONTRIBUTORS

Barry Williams is Professor of Finance at the Faculty of Business, Bond University, Australia, and a visiting researcher at the KOF Swiss Economic Institute, ETH Zurich Switzerland. His research focuses on the determinants of performance and risk of banks, particularly multinational banks.

Shihan Xie is currently an undergraduate majoring in Mathematics and Economics at Nanyang Technological University (NTU), Singapore. She was selected for the SM2 Program by Singapore government in 2008, which offered her full scholarship for her undergraduate study at Singapore. In 2011, she studied at the University of California, Los Angeles as an exchange participant. She started research in macroeconomics under the supervision of Assistant Professor Wai-Mun Chia in her second year.

Nobuaki Yamashita is a Senior Lecturer in School of Economics at Latrobe University, Melbourne, Australia.

Introduction

Bond University's Globalisation and Development Centre partnered with Nanyang Technological University's Economic Growth Centre to host a collaborative workshop on Economic and Policy Developments in East Asia. The event was held in October 2011 with papers presented by academics and policy-makers from Australia, Japan, New Zealand and Singapore. A variety of topics based around three key themes were discussed: macroeconomics and trade, labour and social issues, and taxes and government spending. Keynote addresses were given by Professor Norman Gemmell, the then Chief Economist at the New Zealand Treasury, and Professor Charles Horioka from Osaka University's Institute of Social and Economic Research.

The papers collected in this Special Issue were selected for their potential importance to researchers and commentators on the economies in our Asia-Pacific region. The papers are all empirically oriented and include both cross-country studies and individual country studies. A brief reader's guide follows.

Horioka compares recent trends in private consumption in Japan to its G7 counterparts. The stagnation of private consumption in Japan has been due primarily to the stagnation of household income and wealth as well as the relative stability of its household saving rate. Given Japan's huge public debt and the lack of room to move on monetary policies, he recommends targeted microeconomic policies to lessen the need for precautionary saving. **Gemmell and Au** review the evidence on the relationship between government size, fiscal policy and economic growth. Recent research indicates positive output effects from increases in some public expenditures and negative output effects from higher tax rates. Overall, while the impact of fiscal policy may be sizeable in the short-run, it is moderate in the longer-run. As for the 'government–growth' relationship for the Asia-Pacific, they urge policy-makers to strike a balance between a desire for more public services and the subsequent growth impact of the resulting tax choices.

The papers that follow are cross-country studies, with a special focus on the Asia-Pacific. **Falvey, Foster, and Khalid** examine the effect of capital formation, the share of the government, the economy's openness to trade and its price distortions on income growth. They find that while trade liberalisation facilitates growth, the investment share is the most important conduit. In the Asian region, they find that the beneficial effects of trade liberalisation are offset by the growth in the government share. **Xie, Cheng, and Chia** examine the relationship between trade, finance, specialisation and business cycle synchronisation of 12 Asia-Pacific economies. They argue that trade and financial integration among these economies as well as deeper exchange rate cooperation has been effective in promoting regional economic integration. **Gaston and Rajaguru** examine how migration has affected public social expenditures in OECD countries. They find that while increased immigration of low-skilled workers has reduced social expenditures in the European Union, the effect in the Asia-Pacific has been more benign. **Campbell and Saha** observe that when countries transition to a more democratic rule, the level of corruption often increases. In more mature democracies, corruption becomes less problematic. For Asia-Pacific countries, they find that the beneficial effects of democratic reforms on corruption only occur at high levels of democracy.

Next are the special country studies. **Mukhopadhaya** investigates the rise of income inequality in China. He finds that the dominant contributors to inequality are wages and property income. Consequently, further increases in urbanisation are likely to further increase inequality, as well as the attendant social pressures. **Yamashita and Jayasuriya** examine how changes in the Chinese real exchange rate affect its exports. Their empirical estimates cast doubt on the effectiveness of exchange rate adjustments for reducing Chinese export volumes. **Williams** examines the factors that determine Indonesian bank risk both before and after the Asian financial crisis. He argues that the regulations ensuring that banks are well-capitalised are essential, but counsels against regulatory laxity.

Finally, I would like to acknowledge the support, both financial and logistical, provided by Bond University and Nanyang Technological University. In particular, I would like to thank Ahmed Khalid and Euston Quah for initiating and ensuring the success of the collaborative workshop. Also, heartfelt thanks to Rod Falvey and Sekar Rajaguru for their help with this Special Issue. Last, but not least, I am grateful to Leong Liew for his encouragement and support.

Noel Gaston
Principal Adviser Research
Productivity Commission
Melbourne, Victoria 3000, Australia

Recent trends in consumption in Japan and the other G7 countries

Charles Yuji Horioka[a,b,†]

[a]*Institute of Social and Economic Research, Osaka University, Ibaraki, Japan;* [b]*National Bureau of Economic Research, Inc., Cambridge, USA*

In this paper, we present data on recent trends in private consumption and in possible determinants of private consumption (such as GDP, household incomes, household saving rates, household wealth, and employment conditions) in the group of seven (G7) countries and find that there has been significant variability among the G7 countries not only in their private consumption growth rates but also in the determinants of private consumption growth during the 2002–2007 period. With respect to Japan, we find that private consumption has been relatively stagnant during the 2002–2007 period and that the stagnation of private consumption has been due to the stagnation of household income and of household wealth and the relative stability of the household saving rate.

1. Introduction

The Japanese economy has been in a prolonged recession for most of the past two decades (Japan's so called "Lost Decades"), and private consumption has been stagnant for most of this period along with the other components of GDP. However, as Horioka (2006) shows, the stagnation of public and private investment has been even more pronounced than the stagnation of private consumption.

Even during the relatively prosperous period between the Asian financial crisis of 1997–1998 and the global financial crisis of 2008–2009, the Japanese economy has been relatively stagnant, with private consumption being no exception. In this paper, we present data on recent trends in private consumption growth in Japan and the other Group of Seven (G7) countries (Canada, France, Germany, Italy, the United Kingdom, and the United States) during the 2002–2009 period and explore the reasons for why private consumption was stagnant in Japan compared to the other G7 countries. We compare Japan to the other G7 countries because of their importance in the world economy and because we wanted to compare Japan to countries at a similar stage of economic development and with similar market systems.

This paper is organized as follows: In section 2, we present data on recent trends in private consumption in the G7 countries, and in section 3, we present data on recent trends in possible determinants of private consumption (such as GDP, household incomes, household saving rates, household wealth, and employment conditions) in the G7 countries in order to

---

[†]The author's primary affiliation at present is School of Economics, University of the Philippines, Manila, Philippines.

Table 1. Growth rates of GDP, household income, and consumption.

Country	2002–2007			2007–2009	
	GDP	Net Household Disposable Income	Private Consumption	GDP	Private Consumption
Canada	2.61	3.52	3.74	−0.98	1.67
U.S.	2.75	2.61	2.98	−1.35	−0.73
U.K.	2.68	1.14	2.44	−2.50	−1.38
France	2.00	1.94	2.09	−1.41	0.21
Japan	2.10	1.00	1.30	−3.76	−1.33
Italy	1.14	0.51	1.05	−3.29	−1.30
Germany	1.55	0.40	0.33	−1.91	0.27
Mean	2.12	1.59	1.99	−2.17	−0.37

shed light on the reasons for differences among the G7 countries in recent trends in private consumption. Section 4 is a brief concluding section that summarizes and makes policy prescriptions.

To preview the main findings of this paper, we find that there has been significant variability among the G7 countries not only in their private consumption growth rates but also in the determinants of private consumption growth during the 2002–2007 period, with the relative importance of GDP growth, household income growth, household saving rates, household wealth, and employment conditions varying from country to country. With respect to Japan, we find that private consumption has been relatively stagnant during the 2002–2007 period and that the stagnation of private consumption has been due to the stagnation of household income and of household wealth and the relative stability of the household saving rate.

2. Trends in private consumption growth

Table 1 shows, among other things, data on the average annual real growth rate of private consumption in the G7 countries during the 2002–2007 and 2007–2009 periods (with the countries arranged from highest to lowest with respect to growth rates in 2002–2007). As can be seen from the table, there were substantial differences among the G7 countries in private consumption growth rates in both periods. During the 2002–2007 period, private consumption increased fastest in Canada (3.74 percent) and the United States (2.98 percent), relatively fast in the United Kingdom (2.44 percent) and France (2.09 percent), and slowest in Japan (1.30 percent), Italy (1.05 percent), and Germany (0.33 percent).

During the 2007–2009 period, the average annual private consumption growth rate was lower than during the 2002–2007 period in all of the G7 countries due to the advent of the global financial crisis, with four of the G7 countries (Italy, Japan, the United Kingdom, and the United States) showing negative private consumption growth rates and only three of the G7 countries (Canada, France, and Italy) showing positive private consumption growth rates. However, the rank ordering of the G7 countries with respect to private consumption growth remained largely unchanged, with Canada still showing the highest average annual private consumption growth rate, France still ranking relative high, and Italy and Japan still ranking relatively low. Germany rises in the rankings, while the United Kingdom and the United States fall in the rankings.

Thus, private consumption growth rates varied considerably among the G7 countries during both time periods, but the differences among the G7 countries were relatively stable.

3. Determinants of private consumption growth

In the previous section, we found that there have been substantial and stable differences among the G7 countries in private consumption growth rates. In this section, we attempt to shed light on the reasons for these substantial differences. However, we confine our analysis to the 2002–2007 period for two reasons—first, because sectoral data (in particular, data on the household sector) are still not yet available for the most recent period, and second because the 2002–2007 period was a relatively prosperous period between the Asian financial crisis and the global financial crisis and it is important to understand why private consumption growth was relatively stagnant in Japan even during this period of global prosperity.

3.1. *GDP growth*

Arguably, the most important determinant of private consumption growth rates is the GDP growth rate. Table 1 shows data on real GDP growth rates alongside data on real private consumption growth rates in the G7 countries during the 2002–2007 and 2007–2009 periods. As can be seen from this table, there is, in fact, a high correlation between private consumption growth rates and GDP growth rates. Moreover, private consumption growth rates roughly equal GDP growth rates in many countries, including France (2.09 vs. 2.00 percent), Italy (1.05 vs. 1.14 percent), the United Kingdom (2.44 vs. 2.68 percent), and the United States (2.98 vs. 2.75 percent). However, private consumption growth rates exceed GDP growth rates by a considerable margin in some countries such as Canada (3.74 vs. 2.61 percent) and fall short of GDP growth rates by a considerable margin in some countries such as Germany (0.33 vs. 1.55 percent) and Japan (1.30 vs. 2.10 percent) (all figures pertain to the 2002–2007 period). Thus, GDP growth rates are apparently not the only determinant of private consumption growth rates.

3.2. *Household income growth*

Another determinant of private consumption growth rates is the growth rate of net household disposable income, and it is quite possible that it is a more important determinant of private consumption growth rates than GDP growth rates because households finance their consumption primarily from net household disposable income. Table 1 shows data on the average annual real growth rate of net household disposable income (deflated by the price deflator for private consumption) in the G7 countries during the 2002–2007 period in addition to showing data on the average annual real growth rates of private consumption and GDP during the same time period, and as can be seen from this table, there is a high correlation between GDP growth rates and household income growth rates, with the two being roughly equal in many countries including France (2.00 vs. 1.94 percent) and the United States (2.75 vs. 2.61 percent).

However, there are some notable exceptions: the average annual household income growth rate was considerably higher than the average annual GDP growth rate (3.52 vs. 2.61 percent) in Canada during the 2002–2007 period, and the fact that the average annual private consumption growth rate was higher than the average annual GDP growth rate in Canada (3.74 vs. 2.61 percent) during the 2002–2007 period can be explained by the fact

Table 2. Household saving rates.

Country	2002	2003	2004	2005	2006	2007	Change, 2002–2007
Canada	3.53	2.70	3.24	2.18	3.63	2.57	−0.96
U.S.	3.65	3.76	3.37	1.48	2.47	1.73	−1.93
U.K.	−0.05	0.43	−1.70	−1.26	−2.95	−4.27	−4.21
France	13.66	12.46	12.36	11.37	11.44	11.87	−1.79
Japan	5.09	3.88	3.63	3.85	3.65	3.78	−1.31
Italy	11.36	10.34	10.30	9.96	9.19	8.22	−3.14
Germany	10.06	10.41	10.55	10.63	10.71	10.92	0.87
Mean	6.76	6.28	5.96	5.46	5.45	4.97	−1.78

that the average household income growth rate was higher than the average GDP growth rate in that country during this period.

Conversely, the average annual household income growth rate was considerably *lower* than the average annual GDP growth rate in Germany (0.40 vs. 1.55 percent) and Japan (1.00 vs. 2.10 percent) during the 2002–2007 period, and the fact that the average annual private consumption growth rate was lower than the average annual GDP growth rate in Germany (0.33 vs. 1.56 percent) and Japan (1.30 vs. 2.10 percent) during the 2002–2007 period can be explained by the fact that the average annual household income growth rate was lower than the average annual GDP growth rate in these countries during this period. Thus, not surprisingly, household income growth rates appear to be much better at explaining private consumption growth rates than GDP growth rates.

3.3. *Household saving rates*

Another possible determinant of consumption growth rates is the household saving rate. Private consumption growth rates will exceed household income growth rates if the household saving rate is declining over time and conversely. In order to shed light on the importance of trends over time in the household saving rate as a determinant of private consumption growth rates, we present data on trends over time in the household saving rate and on the net change in household saving rate in the G7 countries during the 2002–2007 period in Table 2.

As can be seen from this table, the level of the household saving rate varies greatly among the G7 countries, being relatively high in France, Germany, and Italy (8.22 to 13.66 percent), relatively low in Japan, Canada, and the United States (1.48 to 5.09 percent), and negative (−0.05 to −4.27 percent) in the United Kingdom in all years but one (2003, when it was 0.43 percent). More importantly, the G7 countries also show substantial variation in the net change in the household saving rate during the 2002–2007 period, with only Germany showing an increase (0.87 percentage points), Canada, Japan, France, and the United States showing relatively moderate declines (−0.96, −1.31, and −1.93 percentage points, respectively), and Italy and the United States showing relatively sharp declines (−3.14 and −4.21 percentage points, respectively).

The relatively sharp declines in the household saving rates of Italy and the United Kingdom can explain why private consumption growth rates exceeded household income growth rates in Italy and the United Kingdom (1.05 vs. 0.51 percent in Italy and 2.44 vs. 1.14 percent in the United Kingdom). Thus, trends in household saving rates can explain

Table 3. Net household wealth to household income ratios.

Country	2002	2007	Change, 2002–2007
Canada	5.127	5.485	0.358
U.S.	5.143	6.157	1.014
U.K.	7.156	9.008	1.852
France	5.713	8.063	2.350
Japan	7.194	7.353	0.159
Italy	7.475	8.570	1.095
Germany	5.336	6.276	0.940
Mean	6.163	7.273	1.110

the divergence between private consumption growth rates and household income growth rates in some cases.

This factor was not so important in Japan because the decline in its household saving rate was not so sharp (−1.31 percentage points), as a result of which its private consumption growth rate was only slightly (0.30 percentage points) higher than its household income growth rate during the 2002–2007 period. To put it another way, one reason for the stagnation of consumption in Japan during the 2002–2007 period is the fact that the household saving rate declined only moderately during this period, due perhaps to increasing precautionary saving brought about by increased pessimism about the future.

3.4. *Household wealth*

Private consumption growth will also be influenced by changes in household wealth, with increases (decreases) in household wealth due to capital gains (losses) on equities, land, and other assets causing private consumption to increase (decrease) by more than would be expected by GDP growth, household income growth, and trends in household saving rates.

Table 3 shows data on the ratio of net household wealth to net household disposable income in 2002 and 2007 and the net change in this ratio during the 2002–2007 period in the G7 countries. As can be seen from this table, household wealth increased sharply in France (by 235.0 percentage points of household income) and the United Kingdom (by 185.2 percentage points of household income), moderately in Italy (by 109.5 percentage points of household income), the United States (by 101.4 percentage points of household income), and Germany (by 94.0 percentage points of household income), and least sharply in Canada (by 35.8 percentage points of household income) and Japan (by 15.9 percentage points of household income).

Thus, the sharp increase in household wealth in the United Kingdom (by 185.2 percentage points of net household disposable income) during the 2002–2007 period can explain the strong private consumption growth in the U.K. (2.44 percent), and in particular, why the average annual private consumption growth rate during the 2002–07 period was much higher than the average annual household income growth rate during the same period (2.44 vs. 1.14 percent).

By contrast, the stagnation of household wealth in Japan (it increased by only 15.9 percentage points of household disposable income during the 2002–2007 period) can explain why private consumption growth was relatively weak during this same period (1.30 percent).

Table 4. Unemployment rates.

Country	2002	2007	Change, 2002–2007
Canada	7.7	6.0	−1.7
U.S.	5.8	4.6	−1.2
U.K.	5.2	5.4	0.2
France	7.9	8.0	0.1
Japan	5.4	3.8	−1.6
Italy	8.7	6.1	−2.6
Germany	8.3	8.3	0.0
Mean	7.0	6.0	−1.0

3.5. Employment conditions

Private consumption growth will also be influenced by employment conditions, with an improvement in (deterioration of) employment conditions leading to higher (lower) private consumption growth than predicted by other factors.

Table 4 shows data on unemployment rates in 2002 and 2007 and the change in the unemployment rate during the 2002–2007 period in the G7 countries. As can be seen from this table, employment conditions improved in most G7 countries during the 2002–2007 period, with unemployment rates declining by 2.6 percentage points in Italy, 1.7 percentage points in Canada, 1.6 percentage points in Japan, and 1.2 percentage points in the United States, not changing at all in Germany, and increasing by 0.1 percentage points in France and 0.2 percentage points in the United Kingdom during the 2002–2007 period.

A comparison of column (3) of Table 1 and column (3) of Table 4 shows that there is little correlation between private consumption growth rates and changes in unemployment rates. The fact that Canada showed the second largest improvement in unemployment rates (1.7 percentage points) as well as the highest growth rate of private consumption (3.74 percent) during the 2002–2007 period suggests that there is a positive correlation between the two, but the fact that Italy showed by far the largest improvement in unemployment rates (2.6 percentage points) even though it showed the second *lowest* growth rate of private consumption (1.05 percent), whereas the United Kingdom was one of only two countries showing a deterioration in their unemployment rates (by 0.2 percentage points) even though it showed the third *highest* growth rate of private consumption (2.44 percent) suggests that there is a negative correlation between the two.

Japan ranked third with respect to the improvement in unemployment rates (a decline of 1.6 percentage points) but only fifth with respect to the growth rate of private consumption (1.30 percent), suggesting that the improvement in employment conditions did not do much to boost private consumption growth in Japan.

3.6. Conclusion concerning the determinants of private consumption growth

In this paper, we showed that private consumption growth is determined by trends in GDP growth, household income growth, household saving rates, household wealth, and employment conditions but that the relative importance of these factors differs greatly from country to country.

For example, in the case of Japan, we found that the stagnation of consumption during the 2002–2007 period was due to the stagnation of household income (which was much more stagnant than GDP), the stagnation of household wealth, and the relative stability of the household saving rate (which was presumably due in large part to increased pessimism about the future).

Similarly, private consumption was the most stagnant in Germany due primarily to the stagnation of household income (which was much more stagnant than GDP) and due partly to a moderate increase in its household saving rate.

France showed an intermediate growth rate of private consumption because its household income growth rate was also intermediate, but its private consumption growth rate was somewhat higher than its household income growth rate presumably because France showed by far the largest increase in household wealth.

By contrast, the strong growth of private consumption in Canada and the United States was due primarily to the strong growth of household income (far in excess of GDP growth in the case of Canada) and due partly to moderate declines in their household saving rates and (in the case of Canada) a sharp improvement in employment conditions.

The most interesting cases are the cases of Italy and the United Kingdom, which showed considerably higher growth rates of private consumption than of household incomes due in large part to the sharp decline in their household saving rates and (especially in the case of the United Kingdom) sharp increases in household wealth.

4. Summary and policy implications

In this paper, we presented data on recent trends in private consumption and in possible determinants of private consumption (such as GDP, household incomes, household saving rates, household wealth, and employment conditions) in the G7 countries and found that there has been significant variability among the Group of Seven (G7) countries not only in their private consumption growth rates but also in the determinants of private consumption growth during the 2002–2007 period, with the relative importance of GDP growth, household income growth, household saving rates, household wealth, and employment conditions varying from country to country.

With respect to Japan, we found that private consumption has been relatively stagnant during the 2002–2007 period and that the stagnation of private consumption has been due to the stagnation of household income and of household wealth and the relative stability of the household saving rate.

This suggests that the best way of stimulating private consumption and of bringing about a recovery of the Japanese economy as a whole would be to boost household income and household wealth. However, given that Japan's government debt is already dangerously high (in excess of 200 percent of GDP, making Japan's government debt the highest among the developed countries as a ratio of GDP) and that there is little scope for further monetary easing, it seems that targeted policies would be more realistic and more effective than macroeconomic policies. For example, policies that redistribute income toward the low-income and others with high marginal propensities to consume, such as policies that create more job opportunities and more opportunities for vocational training for young workers (whose unemployment rates are still very high) and policies that improve the wages and other benefits and working conditions of part-time and temporary workers (whose share has been increasing), would be effective in boosting private consumption and the economy as a whole.

Finally, since we found that the stability of household saving rates is a contributing factor to the stagnation of private consumption in Japan, improving social safety nets and improving access to consumer credit would also boost private consumption by reducing precautionary saving (see Horioka and Yin (2010) and Horioka and Terada-Hagiwara

(2012) for cross-country evidence on the impact of social safety nets and consumer credit on household saving and consumption).

The author hopes that these policy measures will be adopted as soon as possible so that private consumption as well as the Japanese economy as a whole can receive a boost, enabling it to extricate itself from two "lost decades" of stagnant growth and high unemployment.

Data Sources

Data on consumption, GDP, and net household disposable income are from OECD (2010).

Data on unemployment rates (Annex Table 13), household saving rates (Annex Table 23), and net household wealth to household income ratios (Annex Table 58) are from OECD (2011).

Acknowledgements

This research was conducted as part of the Social Resilience Project 2011 of the Pacific Economic Cooperation Council (PECC) and the Japan Institute of International Affairs (JIIA), and the author is grateful to Dr. Yoko Niimi, Ambassador Yoshiji Nogami, the other participants of the Pacific Economic Cooperation Council (PECC) International Workshop on Social Resilience Project 2011, held on July 12, 2011, at Plaza Hall, Kasumigaseki Building, Tokyo, Japan, and of the Twentieth General Meeting of the Pacific Economic Cooperation Council (PECC): State of the Region, held on September 29, 2011, at the Madison Hotel, Washington, D.C., U.S.A., the Guest Editor Noel Gaston, and an anonymous referee for their helpful comments.

References

Horioka, Charles Yuji. 2006. "The Causes of Japan's 'Lost Decade': The Role of Household Consumption." *Japan and the World Economy* 18 (4): 378–400.
Horioka, Charles Yuji and Akiko Terada-Hagiwara. 2012. "The Determinants and Long-term Projections of Saving Rates in Developing Asia." *Japan and the World Economy* 24 (2): 128–137.
Horioka, Charles Yuji and Ting Yin. 2010. "Household Savings Rates and Social Benefit Ratios: Country Comparisons." In *Effects of Social Policy on Domestic Demand: Annual Conference 2009*, edited by Masahiro Kawai and Gloria O. Pasadilla, 63–75. Tokyo, Japan: Asian Development Bank Institute (ADBI).
Organisation for Economic Cooperation and Development (OECD). 2010. *National Accounts of OECD Countries*, Paris: OECD.
Organisation for Economic Cooperation and Development (OECD). 2011. *OECD Economic Outlook*, no. 89, Paris: OECD.

Government size, fiscal policy and the level and growth of output: a review of recent evidence

Norman Gemmell[a] and Joey Au[b]

[a]*School of Accounting and Commercial Law, Victoria University of Wellington, Wellington, New Zealand;* [b]*Chief Economist's Unit, The Treasury, New Zealand*

Theoretical developments, improved methodologies and more extensive data have helped generate a dramatic increase in the literature testing for the impact of government size and fiscal policy on economic growth in recent years. We review a range of the more recent evidence and examine (1) the consistency or robustness of the results, (2) how these results differ from the earlier literature and (3) their usefulness as a guide to policy reform in practice. We find that the last decade has produced more robust evidence and more plausible orders of magnitude on the impact of fiscal policy on growth. However, the value of this evidence remains limited as a basis for quantifying macro-economic responses to fiscal policy reform in practice.

1. Introduction

Economists have long been interested in the twin questions of whether economic prosperity is fostered by larger or smaller governments, and by more interventionist or more laissez faire government policies. As a consequence, policy advice to governments has often hinged on perceived answers to these questions. For Scandinavian economies, for example, the 1990s saw considerable debate over the long-run growth consequences of government intervention and the appropriate policy advice (see, for example, Korpi 1996). Similarly, the rapid growth from the 1970s in several East Asian countries stimulated debate over the role of government in that process; see, for example, Young (1992) and Rodrik (1994). Much evidence on these 'government and growth' issues has since been collected and analysed, often distinguishing between high and low income, or high and low growth, economies.

The Asia Pacific (AP) region contains economies displaying each of these high/low features. This includes established OECD countries such as Australia and New Zealand with relatively high per capita income levels, by AP standards, over many decades, joined by Japan early in the post-World War II (WWII) period, and later Korea. The growth experiences of those economies have been very different since WWII. Further, the so-called Asian Miracle witnessed numerous Asian economies (initially Hong Kong, Korea, Singapore, Taiwan) experience rapid GDP per capita increases from low levels, while others remained stubbornly 'low growth', especially the small island economies of the Pacific. As a consequence several AP countries are either old or new members of the OECD, and the continued economic success of several non-OECD AP countries is likely to lead to further AP economies matching or overtaking the income levels of today's OECD members.

A natural question to ask regarding those AP economies is how far the OECD evidence on the 'government and growth' relationship applies to them? While this paper does not address that question directly, it does provide a review and assessment of the current state of the literature on the 'government and growth' debate for OECD countries. Such evidence is at least likely to provide relevant food for thought among policy-makers in AP countries that are already OECD members, or aim to achieve similar income levels. It is also especially relevant for the currently rapidly growing countries of China and India as these two countries choose very different, but so far similarly successful, paths to higher per capita income levels. If those countries follow the OECD example of rising government expenditure levels in association with increased average incomes, will this help or hinder their subsequent economic prosperity?

There have, of course, been a number of reviews of the empirical literature testing for the impact of fiscal policy in general, and government size in particular, on income levels and growth rates, of which Slemrod (1995) is probably the most comprehensive.[1] His review largely focused on cross-country evidence at the aggregate or macro-level up to the mid-1990s. The question addressed by Slemrod (1995) was simple: what is 'the evidence about the influence of government tax and expenditures on economic prosperity and growth'? (373).[2] In answering this question, Slemrod was generally sceptical of the evidence, arguing that:

> '... *the empirical findings are not robust to various reasonable specifications and, of most concern, do not address identification problems* ...' (380) *and* '[*t*]*his review of existing cross-country literature suggests that there is no persuasive evidence that the extent of government has either a positive or negative impact on either the level or the growth rate of per capita income* ... *top-down studies find a negligible effect*'. (401)

Much has changed since Slemrod's review, with a variety of traditional and new methodologies subsequently being applied to more extensive and different datasets. In particular, within the so-called 'top-down' or aggregate/macro-level approaches, cross-section studies have largely given way to panel analyses across or within countries, and country-specific time-series evidence. This is the motivation for the current review which returns to Slemrod's original question. Specifically, to help answer it we pose three more detailed questions:

(1) How robust or consistent are the results from more recent studies?
(2) Do the results from these studies justify a less sceptical verdict than emerged from Slemrod's review? and
(3) Are these results sufficient to be useful as a guide to fiscal policy reform in practice?

To summarise our assessment, we argue that theory on the output effects of fiscal policy has developed considerably since the time of Slemrod's writing and this theory has increasingly been taken seriously in specifying empirical tests. Together with improvements in econometric methods and new datasets, these developments have allowed better interrogation of panels of data. Our conclusion is that, despite some remaining 'big issues', results from aggregate-level studies are now much more robustly in favour of identifiable effects of government size on income levels and growth rates, provided these conclusions are carefully circumscribed in ways that we will make clear. In addition, plausible orders of magnitude are beginning to emerge, though their value remains limited as an evidence-base for quantitative predictions of the output effects from fiscal policy reforms in practice.

2. Reasons to be sceptical of the evidence

Slemrod (1995) was sceptical of the available cross-section evidence, largely for two reasons. Firstly, while most arguments at the time proposed that bigger governments were harmful for income levels ('prosperity' in Slemrod's terms) or growth rates, unconditional correlations across countries, and trends within countries over time, typically revealed *positive*, rather than negative, correlations or were unclear. Secondly, Slemrod argued that, based on analysis of simple but plausible conceptual relationships among the variables involved, cross-section evidence could not be expected to reveal the empirical relationships sought by studies based on macro-level data. In this and the next section we explore each of those arguments in turn.

To begin, it is helpful to be reminded of the evidence on which Slemrod's conclusions were based. He examined cross-plots of country levels of GDP per capita in 1990 with country ratios of government expenditure to GDP, G/Y, and tax revenue to GDP, T/Y, in 1990. He considered a large sample of developing and developed countries and an OECD sub-sample; see Slemrod (1995, Figures 3–6). Slemrod found a wide array of observations in the GDP per capita, G/Y, space with a likely positive but weak association across all countries. For OECD countries, there was probably less support for a positive association between GDP per capita and G/Y but any attempt to fit a linear relationship to those variables appeared likely to be sensitive to outlying observations such as Japan, Turkey and Greece. Similar conclusions emerged from Slemrod's examination of cross-country patterns for GDP per capita versus the tax ratio, T/Y.

To replicate and update Slemrod's (1995) analysis, Figure 1 plots cross-country GDP per capita levels against G/Y for a sample of 30 OECD countries (including four AP economies:

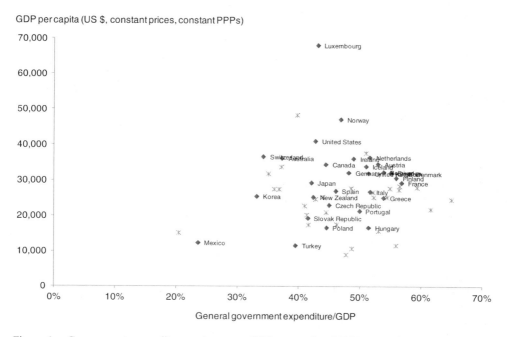

Figure 1. Government expenditure ratio versus GDP per capita: OECD countries, 1995 and 2009.
Note: country names for 1995 'x' observation names have been omitted for clarity.
Source: OECD National Accounts.

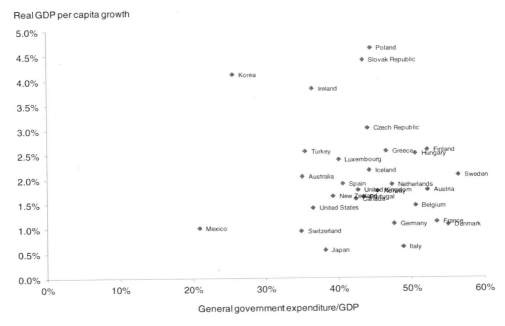

Figure 2. Government expenditure ratio versus average real per capita GDP growth rate 1995–2009: OECD countries.
Source: OECD National Accounts, authors' calculations.

Australia, Japan, Korea, New Zealand), using values for 1995 and 2009. It is clear from the data that the earlier patterns (or lack of) identified by Slemrod (1995) are essentially unaltered by an updated dataset.[3] If instead the general government (total) *tax revenue* to GDP ratio is examined against GDP per capita levels across the same OECD sample (not shown), it proves similarly difficult to identify a positive or negative association.[4] At a minimum, it does not confirm the priors of those who expect higher taxes to be associated with *lower* prosperity.

Slemrod (1995) also states that he is 'not aware of any serious academic study that purports to demonstrate a significant negative causal relationship between the extent of government involvement and the level of prosperity. There are, however, studies that purport to show a negative, and presumably causal, relationship between measures of government involvement and the *growth rate* of real per capita income ... ' [377; emphasis added]. The evidence on this univariate 'growth rate/government size' association is also 'hardly striking' (378) according to Slemrod's 1970–1990 growth data.

For this case there was more, though still limited, support for a negative association across OECD countries than when a wider sample of countries was included. Figure 2 provides an update of the evidence for the OECD. This also appears to show no clear association between a country's average annual growth rate of real per capita GDP over 1995–2009 and its average ratio of G/Y over the same period. These conclusions hold if T/Y is substituted for G/Y in Figure 2.[5]

Some modelling approaches, such as the growth accounting framework, predict a relationship between *changes* in government size and income growth rates. Figures 3 and 4 examine changes in G/Y and T/Y respectively for our sample of OECD countries, considering changes between average values of government size during 1995–1998 and during

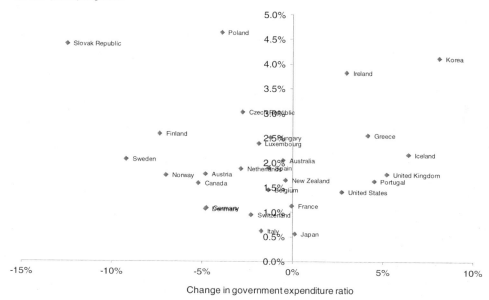

Figure 3. Change in government expenditure ratio 1995–1998 to 2006–2009 versus average real per capita GDP growth rate 1995–2009: OECD countries.
Source: OECD National Accounts, authors' calculations.

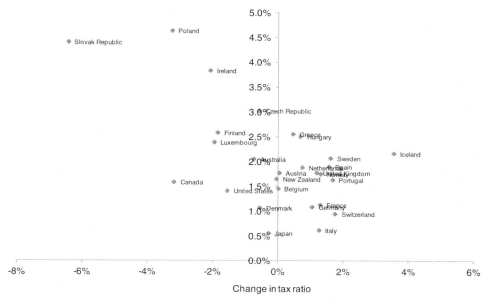

Figure 4. Change in tax ratio 1995–1998 to 2006–2009 versus average real per capita GDP growth rate 1995–2009: OECD countries.
Source: OECD National Accounts, authors' calculations.

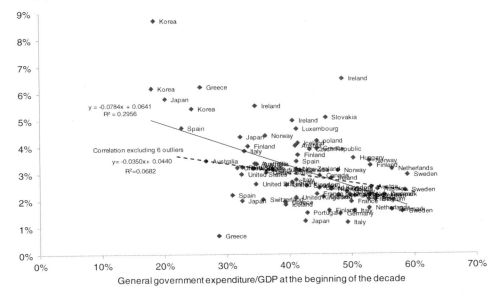

Figure 5. Government expenditure ratio versus average real GDP growth rate: OECD countries.
Source: OECD Economic Outlook database, The Treasury and authors' calculations.
Note: Not all countries have a data point for each of the four decades due to data availability.

2006–2009. The changes in G/Y and T/Y (in percentage points over the period) are plotted against annual per capita real GDP growth over 1995–2009. Once again, observations are widely dispersed and associations between these variables are unclear. Notably, a number of countries with very similar growth rates display large differences in the change (sign and magnitude) of the government share variables. While there is a suggestion in Figure 4 of a negative association between changes in T/Y and per capita GDP growth, the relationship is likely to be sensitive to outlying countries like the Slovak Republic.[6]

Returning to the relationship between government size and income growth, Figure 5, based on more detailed and comprehensive data from New Zealand Treasury (2011), provides an update of this relationship for a wider group of countries. The chart plots the growth rate of GDP over each of the four decades during 1969–2008, against the ratio of general government expenditure to GDP at the start of each decade. Each data point in Figure 5 represents one country in one of the four decades. In line with the evidence of Gwartney, Lawson, and Holcombe (1998), Figure 5 provides more support for a negative association between government size (as measured by the expenditure/GDP ratio) and subsequent economic growth than is observed in Slemrod's data or our OECD update. However, despite the temporal precedence of government size at the start of a decade and subsequent decadal GDP growth rates, this evidence is certainly not sufficient to establish causation.[7] Furthermore, the negative association is again sensitive to a few outlying observations.[8] It may also simply reflect 'unobserved' differences between countries such as different institutions other than government.

Figure 6 replicates Figure 5 but focuses on OECD countries in the AP region (Japan, Korea, New Zealand and Australia). While the number of data points per country is only four or less, in general we observe a negative association across the four AP countries between the size of government and subsequent GDP growth. However, as the lines drawn

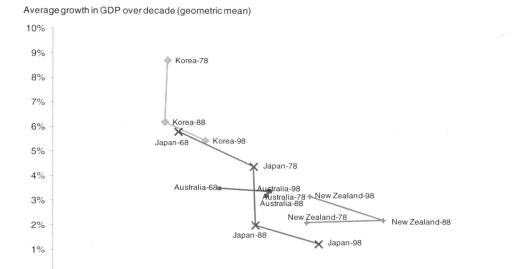

Figure 6. Government expenditure ratio versus average real GDP growth rate: Asia Pacific OECD countries.
Source: OECD Economic Outlook database, The Treasury and authors' calculations.
Note: Not all countries have a data point for each of the four decades due to data availability. Country numbers (e.g. '78') refer to the G/Y ratio year and start year for GDP growth.

between successive decade averages in Figure 6 demonstrate, the time-series patterns are far from uniform and not always clearly negative. *If* negative *ceteris paribus* relationships between the two variables are embedded within the time-series for each country, clearly 'other factors', such as country-specific institutions, must be invoked that can account for the various observed 'shifts' in those relationships.

3. What relationships could be expected?

The theory on the relationship between government size and long-run income levels or growth rates has developed a great deal since the early 1990s, with the seminal paper by Barro (1990) acting as a catalyst for much subsequent theoretical work. It is beyond the scope of the present paper to review this voluminous literature but it is useful to consider the relationship between output growth and government size that the Barro (1990) and similar models predict. Barro distinguishes between two types of public expenditures: those that are either 'productive' (enter private sector production functions) or are 'unproductive' (enter agents' utility functions). These expenditures must be financed by two types of taxation: those (such as income taxes) that are distortionary with respect to investment decisions, including human capital investment, and taxes which do not distort investment decisions.[9] Based on these distinctions, Barro (1990) yields the decomposition of predicted long-run growth affects associated with the combinations of taxes and expenditures shown in Table 1.

The table shows that the predicted long-run growth effect on output depends not only on the type of public spending but also the type of tax used to finance that spending. By recognising that, whatever the impact of public spending on output levels may be, the

Table 1. Predicted long-run growth effects: Barro (1990) model.

		Public spending	
Financed by an increase in:		Productive	Unproductive
Taxes	Distortionary	Positive (negative) at low (high) government size	Negative
	Non-distortionary	Positive	Zero

financing of that spending can also have output effects, these models formalise the role of the government budget constraint (GBC). More recent theoretical models tend to reinforce these conclusions.[10]

The role of the GBC in these models has important implications for empirical testing because, as Table 1 demonstrates, the *combination* of particular tax and public spending categories matters for predicted growth outcomes. Therefore, *which* taxes or expenditures are included in, or excluded from, regression models seeking to explain output levels or growth rates, can be expected to affect parameter estimates. However, many empirical tests for government-output effects have ignored this GBC aspect. Indeed, even where the GBC is recognised as important in principle for empirical testing, implementing it is not always straightforward.

Perhaps the most controversial aspect of aggregate-level studies of government-growth effects is how to model the likely endogenous relationships involved. That is, as well as government spending or taxation potentially impacting on income levels or growth rates, higher income levels may impact on government size – for example, via increasing demand for government services or transfers at higher income levels. This is at the heart of Slemrod's (1995) criticism of the 'identification problems' with this literature, quoted above. In the following sub-section, we use a simple illustration to demonstrate the ambiguous expected relationships that can arise.

3.1. *A simple model of government and growth*

To fix ideas, consider a simple linear case in which government expenditure is income elastic – demands for the goods and services delivered via public expenditure rise faster than income, Y.[11] This demand relationship can be represented by Equation (1) below, where t indexes time, $g = G/Y$ and a, b are parameters.

$$g_t = \left(\frac{G}{Y}\right)_t = a + bY_t. \qquad (1)$$

The parameter b is positively signed if government expenditure is income-elastic such that G changes more than proportionately in association with a given percentage change in income, Y. In the absence of deficit financing, the GBC requires that all expenditure in each period is financed from tax revenues such that $g_t = r_t$, where r_t is the average tax rate, T/Y.

For simplicity, assume a tax system where tax revenues rise with incomes.[12] Where the tax system is progressive (average tax rates rise with income levels), as in most OECD countries, this tends to yield a relationship between tax revenue, R, and income, such that both effective marginal and average tax rates rise with incomes.[13] At the aggregate level we can specify this as a reduced form relationship in which the effective marginal tax rate,

m_t, is proportional (α) to the effective average tax rate, r_t.[14] Hence we can write:

$$r_t = \left(\frac{R}{Y}\right)_t = \alpha m_t, \tag{2}$$

where $0 < \alpha < 1$ in a progressive tax system. Since $g_t = r_t$, then, from Equation (1), both average and marginal tax rates will rise with incomes if $b > 0$ in Equation (1).

To capture the hypothesis that government spending and/or taxes affect income growth, further assume, in a simplification of the Barro (1990) model, that changes in income are affected by these government size measures in the previous period. This can arise from the combined (positive and/or negative) effects of changes in government expenditures and the (presumed negative) effect of changes in effective marginal tax rates. Hence:

$$\Delta Y_t = Y_t - Y_{t-1} = c + d_1 g_{t-1} + d_2 m_{t-1}, \tag{3}$$

where c is an autonomous rate of change of income, determined outside this model. Using Equation (2), Equation (3) can be rewritten as:

$$\Delta Y_t = c + d_1 g_{t-1} + \left(\frac{d_2}{\alpha}\right) r_{t-1} = c + d g_{t-1}, \tag{3'}$$

where $d = \{d_1 + d_2/\alpha\}$ captures the *net* effect of government spending and taxes on the change in income. Though we might expect $d_2 < 0$ if taxes have a negative growth impact (via incentive effects), d_1 is harder to sign but will depend on the positive, zero or negative growth effects associated with various types of public expenditure. Infrastructure expenditure, for example, may boost income levels while others, such as welfare subsidies, may reduce them. Hence, the sign of d in Equation (3') is ambiguous.

Using Equations (1), (2) and (3') it can be shown that:

$$r_t = g_t = a' + b(1 + bd)Y_{t-1}, \tag{4}$$

where $a' = \{a(1 + bd) + bc\}$. With the parameter d ambiguously signed, and $b > 0$, the parameter on Y_{t-1}, $b(1 + bd)$, is therefore also ambiguously signed.

Though simple, Equation (4) illustrates a number of insights into the relationship between GDP and government size. Firstly, in the absence of deficit financing (strictly, in the absence of fiscal deficits rising or falling with income levels), any observed association between income levels and government expenditure/income ratios, g_t, can be expected also to be observed for the equivalent relationship with tax revenue/income ratios, r_t.

Secondly, since $b(1 + bd)$ in Equation (4) may be positively or negatively signed but $b > 0$ in Equation (1) then expected relationships between the government size variables (g_t or r_t) and income levels depend crucially on the particular income lag structure chosen – Y_t or Y_{t-1}. However, consider the typical case where income is growing over time; that is, $Y_t > Y_{t-1}$. In this case any negative effect on growth from government size (if $d < 0$, in Equation (3)) is insufficient to outweigh the positive impact of $c > 0$ in Equation (3').

It can be shown that, for this (typical) case, even if $d < 0$, $b(1 + bd) > 0$ and hence we can expect to observe a positive association between g_t and Y_{t-1} in Equation (4) as well as between g_t and Y_t shown in Equation (1).[15] Different countries may, of course, have different values of the parameter d depending, for example, on the form of public expenditure, the quality of the institutions delivering it. The key point here however is that, even for common negative values of d across countries, the negative association between (lagged) government spending and/or taxes and current income levels, for given lagged values of income (as captured in the structural relationships in Equations (3) and (3′)), would not be identified by either current or lagged relationships between government size and income levels as shown in the simple forms in Equations (1) or (4).[16]

To illustrate how different possible causal impacts of government size on income changes (captured by d) might show up when cross-country relationships between income levels and government size are examined, we explore three cases: a negative, zero and positive value of d. Figure 7 illustrates these cases (which may be thought of as different countries) based on values of the parameters as follows: $a = 0.1$; $b = 0.001$; $c = 50$ and $d = -100, 0, +100$. Four time periods are considered with initial values of $Y_0 = 100$, $g_0 = 0.2$. For the case of no impact of government size on growth ($d = 0$), income is assumed to rise exogenously by 50 units per period. Both panels in Figure 7 plot resulting income levels against the expenditure share, g ($= G/Y$) over the four periods. The left-hand panel compares the case of $d = 0$ with $d = 100$, and the right-hand panel compares $d = 0$ with $d = -100$.

It can be seen that all three countries display identically positively sloping relationships between income levels and government size, as measured by the spending share in income. Simple within-country time-series, or cross-section (for a single period), or combined analysis in a panel would identify a positive association between government size and income levels. This is despite the fact that, in any causal sense, government size is variously harmful, irrelevant or enhancing for income levels over time for the three countries. Rather, what distinguishes the three countries is the *rate of progress* of income levels due to government size effects, d. A key insight from Figure 7, therefore, is that a cross-country analysis of income levels is incapable of identifying any causal impact of government size on (subsequent) income levels. This is compounded when it is recognised that autonomous influences on government size, represented by the parameter a in Equation (1), and contained within a' in Equation (4), are likely to differ across countries such that there could be a series of positively sloping lines for different countries in Figure 7.

Figure 8 shows the implied relationships between *changes* in income levels and government size for the same three countries. As expected there is a difference in slope between the three countries, with negative, zero and positive slopes for the $d = -100, 0, 100$ examples respectively. Notice that the three lines are 'shifted' relative to each other, as well as revealing slope differences, even though all other parameters except d are common across the three countries. It might be thought that these slope differences (between cases of 'no government effect', and 'some government effect', on output) would allow these relationships to be identified in $(\Delta Y, g)$ space. However, once again, with different values of d likely across countries, any set of cross-section, time-series observations, such as in Figure 5, is unlikely to display a simple pattern. As in Figure 7, different autonomous sources of growth in different countries (parameter c values) would produce further diversity in the $(\Delta Y, g)$ space in Figure 8.

These graphs highlight a further insight from Equation (4) – namely countries may differ in the values of any or all of the four critical parameters: a, b, c and d (as well as further parameters in a more fully specified model).[17] To the extent that they do, further combinations of line shifts and slopes in Figures 7 and 8 will occur, making identification of reliable aggregate cross-country relationships harder. While in principle, we might hope to control for other non-government-related factors affecting income levels and growth rates, in practice it is likely to be difficult. This is not simply a matter of poor 'signal to noise' ratios due to random unobserved heterogeneity across countries, but also reflects differences in

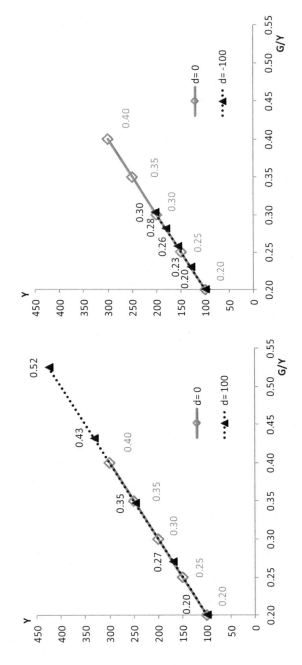

Figure 7. Illustrating government size and output levels.

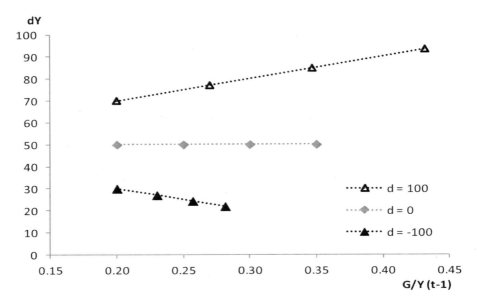

Figure 8. Illustrating government size and output growth.

the underlying hypothesised relationships across countries (such as differences in the mix of growth-enhancing and growth-retarding types of public spending or the distortionary impacts of different types of taxes). Though the illustrations above have not included budget deficits, where these are relevant they can be thought of as simply another form of distortionary taxation.

To sum up, this simple illustration emphasises why cross-country, or pooled cross-country/time-series data on government size and income levels or growth rates can readily present confused, apparently inconsistent patterns, with what would appear to be 'noise'. It also stresses the importance of careful theorising before seeking to identify relationships empirically. For example, reduced form relationships that do not pay careful attention to the lag structure that emerges from the theory are likely to be mis-specified.

While much of the early (approximately, pre-1990) empirical literature based on period averages of cross-country data yielded a confused picture, more recent studies have sought to deal with some of the problems identified above. For example, panel econometric methods are now better able to deal with cross-country heterogeneity, methods of controlling for fiscal and non-fiscal determinants of growth have improved, and improved tests for, and treatment of, endogeneity concerns between income and government size. In general, as Figures 7 and 8 illustrate, it is likely to be easier to identify the associations between government size and income *growth rates* rather than with income *levels*, provided care is taken in allowing for country-specific effects.

4. Evidence from recent studies

Gemmell (2004) argued that empirical 'fiscal policy and growth' evidence could usefully be categorised as 'first, second and third generation' studies. First generation studies (approximately, pre-1990) were generally motivated, at least formally, by little or no theory. To the extent that they were, this often took the form of various, broadly defined, public choice arguments or hypotheses that predicted a negative association between government size and economic prosperity. Empirical methods were generally cross-section in nature and poorly specified regressions with results, not surprisingly, non-robust. In our view they are worth little as a guide to expected or observed relationships.

Second generation empirical studies (mainly during the 1990s) began to be informed by emerging endogenous growth theory and refinements of the neoclassical model, following Barro (1990), King and Rebelo (1990), Baxter and King (1993) and others. These and other papers provided clearer theoretical foundations both for the basic hypothesis that government fiscal policy could affect long-run, steady-state growth rates, and identified specific channels through which this might occur. Alternative models predicted only transitional effects but these, it was shown, could be expected to last over several decades for plausible values of key parameters (Turnovsky 2004).

Empirical studies, however, continued to be based loosely at best on theoretical insights, generally continued to use cross-section econometric methods applied to limited datasets, and tended to use regression specifications with many fiscal variables apparently selected on an *ad hoc* basis rather than derived from specific theoretical frameworks. Again, results appeared non-robust, though Kneller, Bleaney, and Gemmell (1999) argued that at least some apparent non-robustness reflected failure to account properly for the GBC which led authors to misinterpret their own estimates.

Gemmell (2004) defines the 'third generation' of long-run cross-country studies (generally post-2000) as those that meet three conditions. They: (i) recognise the implications for testing of the GBC; (ii) allow for potential growth differences from the tax/spending *decompositions* suggested by theory; and (iii) use panel or time-series rather than cross-section methods.[18] Gemmell, Kneller, and Sanz (2011a) argue that this third generation evidence appears more robust than suggested by earlier approaches, but doubts regarding the reliability of even this evidence persist. This stems from a number of features that still afflict aggregate-level evidence on fiscal policy and growth including: (a) limited evidence for public expenditures compared to tax (the opposite is generally true for evidence on short-run 'fiscal shocks' – see below); (b) conceptual and measurement problems regarding appropriate 'tax rates'; and (c) difficulties distinguishing supply-side, from demand-side, effects of fiscal policy; see Romer and Romer (2010).

Below we summarise some recent evidence from research into the long-run impacts of fiscal policy on growth, not all of which would qualify as 'third generation'. Firstly, in the next sub-section, we briefly describe recent empirical approaches to measuring short-run impacts of fiscal policy.

4.1. *Short-run evidence from vector auto regression studies*

Due to limited space, this paper focuses on the evidence concerning longer-run impacts of government on growth, but a number of developments in short-run modelling have had influences on the methodologies used to examine these long-run relationships.[19]

Blanchard and Perotti (2002) introduced the Structural Vector Auto Regression (SVAR) approach to the study of the output effects of fiscal policy and marked a watershed in this empirical literature. In particular, despite long neo-classical and Keynesian traditions supporting possible output effects over the short-run from fiscal policy stimuli or 'shocks', reliable evidence measuring these effects was limited prior to around the year 2000. As Blanchard and Perotti (2002, 1329) note:

> the evidence from large-scale econometric models has been largely dismissed on the grounds that, because of their Keynesian structure, these models assume rather than document a positive effect of fiscal expansions on output.[20]

Subsequent developments in SVAR modelling have been considerable, both in terms of methodological improvements and the scope of empirical estimates for individual and groups of countries. In addition, so-called 'event studies', such as war episodes, and 'narrative approaches' have begun to provide a range of possible approaches to the identification of the output responses to fiscal policy, both short-run and longer-run.[21] While a review of the results of the numerous studies using these approaches is beyond the scope of the present paper, a number of features already strand out.

Firstly, because the short-run predictions of neo-classical and New Keynesian models differ in a number of respects, these approaches are, in principle, capable of testing their predictions empirically. Secondly, they provide better methods of testing or controlling for endogeneity (at least in a statistical sense) than has so far been possible in most of the aggregate long-run growth literature. They might, therefore, hope to provide insights into causal impacts rather than simple 'associations'.

Thirdly, most of the evidence from the SVAR literature (and to some extent also for the narrative/event approaches) relates to effects from public expenditure shocks, with less evidence for taxation. To the extent that taxation impacts are examined the same methodological problems mentioned above regarding endogeneity and measurement of tax rates applies. Indeed for tax shocks, results are more often non-robust and/or counter-intuitive; see, for example, Auerbach and Gorodnichenko (2010) and Fielding, Parkyn, and Gardiner (2011) for US and New Zealand evidence respectively. Arguably problems of endogenous tax revenues and tax rate measurement are harder to overcome in this literature since the ability of SVAR approaches to model feedback to tax revenues from other variables in the VAR, requires an endogenous revenue variable, rather than a marginal or average tax rate, measure. However, it is the latter that are most likely to capture the direct or exogenous output effects from discretionary *tax policy* changes.

Fourthly, in order to test for short-run fiscal impacts many SVAR models apply methods that impose convergence to a 'no impact' long-run equilibrium. Such models are, therefore, incapable of identifying any long-run effects of fiscal policy imbedded in the data. Nevertheless, since most models test for the effects of 'one-off' or temporary expenditure or revenue shock (as opposed to permanent changes) such fiscal policy innovations would not be expected to have long-run impacts. They are, however, compatible with the long-run fiscal-growth literature which generally seeks to estimate effects from persistent changes in fiscal policy. Surprisingly, Auerbach and Gorodnichenko (2010) appears to be the only empirical study to demonstrate how different phases of the business cycle are associated with quantitatively different fiscal responses (large in recessions, small in expansions). There is, of course, no equivalent in the long-run response literature.

4.2. *Long-run evidence from panel studies*

As noted above, recent studies into the longer-run impacts of government on growth have increasingly used panel data methods and have generally focussed on the impact of taxes (as opposed to expenditures) on growth. Table 2, adapted from Kneller and Misch (2011), lists panel studies which have examined the long-run effects and identifies whether they explicitly consider the GBC and/or allow for dynamics; that is, they allow for short/long-run differences. Kneller and Misch's selection criterion required that the parameter estimates obtained by each study were capable of being used to make direct inferences regarding the growth impacts of tax reforms capable of being replicated in practice.[22]

The table shows that a large number of studies continue to ignore the GBC in empirical specifications, making interpretation difficult and the actual tax reform harder to identify

Table 2. Overview of recent panel studies.

Paper	Data	GBC explicitly considered?	Short-run effects considered?
Cross-country			
Aiginger and Falk (2005)	All OECD, 1970–1999, 5-year averages	no	no
Angelopoulos, Economides, and Kammas (2007)	23 OECD, 1970–2000, 5-year averages	no	no
Arin (2004)	G7, 1965–2000, 5-year averages/annual cyclically adj.	no	no
Arin, Berlemann, and Koray (2011)	UK, US, Scandinavia, 1960–2004, annual/3-year averages	no	no
Arnold (2008)	21 OECD, 1971–2004, annual	yes	yes
Romero-Ávila and Strauch (2007)	EU-15, 1971–2001, annual/cyclically adj.	no	no
Benos (2009)	14 EU, 1990–2006, annual	yes	no
Bleaney, Gemmell, and Kneller (2001)	OECD, 5-year averages and annual data	yes	yes
Castro (2006)	EU-15 (except Lux.), 1970–2000, 5-year averages	no	no
Colombier (2009)	21 OECD, 1970–2001	no	no
Doménech and García (2001)	OECD, 1960–1995, 5-year averages	no	no
Gemmell, Kneller, and Sanz (2011a, 2011b)	17 OECD, late 1970s–2004, annual	yes	yes
Kneller, Bleaney, and Gemmell (1999)	22 OECD, 1970–1995, 5-year averages	yes	no
Muinelo-Gallo and Roca-Sagales (2011)	45 middle/high income countries, 1972–2006, 5-year averages	yes	no
Padovano and Galli (2002)	25 developed countries, 1970–1998, 10-year averages	no	no
Widmalm (2001)	23 OECD, 1965–1990, 5-year averages	no	no
Sub-national			
Bania, Gray, and Stone (2007)	49 US states, 1962–1997, 5-year averages	no	no
Dahlby and Ferede (2008)	Canadian provinces, 1977–2006, 5-year averages	no	no
Denaux (2005)	North Carolina Counties, 1980–1995	no	no
Denaux, Cunningham, and Allen (2005)	48 US states, 1969–1988	no	no
Miyakoshi et al. (2007)	Japanese prefectures, annual	no	no
Reed (2008)	48 US states, 1970–1999, 5-year averages	no	no

Source: Adapted from Kneller and Misch (2011, 27).

and replicate. An even larger number of panel studies still do not consider the dynamic effects of tax reforms such that the timeframe over which so-called 'long run' effects occur is often unclear. Nevertheless, there are a number of exceptions, most notably Arnold (2008) and Gemmell, Kneller, and Sanz (2011a).

Results from some of those panel studies on the long-run impact of personal and corporate income taxes, and the broader category of 'distortionary taxes' are summarised in Table 3, as sourced and adapted from Kneller and Misch (2011). These consistently estimate the long-run effect of personal taxation on output levels or growth rates to be negative. Several measures of the personal income tax burden were examined including effective rates, implicit average rates, top statutory rates and the share of personal income tax in total tax revenue. For corporate taxation, the estimated effects on output in general are similarly negative and the estimates are often larger than for personal taxes. Nevertheless, some studies such as Angelopoulos, Economides, and Kammas (2007) find somewhat perverse results for corporate taxation (e.g. incorrect signs).

For distortionary taxes overall, the effect of an increase in taxation on growth can appear relatively, perhaps implausibly, large. For example, Bleaney, Gemmell, and Kneller (2001) estimate tax-growth parameters at around -0.4 (an increase in the ratio of distortionary tax revenues to GDP of 1% is associated with a fall in long-run growth rates of 0.4 percentage points). However, this effect occurs in conjunction with a similarly sized effect of opposite sign from productive public expenditure increases (estimated distortionary tax-growth effects differ depending on which type of public spending is included in regressions). The combined effect of these two (tax, expenditure) changes appears to approximately cancel out in practice such that observed net effects on long-run growth are small. More recent estimates for similar specifications and samples reveal smaller parameters – around -0.07 to -0.15 (Gemmell, Kneller, and Sanz 2011a, 2011b). Overall, the greater consistency of the results from recent panel studies gives us more confidence that at least the *direction* of the long-run growth effects can be predicted with a reasonable degree of certainty. Furthermore, the size of the effect on output is also now more similar between different panel studies with differences potentially explained by differences in samples, measurement of fiscal variables or the assumed offsetting change.

4.3. *Evidence from two recent studies*

Of the research mentioned above, two recent studies offer evidence that seeks to shed light simultaneously on the short-run and long-run responses of output to fiscal policy. Romer and Romer (R&R, 2010) use both ordinary least squares (OLS) and fiscal VAR methods applied to quarterly US data (1947–2005) to examine short-run fiscal responses and their persistence over longer periods. Gemmell, Kneller, and Sanz (2011a) use the methodology of long-run growth regressions applied to annual data for a panel of OECD countries (1970–2004), allowing for dynamic responses that can vary across countries in the short-run.

Each study benefits and suffers from the strengths and weaknesses of their respective approaches as described above, but both tell a broadly similar story — of statistically significant initial output responses to tax shocks that appear to persist over a number of years. However, the 'motivation' for tax changes and the GBC matter; for example, whether fiscal changes involve attempts to reduce fiscal deficits, fund additional spending or achieve higher growth. We discuss the results from each of those studies by focusing on the key conclusions that emerge from them.

Table 3. Summary of recent panel estimates of growth effects of taxation.

Study	Angelopoulos et al. (2007)	Arin (2004)	Dahlby and Ferede (2008)	Gemmell, Kneller, and Sanz (2011b)	Gemmell, Kneller, and Sanz (2011b)	Arnold (2008)	Arnold (2008)	Arnold (2008)	Arnold (2008)	Arnold (2008)	Arnold (2008)
Personal income taxation											
Tax measure	'effective'	IATR	top statutory	top statutory	top statutory	% total tax	% total tax	% total tax	% total tax	% total tax	% total tax
Log/level	levels	levels	levels	levels	levels	log-levels	log-level	log-level	log-level	log-level	log-level
Coefficient low	−0.174	−0.199	−0.065	−0.033	−0.039	−1.13	−0.2	−1.01	−0.96	−1.35	
high	−0.118		−0.054	−0.018	−0.034						
Corporate income taxation											
Tax measures	top statutory		top statutory	statutory	effective	% total tax	% total tax	% total tax	% total tax		
Log/level	levels		levels	levels	levels	log-level	log-level	log-level	log-level		
Coefficient low	0.047		−0.158	−0.129	−0.161	−2.01	−1.18	−2.04	−2.4		
high			−0.108	−0.035	−0.056						
Study	Romero-Ávila and Strauch (2008)	Benos (2009)	Gemmell, Kneller, and Sanz (2011a)	Gemmell, Kneller, and Sanz (2011b)	Bleaney, Gemmell, and Kneller (2001)	Bleaney, Gemmell, and Kneller (2001)	Kneller, Bleaney, and Gemmell (1999)	Kneller, Bleaney, and Gemmell (1999)	Kneller, Bleaney, and Gemmell (1999)	Arnold (2008)	
Distortionary taxation											
Tax measures	IATR	IATR	IATR	IATR	IATR	IATR	IATR	IATR	IATR	% total tax	
Log/level	logs	levels	levels	levels	log-level	log-level	log-level	log-level	log-level	log-level	
Coefficient low	−0.04	−1.516	−0.139	−0.132	−0.854	−0.427	−0.467	−0.463	−0.446	−0.98	
high	0.05	−0.077	−0.073	−0.033	−0.411	−0.393	−0.410	−0.410	−0.427	−0.28	

Source: Adapted from Kneller and Misch (2011, 28–32).

Table 4. GDP level effects of 1% distortionary tax changes (in percent).

Number of years after tax change	1	5	10	15	20
OECD average	−0.6	−2.0	−3.2	−4.4	−5.5
Canada	−1.8	−2.3	−3.4	−4.6	−5.8
US	−1.5	−4.2	−5.8	−7.3	−8.4
France	−0.7	−0.7	−1.9	−3.0	−4.2
UK	−0.5	−1.6	−2.4	−3.6	−4.7
Australia	−1.0	−1.0	−2.1	−3.3	−4.5
New Zealand	−0.4	−1.6	−2.8	−4.0	−5.1
US					
Romer and Romer (2010)	−1.0	−2.0*	—	—	—
Turnovsky and Chatterjii (2002)	−0.6	−1.3	−1.8	−2.2	−2.5

Note: *Maximum estimated impact is 2.9% after 3 years.
Source: Adapted from Gemmell, Kneller, and Sanz (2011a, F51).

(1) *Tax changes have observable impacts on aggregate output.*
For the US, R&R (2010, 799) find that

> results indicate that tax changes have very large effects on output. ... an exogenous tax increase of one percent of GDP lowers real GDP by almost three percent. Our many robustness checks for the most part point to a slightly smaller decline, but one that is still typically over 2.5 percent. In addition, ... investment falls sharply in response to exogenous tax increases.

Though these effects relate to relatively short periods (R&R's maximum impacts occur after 12 quarters and simulations are only reported for up to 20 quarters), there is no suggestion that the observed effects decay to zero after the simulated 5 years. They are also broadly consistent with the results for a sample of OECD countries reported by Gemmell, Kneller, and Sanz (2011a), reproduced here as Table 4. The effects shown there are effects on the level of GDP for a 1% of GDP increase in distortionary tax revenues, derived from growth regressions, for up to 20 years after the tax change. While the estimates for the US are somewhat larger than the R&R estimates, for OECD countries on average results are broadly similar. (Note R&R's tax changes include all Federal tax changes but should be broadly comparable to the Gemmell et al. 'distortionary' tax changes).[23]

(2) *Failure to deal with endogeneity will lead to underestimates of tax-growth effects.*
R&R (2010) establish, firstly, that it is important to strip out exogenous changes in tax revenue from all observed changes, where the former are those legislated tax changes that were not motivated by prior changes in output (e.g. due to recessionary factors). Total tax revenues (R&R work with a cyclically adjusted total) may, therefore, be decomposed into those due to legislated tax changes and the sub-set of 'exogenous' legislated tax changes, with the remainder reflecting endogenous revenue responses. These series were created using their 'narrative approach' which involved scrutinising Federal Budget documents to identify both the magnitude of, and motivation for, legislated tax changes. Figure 9, reproduced from R&R (2010), shows that the 'exogenous' distinction matters a great deal for the resulting measures of tax change. They also show that a comparable measure capturing *all* legislated tax changes (as opposed to only those designated as exogenous) follows a quite different pattern from either of the other two revenue measures.

When the output effects associated with the 'exogenous' tax measures are compared with those obtained from the total 'cyclically adjusted revenues' measure, the

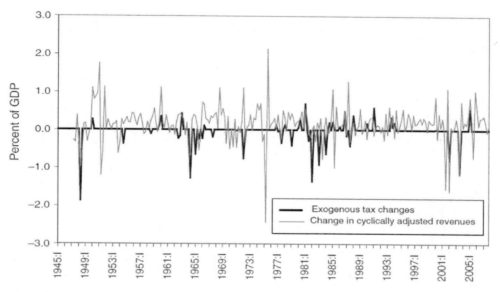

Figure 9. Romer and Romer's (2010) tax change measures.
Source: Romer and Romer (2010, 779).

estimated output effects are much larger, and identified more precisely, with the former. That is, failure to account for the endogeneity embedded in actual revenue data is more likely to lead to the false conclusion that taxes have only small, or no, effects on output. For their OECD sample, Gemmell, Kneller, and Sanz (2011a, F59) also report some evidence of larger estimated tax effects on output growth when using methods that deal better with endogeneity aspects.

(3) *Allowing for each element of the government budget matters.*

As we noted earlier, the fact that the government budget is an accounting identity means that changes in one element must be matched by an equal and opposite net change across all other elements. Despite this, many authors of fiscal-growth studies interpret their results in terms of, for example, 'the effect of a tax change'. This only makes sense if the specific tax change, and the opposing changes are specified (except in the unlikely case where all possible opposing changes have identical effects). Thus, a reduction in tax rates which lowers tax revenue must be associated with a larger fiscal deficit or lower public spending, or both. The results of both R&R and Gemmell et al. confirm that this particular distinction is especially important for the estimated growth effects of fiscal policy changes.

R&R (2010, 786–7) report that when exogenous tax increases are 'motivated' by a need/desire to reduce fiscal deficits, as distinct from a motivation to raise long-run growth rates, the output effects are quite different. For the latter category, output effects are almost identical to those for exogenous tax changes overall; i.e. around a 3% reduction in output in response to a 1% increase in tax revenue. However, where deficit reduction is the motivation, around a 1–2% *increase* in output is observed when taxes rise by 1% with the impact tending, if anything, to increase, rather than decline, over time. This evidence, therefore, suggests strongly that reducing US fiscal deficits is growth-enhancing even though this involves raising taxes: deficits (together with pre-reformed taxes) are more growth-retarding than the combination of higher post-reform taxes and lower deficits.

This result is mirrored in Gemmell, Kneller, and Sanz (2011a, F41) for the OECD. Their results demonstrate that, when splitting the government budget into five elements (more/less distortionary taxes, productive/unproductive spending and deficits), the estimated growth effects observed depend on the various *combinations* of budget change, as indicated in Table 4. For example, on average across the OECD sample, raising more distortionary (mainly income) taxes to fund cuts in less distortionary (mainly consumption) taxes or to increase unproductive government expenditure appears to be around twice as harmful for long-run growth rates compared to when the tax increase funds a reduction in fiscal deficits. The authors argue that a rough ranking of taxes and deficits (from largest to smallest) in terms of their growth effects is: more distortionary taxes → deficits → less distortionary taxes, where each option finances the same total and mix of public spending.

(4) *Observed fiscal policy (tax/expenditure/deficit) changes overall do not have large effects on observed long-run GDP growth rates.*

Jones (1995) and Karras (1999) argued that evidence of non-stationarity in investment/GDP ratios (Jones) and total tax/GDP ratios (Karras) in many countries is at odds with evidence of stationarity in GDP growth rates, if the former were thought to cause the latter. Indeed, Jones argues that the former cannot plausibly explain the latter, unless *'by some astonishing coincidence all of the movements in variables that can have permanent effects on growth rates have been offsetting'* (Jones 1995, 496). This might appear to be a damning critique of the argument that fiscal policy has persistent or 'permanent' impacts on GDP growth rates.[24] However, there are at least two reasons why stationary long-run growth rates may be consistent with the evidence of persistent effects from fiscal policy from R&R (2010), Gemmell, Kneller, and Sanz (2011a) and others.

Firstly, OECD evidence suggests a clear tendency for so-called 'productive' public spending to be positively associated with long-run GDP growth rates, while distortionary taxes are negatively associated, such that in combination there are negligible long-run growth effects (Gemmell, Kneller, and Sanz 2011a, F50). With all changes in net tax revenues being offset by spending and/or deficit changes it is not surprising that the net growth effects largely 'wash out'. This is quite consistent with a finding that reforms involving a particular type of tax funding of a particular composition of public expenditure can have a non-zero impact on GDP over the short- or long-run.

Secondly, the evidence suggests that many changes in fiscal variables, and especially exogenous changes, have often not persisted. Hence, even if in principle such fiscal changes would have persistent effects on GDP levels or growth rates, short-run reversals of these fiscal changes will similarly reverse the initial impact on GDP. R&R's (2010) US data in particular show that substantial quarterly increases in tax revenues (as a percentage of GDP) are frequently followed by reverse movements soon thereafter, while their measure of exogenous tax changes display relatively few, intermittent and temporary changes in either direction (see Figure 9).

5. Limitations

The evidence reviewed in Section 4 would appear to suggest stronger support than previously acknowledged for at least some of the alleged relationships between government size or other aspects of fiscal policy and output at the macro-level. Nevertheless, there are a number of reasons to exercise some caution in interpreting the results of even the more robust recent evidence as confirming non-zero output effects of fiscal policy, especially over the longer-run.

Issues of interpretation continue to pose difficulties with the current evidence principally for two reasons. Firstly, specifying the GBC suitably in empirical studies can be problematic yet interpretation of parameters depends crucially on knowing how the GBC is affected by different specific fiscal policy changes. Secondly, interpretation of results that may be subject to endogeneity problems continues to pose some difficulties for authors of aggregate-level studies and allows some scepticism of their results to persist.

Sceptics, however, typically query whether estimated parameters on fiscal variables in output or growth regressions that demonstrate statistically significant non-zero estimates, genuinely capture non-zero effects. This fails to recognise that, to the extent that *tax* measures (often revenue-based) are subject to endogeneity, this is expected to bias the estimated parameter towards zero. Romer and Romer's (2010) evidence, for example, supports the view that endogeneity leads to *under*-estimates of the absolute value of tax effects on output and other macro-aggregates. For government expenditures the issue is less straightforward since the sign of any bias depends on the how particular expenditures are expected to change in response to rising income levels.

Identifying and using the 'right' tax rates remains problematic. In the case of fiscal VARs, modelling of *tax* shocks is especially unsatisfactory because of their reliance on revenue-based tax measures. While modelling the endogenous response of tax *revenue* to an exogenous expenditure change may be the appropriate procedure to capture the feedbacks on fiscal budgets and output via demand pressures, it is not the appropriate way to capture responses to exogenous tax shocks. Perhaps it is not surprising then that several VAR studies have found perverse (i.e. positively signed) output effects from tax increases. Tellingly, Romer and Romer's (2010) fiscal VAR for the US obtains the expected negative sign using their measure of 'exogenous' tax revenue changes but not for their measure of total revenue changes.

In the case of long-run growth regressions, tax rates are also often measured from a revenue-based variable so hampering interpretation of results. However, as Gemmell, Kneller, and Sanz (2011a, 2011b) demonstrate, results using better measures of effective marginal and average tax rates – for personal and corporate income taxes – continue to support previous evidence of long-run negative, if quantitatively small, tax-growth effects. Nevertheless, evidence on the output or growth effects of reliably exogenous effective marginal (or average) tax rates remains limited.

A surprising aspect of much of the VAR and growth regression evidence is the lack of an *international dimension* with many models either implicitly or explicitly 'closed economy'. This is despite the increasing evidence over the last several decades of global flows that can be expected to give rise to 'fiscal leakages' and increased co-determination of fiscal policy settings such as corporate tax rates across countries (see, for example, Devereux, Lockwood, and Redoano 2008). Beetsma and Giuliodori (2011) and Gemmell, Kneller, and Sanz (2011b) are two of the small number of recent studies that explicitly seek to incorporate these international aspects.

Another limitation arises as a consequence of the widespread use of 'tax revenue' or tax revenue/GDP measures. These measures are not direct discretionary policy instruments and hence provide little guidance regarding how *actual* fiscal instruments can be suitably reformed. Finance Ministers, if they are to enact tax policy reform typically need to know: *'if a single tax rate is cut by y%, or several tax rates are simultaneously cut by x, y, z%, what will be the effects on output growth over the next 5 (or more/fewer) years?'* and *'what are the impacts of alternative revenue-neutral tax rate and/or other tax parameter reforms?'*.

Currently available parameter point estimates that could be applied to address such questions are not generally available or are not precise enough to provide narrow prediction 'cones' for effects on GDP. Moreover, most available parameter estimates are averages across episodes, countries or states, and their reliability in a given condition in a specific country, time or region can be unclear. The challenge for evidence-based fiscal policy reform is to quantify tax/spending reform impacts on output in ways that will allow policy-makers to compare alternative fiscal and other policy reforms in a quantitatively robust manner.

Finally, single country SVARs and 'narrative' studies, such as Romer and Romer (2010) who combine both methods, are probably the most reliable methodologies where it is desired to identify fiscal-growth effects up to a horizon of five years or so. However, even here, most studies have largely ignored the possibility that these effects differ depending on the *degree* of disequilibrium in the economy. The recent paper by Auerbach and Gorodnichenko (2010) appears to be the first formally to try to quantify such differences (for the US). They argue, with empirical support, that this distinction may matter a great deal.

6. Conclusions

We began this paper with the objective of answering three questions relating to the relationships between government size, fiscal policy and output levels or growth rates:

(1) how robust or consistent are the results from recent macro-level studies?;
(2) do these results justify a less sceptical verdict than emerged from earlier reviews such as Slemrod (1995) and Myles (2000)?; and
(3) are these results sufficient to be useful as a guide to fiscal policy reform in practice?

In summary, we have argued that the theory on the output effects of fiscal policy has developed considerably since the time of Slemrod's writing and this theory has increasingly been taken seriously in specifying empirical tests. Undoubtedly, improvements in panel datasets (both across countries and within them), and methods to analyse them, have also helped to address some of the criticisms levelled by Slemrod (1995) at the mainly cross-section empirical evidence available at that time. Partly as a result, the last decade or so appears to have produced more robust evidence on the impacts of taxes and public expenditures on GDP at the macro-level.

The last decade has also seen much greater application of time-series, mainly VAR, methods to examine shorter-run impacts of fiscal policy. Together with greater use of dynamic specifications in long-run panel regression studies, this research has now established clearer evidence of short-run output effects from fiscal policy that demonstrate some persistence – at least up to five years and probably longer.

Our overall conclusion is that, despite some remaining 'big issues', results from aggregate-level studies are now much more robustly in favour of identifiable effects of government size on income growth rates, provided these conclusions are carefully circumscribed in ways that we have discussed. In general, positive output effects from increases in at least some public expenditures and negative output effects from higher tax rates are supported. Plausible orders of magnitude are also beginning to emerge suggesting that the impacts of fiscal policy may be sizeable in the short-run (but depend, among other things, on the degree of excess capacity in the economy), and are probably moderate or small in the longer-run. Importantly, long-run *net* fiscal effects on output are often small or negligible when the more sizeable effects of taxes, expenditures or deficits measured *in isolation*, are instead considered in *combination*, as they should be.

Question marks remain over the reliability of estimates of tax effects on output versus public spending effects on output. Within the VAR literature on short-run output responses, evidence on expenditure shocks is both more extensive and seems to be more robust than equivalent evidence for tax shocks. In the long-run growth regression literature the reverse is probably true – it has generally proved easier to identify negative tax-growth impacts than to identify growth impacts from public expenditures. This may partly reflect the fact that the expected sign of the former is unambiguously negative, whereas expenditure effects on growth are ambiguously signed. A major weakness of almost all recent research is that its value remains limited as an evidence-base for robust quantitative predictions of the output responses to changes in the specific tax policy instruments that are typically available to governments undertaking fiscal reform in practice.

Much debate has surrounded how far existing evidence supports neo-Keynesian, neo-classical or endogenous growth model specifications. To some extent the answer to this question depends on the in/out-of steady-state issue mentioned above. However, much of the debate has also sought to shed light on whether, and how far, observed fiscal-growth effects represent demand-side or supply-side responses in the economy. The difficulties of this exercise are summed up by Romer and Romer (2010, 799) who acknowledge:

> *our results are largely silent concerning whether the output effects operate through incentives and supply behavior or through disposable income and demand stimulus. The persistence of the effects is suggestive of supply effects. But other studies have found that monetary policy, which necessarily works through demand, also has highly persistent output effects. The speed of the effects is suggestive of demand effects. But rapid supply responses are not out of the question.*

We began by suggesting that a knowledge of the OECD evidence on the 'government and growth' debate would be beneficial for policy-makers and advisors in AP countries. Clearly the relevance of the evidence from individual or 'average' OECD countries for specific, or groups of, AP economies will be quite different and depend on a variety of institutional differences. However, some lessons would seem to have general applicability.

Firstly, cross-country correlations are likely to provide little assistance and can be positively misleading, especially where interest focuses on understanding the impact of changes in government size *within* a country.

Secondly, when looking for relationships between government size and income variables, the tendency for these two variables to be mutually reinforcing ('endogeneity') often appears to be important, and ignoring this can readily lead to false conclusions from the data. If AP countries experience the increased demands for some publicly supplied services in association with income growth that has been observed in some OECD countries, then this will similarly complicate identifying any causal relationships from government size (or growth) to GDP. A balance may need to be struck between a desire for more and better public services and the subsequent growth consequences of the resulting public spending and tax choices.

Thirdly, the fairly wide-ranging support for adverse effects of taxes on aggregate output (in addition to more extensive micro-level evidence on behavioural responses to taxes) suggests that policy-makers in AP countries should be cautious about raising potentially growth-retarding distortionary taxes. However, the small *net* growth impacts of larger public expenditures, deficits and tax revenues estimated for OECD countries caution against expecting a sustainable increase in government size (i.e. one that is not financed longer-term by increased deficits) to have substantial long-run effects, either growth-enhancing or retarding.

Finally, evidence is still scarce on how far the *institutions* of government, the *quality* of those institutions (including such things as corruption among government officials) and the degree of non-fiscal government interventions such as business regulation affect aggregate income levels or growth rates. Most OECD countries have developed those institutions over a long period of time and at least some evidence suggests that institutions such as the 'rule of law' and government corruption are among the 'necessary but not sufficient' conditions required for public spending to affect private sector investment or productivity positively.[25] AP countries may, therefore, do more to achieve or maintain high economic growth rates by ensuring that key governance-related institutions are maintained or developed than by modest changes to the level or structure of public expenditures and taxes.

Acknowledgements

The authors are grateful for helpful comments on an earlier draft of this paper from Professor Noel Gaston, an anonymous referee of *this journal*, and participants at the First Annual Workshop, on *Economic and Policy Developments in East Asia*, held at Bond University, Gold Coast, Australia (October 2011). The views expressed in this article are those of the authors and do not necessarily represent those of the New Zealand Treasury.

Notes

1. See also Myles (2000).
2. The distinction here between effects on income 'levels' or 'growth rates' is essentially a distinction between short-run, *temporary* effects on income growth which lead to permanent changes in income *levels*, versus persistent effects on income growth that thus have 'permanent' (or at least long-lasting) effects on income *growth rates*.
3. Similar patterns are found if 2007, rather than 2009, is used suggesting that the observed patterns are not specific to the post-2008 global recession period. Furthermore, averaging the data over the 1995–2009 period reveals similar patterns.
4. For the same sample of OECD countries, the T/Y ratio is heavily concentrated within a very small interval, largely falling within 15%–30%.
5. Statistically, weak negative associations are obtained in both cases, not significant at the 5% level.
6. The scatter in Figure 4 does reveal a statistically significant (at 5%) negatively signed relationship between the two variables.
7. For example, persistence within the decadal data for individual countries could yield a positive association between current government size and subsequent growth that essentially mirrors the equivalent contemporaneous association between the two variables.
8. For example, the estimated slope of a linear OLS regression on the data in Figure 5 changes from -0.078 (t-ratio $= -5.68$) when all countries are included, to -0.035 (t-ratio $= -2.28$) when just the six observations (7.6% of the sample) on the extreme left of the figure are omitted: 3 for Korea; 1 each for Japan, Greece and Spain. The regression fit (R^2) also falls from 0.30 to 0.07. This is not intended to suggest that such observations *should* be omitted but merely to demonstrate the sensitivity to inclusion/omission of small numbers of extreme observations.
9. This latter category would include consumption taxes in the absence of labour supply effects.
10. See, for example, the endogenous growth models of Peretto (2003, 2007). Similar 'transitional' (as opposed to steady-state) growth effects of fiscal policy are obtained from neoclassical models; see, for example, Turnovsky (2004).
11. Here we treat as given the institutional structures that determine which goods are delivered via market or non-market mechanisms.
12. For income taxes this is clearly built into the tax code where an income definition forms the tax base; however, an indirect relationship with income levels is also often observed for other taxes, such as expenditure taxes, where the tax base (e.g. consumption expenditure) moves in association with income.
13. For example, the familiar multi-step income tax used in many countries usually involves individual's marginal (and associated average) tax rates rising with income levels.

14. As noted above a statutory income tax involving a progressive multi-rate structure, generally leads to effective average and marginal tax rates rising as all income levels increase. In most such tax structures the relationship between effective average and marginal rates would not be strictly proportional as both would approach the top statutory marginal rate as incomes rise.
15. When d is sufficiently negative to generate $b(1 + bd) < 0$, then Y_t will be lower than Y_{t-1}.
16. The mis-specification of typical cross-country OLS regressions (in which income levels or growth rates are regressed on a measure of government size) can be seen by re-arranging Equation (1) to give: $Y_t = -(a/b) + (1/b)g_t$ or, taking first differences, $\Delta Y_t = (1/b)\Delta g_t = (1/b)g_t - (1/b)g_{t-1}$. Hence regression testing for relationships between current government size and current income levels or changes are likely to pick up these endogenous demand-driven relationships between the variables depicted in Equation (1) rather than, or as well as, the hypothesised causal relationships from government size to income levels or growth.
17. The Barro (1990) model, for example, effectively implies a value of d in Equation (3) that is positive at low income levels, becomes zero then turns negative at high income levels due to the non-linear distortionary effects of rising marginal tax rates. Slemrod (1995) and others have argued that this may, in part, explain the failure of empirical studies to identify robust linear cross-country relationships between income levels and government size.
18. Two earlier studies which broadly meet these criteria are Mofidi and Stone (1990) and Miller and Russek (1997) – the former applied to cross-State data for the US. Note that almost all third generation evidence appears after the critical reviews of Slemrod (1995), Agell, Lindh, and Ohlsson (1997) and Myles (2000).
19. See Dungey and Fry (2009), Ilzetzki, Mendoza, and Vegh (2010) and Beetsma and Giuliodori (2011) for more detailed reviews of methods and evidence.
20. Other evidence prior to 2000 includes time-series regression estimates of business cycle models for individual countries which estimate or simulate fiscal policy shocks (e.g. McGrattan, Rogerson, and Wright 1997), and simple Granger-causality-based tests that provide some, but limited, insights (e.g. Saunders 1993).
21. See, for example, Romer and Romer (2010), Ramey (2011) and Barro and Redlick (2011).
22. For example, where studies ignore the GBC and report parameter estimates for, say, an 'income tax' effect on output growth, this could not be used to investigate the growth effects of possible tax reform scenarios without knowing which other element(s) also changed (or were implicitly assumed to change) in the empirical exercise.
23. The table also reports similar orders of magnitude for simulations of the output effects of capital tax rate changes for the US by Turnovsky and Chatterjii (2002).
24. We prefer the term 'persistent' to 'permanent' here since the generally limited periods of analysis used in most studies do not allow 'persistent' but nevertheless transitional effects (in the sense used in theoretical models), to be readily distinguished from permanent effects.
25. See, for example, Glaeser, Lopez-de-Silanes, and Schleifer (2004) and Mauro (1995).

References

Agell, J., T. Lindh, and H. Ohlsson. 1997. "Growth and the Public Sector: A Critical Review Essay." *European Journal of Political Economy* 13 (1): 33–52.

Aiginger, K., and M. Falk. 2005. "Explaining Differences in Growth Among OECD Countries." *Empirica* 32 (1): 19–43.

Angelopoulos, K., G. Economides, and P. Kammas. 2007. "Tax-spending Policies and Economic Growth: Theoretical Predictions and Evidence from the OECD." *European Journal of Political Economy* 23 (4): 885–902.

Arin, P. 2004. "Fiscal Policy, Private Investment and Economic Growth: Evidence from G-7 Countries." Unpublished manuscript, Massey University, Auckland.

Arin, P., M. Berlemann, and F. Koray. 2011. "The Taxation-Growth-Nexus Revisited." *HWWI Research Papers* 104, Institute of International Economics, Hamburg, Germany.

Arnold, J. 2008. *Do Tax Structures Affect Aggregate Economic Growth: Empirical Evidence from a Panel of OECD Countries*. OECD Economics Department Working Paper No. 643. Paris: OECD.

Auerbach, A. J., and Y. Gorodnichenko. 2010. *Measuring the Output Responses to Fiscal Policy.* NBER Working Paper No. 16311. Boston, MA: National Bureau of Economic Research.

Bania, N., J. A. Gray, and J. A. Stone. 2007. "Growth, Taxes, and Government Expenditures: Growth Hills for U.S. States." *National Tax Journal* 60 (2): 193–204.

Barro, R. 1990. "Government Spending in a Simple Model of Endogenous Growth." *Journal of Political Economy* 98 (5): s103–17.

Barro, R., and C. J. Redlick. 2011. "Macroeconomic Effects of Government Purchases and Taxes." *Quarterly Journal of Economics* 126 (1): 51–102.

Baxter, M., and R. G. King. 1993. "Fiscal Policy in General Equilibrium." *American Economic Review* 83 (3): 315–34.

Beetsma, R., and M. Giuliodori. 2011. "The Effects of Government Purchases Shocks: Review and Estimates for the EU." *Economic Journal* 121 (550): F4–32.

Benos, N. 2009. "Fiscal Policy and Economic Growth: Empirical Evidence from EU Countries." MPRA Paper No. 19174, University Library of Munich, Germany.

Blanchard, O., and R. Perotti. 2002. "An Empirical Characterization of the Dynamic Effects of Changes in Government Spending and Taxes on Output." *Quarterly Journal of Economics* 117 (4): 1329–68.

Bleaney, M., N. Gemmell, and R. Kneller. 2001. "Testing the Endogenous Growth Model: Public Expenditure, Taxation and Growth Over the Long Run." *Canadian Journal of Economics* 34 (1): 36–57.

Castro, C. 2006. "Política Fiscal e Crescimento Económico." *Polytechnical Studies Review* 3 (5/6): 87–118.

Colombier, C. 2009. "Growth Effects of Fiscal Policies: An Application of Robust Modified M-Estimator." *Applied Economics* 41 (7): 899–912.

Dahlby, B., and E. Ferede. 2008. "Tax Cuts, Economic Growth, and the Marginal Cost of Public Funds for Canadian Provincial Governments." Unpublished manuscript.

Denaux, Z. S. 2005. "A Cross-County Evaluation of Fiscal Policy." *Journal of Business and Public Affairs* 32 (1): 14–20.

Denaux, Z. S., D. J. Cunningham, and R. C. Allen. 2005. "Spend More of Tax Less? Which Way to State Economic Growth?" *Journal of Business and Public Affairs* 32 (1): 21–5.

Devereux, M. P., B. Lockwood, and M. Redoano. 2008. "Do Countries Compete Over Tax Rates?" *Journal of Public Economics* 92 (5-6): 1210–35.

Doménech, R., and J. R. García. 2001. "Estructura Fiscal y Crecimiento Económico en la OECD." *Investigaciones Económicas* 15 (3): 441–72.

Dungey, M., and R. Fry. 2009. "Identifying Fiscal and Monetary Policy in a Small Open Economy VAR." *Economic Modelling* 26: 1147–60.

Fielding, D., O. Parkyn, and P. Gardiner. 2011. "Explaining Some Puzzles in the Estimated Response of New Zealand GDP to Fiscal Shocks." Paper presented to the New Zealand Association of Economists, Annual Conference, Wellington, New Zealand, July.

Gemmell, N. 2004. "Fiscal Policy in a Growth Framework." In *Fiscal Policy for Development: Poverty, Reconstruction and Growth*, edited by T. Addison and A. Roe, 149–76. London: Palgrave Macmillan.

Gemmell, N., R. Kneller, and I. Sanz. 2011a. "The Timing and Persistence of Fiscal Policy Impacts on Growth: Evidence from OECD Countries." *Economic Journal* 121 (550): F33–58.

Gemmell, N., R. Kneller, and I. Sanz. 2011b. "The Growth Effects of Corporate and Personal Income Taxes in the OECD." Working Paper No. 49. Globalisation and Development Centre, Bond University, Australia.

Glaeser, E. L., F. Lopez-de-Silanes, and A. Schleifer. 1994. "Do Institutions Cause Growth?" *Journal of Economic Growth* 9 (3): 271–303.

Gwartney, J. D., R. A. Lawson, and R. G. Holcombe. 1998. "The Scope of Government and the Wealth of Nations." *Cato Journal* 18 (2): 163–90.

Ilzetzki, E., E. G. Mendoza, and C. A. Vegh. 2010. *How Big (Small?) are Fiscal Multipliers?* NBER Working Paper No. 16470, Cambridge, MA.

Jones, C. I. 1995. "Time Series Tests of Endogenous Growth Models." *Quarterly Journal of Economics* 110 (2): 495–525.

Karras, G. 1999. Taxes and Growth: Testing the Neoclassical and Endogenous Growth Models. *Contemporary Economic Policy* 17 (2): 177–88.

King, R. G., and S. Rebelo. 1990. *Fiscal Policy and Economic Growth. Developing Neoclassical Implications*. NBER Working Paper no. 3338, Cambridge, MA.

Kneller, R., M. Bleaney, and N. Gemmell. 1999. Fiscal Policy and Growth: Evidence from OECD Countries." *Journal of Public Economics* 74 (2): 171–90.

Kneller, R., and F. Misch. 2011. "What Does Ex-post Evidence Tell us About the Output Effects of Future Tax Reforms?" ZEW - Centre for European Economic Research Discussion Paper No. 11-029, Mannheim, Germany.

Korpi, W. 1996. "Eurosclerosis and the Sclerosis of Objectivity: On the Role of Values Among Economic Policy Experts." *Economic Journal* 106 (439): 1727–46.

Mauro, P. 1995. "Corruption and Growth." *Quarterly Journal of Economics* 110 (3): 681–712.

McGrattan E. G., R. Rogerson, and R. Wright. 1997. "An Equilibrium Model of the Business Cycle with Household Production and Fiscal Policy." *International Economic Review* 38 (2): 267–90.

Miller S., and F. Russek. 1997. "Fiscal Structures and Economic Growth: International Evidence." *Economic Inquiry* 35 (3): 603–13.

Miyakoshi, T., Y. Tsukuda, T. Kono, and M. Koyanagi. 2007. "Public Expenditure Composition and Economic Growth: Optimal Adjustment by Using Gradient Method." Discussion Paper No. 07-17, Osaka University, Japan.

Mofidi, A., and J. Stone. 1990. "Do State and Local Taxes Affect Economic Growth?" *Review of Economics and Statistics* 72 (4): 686–91.

Muinelo-Gallo, L., and O. Roca-Sagales. 2011. "Economic Growth and Inequality: The Role of Fiscal Policies." *Australian Economic Papers* 50 (2-3): 74–97.

Myles, D. 2000. "Taxation and Economic Growth." *Fiscal Studies* 21 (1): 141–68.

New Zealand Treasury. 2011. *Government and Economic Growth. Does Size Matter?* New Zealand Treasury Paper No. 11/01, Wellington.

Padovano, F., and E. Galli. 2002. "Comparing the Growth Effects of Marginal vs Average Tax Rates and Progressivity." *European Journal of Political Economy* 18 (3): 529–44.

Peretto, P. F. 2003. "Fiscal Policy and Long-run Growth in R&D-based Models with Endogenous Market Structure." *Journal of Economic Growth* 8 (3): 325–47.

Peretto, P. F. 2007. "Corporate Taxes, Growth and Welfare in a Schumpeterian Economy." *Journal of Economic Theory* 137 (1): 353–82.

Ramey, V. A. 2011. "Identifying Government Spending Shocks: It's All in the Timing." *Quarterly Journal of Economics* 126 (1): 1–50.

Reed, R. 2008. "The Relationship Between Taxes and US State Income Growth." *National Tax Journal* 61 (1): 57–80.

Rodrik, D. 1994. *King Kong Meets Godzilla: The World Bank and the East Asian Miracle*. Centre for Economic Policy, Working Paper No. 944, London.

Romer, C. D., and D. H. Romer. 2010. "The Macroeconomic Effects of Tax Changes: Estimates Based on a New Measure of Fiscal Shocks." *American Economic Review* 100 (3): 763–801.

Romero-Ávila, D., and R. Strauch. 2008. "Public Finances and Long-term Growth in Europe: Evidence from a Panel Data Analysis." *European Journal of Political Economy* 24 (1): 172–91.

Saunders, P. J. 1993. "A Granger Causality Approach to Investigating the Impact of Fiscal Policy on the US Economy: 1970.I – 1990.III." *Studies in Economics and Finance* 16 (1): 3–22.

Slemrod, J. 1995. "What Do Cross-Country Studies Teach about Government Involvement, Prosperity, and Economic Growth?" *Brookings Papers on Economic Activity* 2: 373–431.

Turnovsky, S. J. 2004. "The Transitional Dynamics of Fiscal Policy: Long-run Capital Accumulation and Growth." *Journal of Money, Credit and Banking* 36: 883–910.

Turnovsky, S. J., and S. Chatterjii. 2002. "To Spend the US Government Surplus or to Increase the Deficit? A Numerical Analysis of the Policy Options." *Journal of Japanese and International Economics* 16 (4): 405–35.

Young, A. 1992. "A Tale of Two Cities: Factor Accumulation and Technical Change in Hong Kong and Singapore." *NBER Macroeconomics Annual* 7: 13–64.

Trade liberalisation and growth: a threshold exploration

Rod Falvey,[a] Neil Foster-McGregor[b] and Ahmed Khalid[a]

[a]*School of Business and Globalisation and Development Centre, Bond University, Gold Coast, Australia;* [b]*Vienna Institute for International Economic Studies, Vienna, Austria*

> Openness and trade liberalisation variables are consistently estimated to have significant positive coefficients in panel growth regressions. Many arguments have been advanced as to why and how more open or liberalised economies might grow faster, but the specific channels this process uses have begun to be investigated only recently. We continue these efforts by including a variable identifying the date of trade liberalisation in a system of equations that captures the determinants of growth in per capita income. Four 'channels' are considered: capital formation, the share of government, the economy's openness to trade and its price distortions. We include the liberalisation variable in the equation explaining each channel, and allow for thresholds on its coefficient depending on the 'years since liberalisation'. These estimated coefficients can also differ by region. In this way, we can identify the channels through which trade liberalisation affects growth and uncover the timing of the adjustments involved.

1. Introduction

Trade liberalisations among developing and transition countries have been particularly widespread in the last three decades. Their motivations include disenchantment with import substitution as a development strategy; the preponderance of empirical evidence (particularly relating to East Asia) suggesting a positive relationship between outward orientation and growth; and the inclusion of trade reforms in the reform packages required for financial support from the World Bank and the IMF.[1] There are many empirical studies examining the relationship between openness or trade liberalisation and economic growth (prominent examples include Dollar, 1992; Sachs and Warner, 1995; Edwards, 1998; Greenaway, Morgan, and Wright, 2002),[2] and the estimates from two recent cases are representative of those obtained in the literature. Wacziarg and Welch (2008) find the difference in growth between a liberalised and non-liberalised country is 1.53 percentage points; while Salinas and Aksoy (2006) using an alternative indicator[3] find that trade liberalisation increases growth by between 1 and 4 percentage points. Despite this evidence supporting a positive relationship between openness or liberalisation and growth, considerable scepticism remains. This is highlighted by Rodríguez and Rodrik (2000) who question the empirical methodology and argue that the measures of openness are really proxies for other policy or institutional variables. They further suggest that there is likely to be a contingent relationship between openness and growth, with the impact depending upon a number of country and external factors.

The potential growth effects of trade liberalisation are well known. Although the immediate impact is likely to be negative as resources are shed in areas of comparative disadvantage, their eventual employment in areas of comparative advantage will see a rise in the growth rate in the medium run as income moves to a higher steady state level. The static gains from trade liberalisation need not be limited to such resource allocation gains. Further gains can arise from: reductions in rent seeking, corruption and smuggling; exploiting economies of scale in exporting industries; and reduced market power in protected markets. Longer run gains in the growth rate must come through improvements in factor productivity and these can also emerge through a variety of channels. Increased imports of capital and intermediate goods not available domestically may directly raise the productivity of manufacturing production (Lee, 1995). Increased trade (both exports and imports) with advanced economies could indirectly raise growth by facilitating knowledge and technology spillovers. Learning by doing may be more rapid in export industries.[4] A liberal trading regime may attract export-platform FDI. The magnitude of these longer-run growth effects will vary across countries, depending on their sectors of comparative advantage.

Although the potential growth-enhancing effects of trade liberalisation are well known, less attention has been paid to how they are realised. An important step in this direction was taken by Wacziarg (2001), who investigated the channels linking trade policy and economic growth. The channels he considered involved government actions, investment and technology transmission. Trade liberalisation may encourage governments to pursue more growth-friendly policies. Since trade reform works by correcting distortions in relative prices, high and variable inflation and exchange controls can confound price signals, making it difficult to disentangle relative price changes from changes in the general price level, thereby blunting incentives to reallocate resources (Rodrik, 1992). If trade liberalisation is to be successful, the private sector must respond to changed incentives. If private agents are sceptical of policy-makers' commitment, they will be slow to incur the (sunk) costs associated with shifting resources between import competing and export sectors. Short-run adjustment will be prolonged and efficiency gains delayed. Credibility is enhanced by more responsible macroeconomic behaviour and a reduction in the role of government. The share of government activity in GDP has been found to have a significant influence on growth, but the likely effects of trade reform on the size of government are ambiguous. A government that wishes to maintain the competitiveness of domestic firms may tax and spend less. But if more open economies are subject to larger economic shocks, then government's role in providing a social safety net through redistribution may increase. Which role dominates may depend on the characteristics of the country concerned. Physical investment will be required for resource reallocation to take place and for the exploitation of technology spillovers. The share of investment in GDP is consistently found to be significant in growth regressions. Here again, the government can have an important facilitating role by moderating government deficit levels so as to avoid the crowding out of private investors in financial markets. Technology transmission comes from increased access to the world's stock of knowledge through increased goods and services trade and FDI.

The primary difficulty in any empirical analysis of the links between trade policy and growth is finding an appropriate policy indicator. The multidimensional nature of trade policy, in terms of the numbers of both products traded and types of policies pursued, makes a single policy indicator problematic. Aggregate measures of even direct trade policy instruments (tariffs and quotas) are difficult to formulate (Anderson and Neary, 2005), and even if they could be, the data on trade policy measures required for quantification are not available for an adequate sample of countries. Wacziarg (2001) attempts to overcome this difficulty by constructing a 'trade policy openness index' (TP). He regresses a country's trade share (exports plus imports as a share of GDP) on a set of variables,[5] including trade policy variables, and then uses the estimated coefficients on the policy variables as weights in constructing a TP, which captures that portion of observed trade shares attributable to the effective impact of trade policy. Three trade policy indicators are available – the share of import duty revenues in total imports; an un-weighted coverage ratio for pre-Uruguay Round non-tariff barriers; and a dummy variable indicating liberalisation status based on the Sachs and Warner (1995) trade liberalisation dates. He also presents results for the policy indicator estimated without the liberalisation status dummy.[6] The system of equations is then estimated using data from a sample of 57 countries between 1970 and 1989 (divided into four periods). The system includes a growth equation, whose determinants include the channel variables but not TP, and separate equations for each of the channels, where TP is included as an explanatory variable. Results using the full index (TP1) indicate a positive effect of openness on growth, with more than half of this effect due to the accumulation of physical capital. Technology transmission and enhanced macro policy account for smaller effects. When liberalisation status is excluded (TP2), the growth effects are smaller, though the proportional effects through the channels are roughly unchanged. However, the macroeconomic policy channel is no longer significant.

In this paper, we extend and complement Wacziarg's approach. We *complement* his approach by using an alternative indicator of trade policy. While probably the best indicator of its type given what data are available, and certainly an improvement on indicators based on the residuals from a gravity equation for example, Wacziarg's TP is handicapped by its heavy reliance for its cross-period variation on the import duty share, an indicator widely criticised even as an average tariff measure. Analysis with alternative indicators would therefore seem warranted before definite conclusions are drawn. Here we restrict attention to a liberalisation status indicator based on the liberalisation dates from Wacziarg and Welch (2008).[7] We can then determine whether the growth effects of trade liberalisation operate through similar channels to those found for Wacziarg's TP indicator of trade policy.

We *extend* Wacziarg's approach by investigating whether the effects of liberalisation take place gradually.[8] We do this through threshold regressions which allow the estimated coefficients on our liberalisation variable in the growth and channel equations to depend on the years since liberalisation. In this way, the effects of trade liberalisation on investment, say, can depend on how deep the economy is into the process of adjustment following the liberalisation. We don't impose the thresholds, they are determined by the data. Ideally we would estimate separate thresholds for each country or for groups of similar countries. Unfortunately there are too few liberalisation episodes for this to be possible, so we are constrained to apply common thresholds to all countries. We are able to take some account of country heterogeneity, however, by allowing the estimated coefficients on the liberalisation variable to differ by 'region'. Regional differences in the patterns of adjustment to trade liberalisation are not unexpected. The success of the early East Asian liberalisers, which helped convince others to liberalise trade, does not appear to have been matched in other regions including later liberalisers in Asia.

The outline of the remainder of this paper is as follows. The next section describes the data and empirical methodology. Section 3 then presents the results of estimating our growth and channel equations individually, allowing for thresholds on the liberalisation variable. The results of estimating all the equations as a system are given in Section 4. Here we discuss the estimated regional effects, along with the inferred effects of liberalisation on growth, broken up by time, channel and region. The final section presents our conclusions.

Table 1. Data description.

Variable	Description	Source
GDP	Gross Domestic Product	World Development Indicators (WDI)
LIB	A dummy variable which takes the value zero in the years prior to liberalisation and 1 in the years after liberalisation	Wacziarg and Welch (2008)
Grow	Annual growth rate of per capita GDP (in constant US$) measured as the change in the logged value of per capita GDP	WDI
Invest	Investment Share: Gross capital formation as a share of GDP	WDI
BMP	Black Market Premium: the percentage difference between the official and black market exchange rates	Pick's Currency Yearbooks and Global Financial Statistics
ΔPop	Growth rate of population measured as the change in the logged value of population	WDI
Govt	Government Share: General government final consumption expenditure as a percentage of GDP	WDI
Trade	Trade Share: Ratio of imports plus exports to GDP	WDI
P15-64	Share of population aged between 15 and 64	WDI
P64+	Share of population aged 65 and over	WDI
RPCap	Relative Price of Capital Goods: Price level of investment relative to the price of consumption	Penn World Tables
FDev	Financial Development: Money and quasi-money as a percentage of GDP	WDI
Rer	Real Effective Exchange Rate: The nominal effective exchange rate (a measure of the value of a currency against a weighted average of several foreign currencies) divided by a price deflator or an index of costs	WDI
CAD	Current Account Deficit	WDI

2. Data and empirical methodology

We use annual data for a panel of 58, predominantly developing countries for the period 1970–2005. The variables, their definitions and sources are given in Table 1. The countries, their allocation to regions and their liberalisation dates are given in Appendix Table A1. Five regions are considered: Asia, Africa (both north and sub-Saharan Africa), Latin America (including the Caribbean), OECD (only Australia, Japan and New Zealand) and a residual 'Other' (primarily Eastern European transition economies).

Our procedure is to first estimate separately a growth equation and individual equations explaining each of the channel variables. To these equations we then add the liberalisation dummy, linearly to begin with and subsequently allowing for thresholds based on the years since liberalisation. Besides being of interest in their own right, we use these equations to fix the thresholds when we estimate separate regional liberalisation effects and the systems of equations using SUR in the final stage.[9]

Table 2. The growth equation.

	(1) Grow	(2) Grow
Invest	0.230***	0.231***
	(0.0371)	(0.0368)
Govt	−0.157***	−0.129***
	(0.0472)	(0.0470)
Trade	−0.00309	−0.00270
	(0.0101)	(0.00998)
BMP	−0.000552	−0.000395
	(0.000411)	(0.000414)
ΔPop	−0.543*	−0.610**
	(0.298)	(0.285)
LIB		0.0166***
		(0.00354)
F-stat	5.14***	5.37***
R-squared	0.304	0.316
Observations	1,227	1,227

Note: Robust standard errors in parentheses; *** indicates $p < 0.01$, ** $p < 0.05$, and * $p < 0.1$.

3. The single equation estimates

We identify four channels through which we expect trade liberalisation to impact upon economic growth.[10] Below we discuss each of these channels in turn, but first we estimate a growth equation including the channels and the liberalisation dummy. Our channels are capital formation (*Invest*), the government share of GDP (*Govt*), the trade share (imports plus exports) of GDP (*Trade*) and the black market premium (*BMP*). To these variables we add the rate of growth of population (ΔPop), country and time fixed effects. The liberalisation variable is included directly in case there are channels that we have missed. The equation estimated is shown below and the results are in Table 2.

$$Grow_{it} = \beta_1 Invest_{it} + \beta_2 Govt_{it} + \beta_3 Trade_{it} + \beta_4 BMP_{it}$$
$$+ \beta_5 \Delta Pop_{it} + \delta_0 LIB_{it} + \gamma_t + \gamma_i + \varepsilon_{it}. \quad (1)$$

Column (1) omits the liberalisation dummy. These results indicate that growth in per capita income is positively related to investment and negatively related to the size of government and the growth in population. Neither the trade share nor the BMP is statistically significant. These outcomes are unaffected by the addition of the liberalisation dummy in column (2), which yields an estimate of the direct effects of a trade liberalisation on growth of about 1.7%.

We now investigate whether these direct growth-enhancing benefits of trade liberalisation depend on the time that has elapsed since the liberalisation took place. To do this we allow the parameter associated with liberalisation to change discretely depending upon the years since liberalisation.[11] This is achieved by estimating the following equation:

$$Grow_{it} = \beta_1 Invest_{it} + \beta_2 Govt_{it} + \beta_3 Trade_{it} + \beta_4 BMP_{it} + \beta_5 \Delta Pop_{it}$$
$$+ \delta_1 LIB_{it} I(YSL_{it} \leq \mu) + \delta_2 LIB_{it} I(YSL_{it} > \mu) + \gamma_t + \gamma_i + \varepsilon_{it}, \quad (2)$$

where μ is the breakpoint. Here the observations are divided into two regimes depending on whether the threshold variable, *YSL*, is smaller or larger than μ. The direct impact of liberalisation on growth will be given by δ_1 in the early years of the post-liberalisation period and by δ_2 in the later years. To estimate this equation we first need to jointly estimate the threshold value μ and the slope parameters. Chan (1993) and Hansen (2000) recommend obtaining the least squares estimate of μ as the value that minimises the concentrated sum of squared errors. Then we can estimate the parameters of our growth equation. Having found a threshold we need to identify whether it is statistically significant. This involves testing the null hypothesis that $\delta_1 = \delta_2$, where rejecting the null allows us to conclude that a threshold exists. One complication is that the threshold μ is not identified under the null hypothesis, implying that classical tests do not have standard distributions and that critical values cannot be read off standard distribution tables. We follow Hansen (1996) and bootstrap to obtain the p-value for the test of a significant threshold. Column (1) of Appendix Table A2 gives the results from estimating a first threshold, which occurs 12 years after the liberalisation, but is not statistically significant. We cannot reject the hypothesis that $\delta_1 = \delta_2$, implying that there is no significant threshold based on years since liberalisation in the direct effect of trade liberalisation on growth.

3.1. *Capital formation*

The accumulation of physical capital was found by Wacziarg (2001) to contribute more than 60 per cent of the total effect of policy openness on growth. We expect investment to respond positively to trade liberalisation for a number of reasons. In the short and medium runs, investment is required to facilitate the resource reallocation towards sectors of comparative advantage that the liberalisation promotes. Investment may also be encouraged through market size and scale economy effects, and because liberalisation may lower the costs of and widen access to imported capital goods. How soon after liberalisation these effects 'kick in' and how long they persist are obvious questions of interest, on which our threshold analysis can shed light.

The specification of our investment equation is based on Bond and Malik (2007), which is an empirical study explaining cross-country variation in the share of investment to GDP using a sample of 61 developing countries. They consider 43 potential explanatory variables, but most of these are country-specific and time invariant[12] and are therefore captured by the country dummies that we include. The explanatory variables that remain are: GDP per capita (Gpc) as a measure of the level of development; the relative price of capital goods (RPCap), included to capture the costs of investment goods; the population age structure, with the shares of the working age population (P15-64) and those of retired age (P64+) entered separately; financial development as measured by a broad indicator (the ratio of M2/GDP) (FDev); and trade liberalisation. The results of the single equation estimation are shown in Table 3.

The share of gross capital formation in GDP is seen to be increasing in per capita income, the relative price of capital goods and trade liberalisation, and decreasing in the share of the retired population and (somewhat unexpectedly) financial development.[13] The negative sign of the M2/GDP coefficient indicates that this variable may be acting more as an indicator of monetary policy crowding out private investment, perhaps in support of a government deficit. Our threshold analysis for this channel (columns (3), (4) and (5) in Table A2) indicates that there are two significant thresholds on the liberalisation effects, at 2 and 7 years since liberalisation, respectively. Taking these thresholds into account for the aggregate sample in column (3) of Table 3, we find that liberalisation leaves the investment

Table 3. The investment channel.

	(1) Invest	(2) Invest	(3) Invest
Gpc	0.125***	0.132***	0.129***
	(0.0102)	(0.0102)	(0.0101)
P15-64	0.0583	0.0751	0.110
	(0.0976)	(0.0964)	(0.0948)
P64+	−0.745***	−0.733***	−0.638***
	(0.202)	(0.201)	(0.204)
RPCap	0.0191*	0.0203*	0.0205*
	(0.0103)	(0.0107)	(0.0106)
FDev	−0.000414***	−0.000320**	−0.000317**
	(0.000142)	(0.000145)	(0.000149)
LIB		0.0159***	
		(0.00436)	
LIB (YSL < 2)			0.00286
			(0.00480)
LIB (2 < YSL < 7)			0.0240***
			(0.00508)
LIB (7 < YSL)			0.0404***
			(0.00613)
F-stat	19.11***	19.25***	19.91***
R-squared	0.619	0.623	0.636
Observations	1,227	1,227	1,227

Notes: See Table 1.

share unaffected until two years have elapsed after which the investment share increases and receives a further boost after seven years.

3.2. Macroeconomic policy

Our indicator of macroeconomic policy is the black-market premium on the official exchange rate (BMP). A high black market premium reflects an overvalued official exchange rate and indicates domestic price distortions, capital and trade controls. In addition, it is often a signal of poor macroeconomic policy accompanied by a high public sector deficit and debt levels. If trade liberalisation encourages governments to adopt more stable and less price-distortionary macroeconomic policies, it may be expected to have a positive impact on growth for the reasons discussed in the Introduction. Our BMP equation includes: real income per capita, the real exchange rate (Rer), the current account deficit (CAD) as an indicator of excess demand, our indicator of financial development (FDev) and the liberalisation dummy. The estimation results are shown in Table 4.

Increases in real income per capita, the real exchange rate or trade liberalisation reduce the black-market premium, while financial development, again unexpectedly, appears to increase it. This is further evidence that M2/GDP acts as an indicator of monetary laxness rather than financial development for our sample. When we look at the threshold results in columns (5) and (6) of Table A2 we find one significant threshold. The pattern of coefficients for the aggregate sample in column (3) of Table 4 indicates that trade liberalisation does significantly reduce the BMP, but only after five years have elapsed.

Table 4. The black market premium channel.

	(1) BMP	(2) BMP	(3) BMP
Gpc	−2.336***	−2.734***	−2.691***
	(0.5543)	(0.2945)	(0.562)
Rer	0.0057	−0.0141	−0.0359
	(0.147)	(0.144)	(0.137)
CAD	0.0187	0.0168	0.0181
	(0.0204)	(0.0205)	(0.0201)
FDev	0.0542***	0.0496***	0.0489***
	(0.0121)	(0.0125)	(0.0125)
LIB		−0.804***	
		(0.295)	
LIB (YSL < 5)			−0.413
			(0.286)
LIB (5 < YSL)			−2.051***
			(0.410)
F-stat	57.10***	56.88***	57.46***
R-squared	0.828	0.829	0.833
Observations	1,227	1,227	1,227

Notes: See Table 1.

3.3. Size of government

Openness and trade liberalisation have been found to impact upon government size, though the direction of any effect is disputed both theoretically and empirically. Our specification of the government share equation is based on Gemmell, Kneller, and Sanz (2008) (GKS). They note that the effects of trade (or globalisation more generally) on the share and composition of government spending are captured in two competing hypotheses: (1) the *efficiency hypothesis* where governments compete to facilitate exports and to attract internationally mobile capital by reducing taxes and shifting expenditure towards privately productive public inputs (education, training, R&D etc.) resulting in a reduced share of government expenditure in GDP; and (2) the *compensation hypothesis* which sees the government under pressure to expand social welfare programmes to compensate individuals for the increased uncertainty associated with higher exposure to international trade, resulting in an increased share of government in GDP. They note that the empirical testing of these hypotheses has often been inconclusive. In their study for OECD countries, GKS estimate an equation including 'a common set of control variables, based on standard models of demand for government expenditure … These are per capita income, relative public private sector prices and the size and structure of the population'. We include the same variables, with the exception of the relative price variable, the data for which are unavailable for many of the non-OECD countries in our sample.

Our variables include: GDP per capita; total population (Pop); the share of working age and retired age population; and the liberalisation dummy. All are statistically significant in Table 5 (except per capita income in column (1)) and increases in each of these reduce the share of government. In columns (7) and (8) of Table A2 a single threshold is found, seven years after liberalisation. In column (3) of Table 5 the coefficient on the liberalisation variable is significant and negative in both regimes for the aggregate sample, but is more

Table 5. The government share channel.

	(1) Govt	(2) Govt	(3) Govt
Gpc	−0.00746 (0.00578)	−0.0172*** (0.00617)	−0.0189*** (0.00614)
lnPop	−0.120*** (0.0163)	−0.123*** (0.0160)	−0.122*** (0.0164)
P15-64	−0.149** (0.0652)	−0.164** (0.0638)	−0.145** (0.0641)
P64+	−0.597*** (0.158)	−0.668*** (0.146)	−0.629*** (0.159)
LIB		−0.0182*** (0.00309)	
LIB (YSL < 7)			−0.0197*** (0.00303)
LIB (7<YSL)			−0.00733* (0.00420)
F-stat	45.46***	46.89***	47.23***
R-squared	0.792	0.799	0.802
Observations	1,227	1,227	1,227

Notes: See Table 1.

than halved in the later regime. This suggests that liberalisation has only a small permanent effect on the share of government on average, an outcome consistent with that in GKS.

3.4. Trade openness

Trade openness can increase a country's access to productivity-enhancing technology and can thus encourage technology diffusion and transmission. This could occur through domestic producers imitating foreign knowledge or by allowing domestic producers to use foreign knowledge in their production processes. Technology diffusion could also occur through access to imported goods, learning by exporting, etc. If liberalisation increases the level of openness (as measured by trade shares), it might be expected to enhance growth.

Much of the literature aimed at explaining the trade share has been motivated by using the residuals from the trade share equation as a trade policy indicator. This approach has not been particularly successful and the construction of a trade policy index is not our purpose in estimating this equation. However, we do use similar explanatory variables. These are: GDP per capita; population as an indicator of market size; the real exchange rate, the current account deficit and liberalisation. The results are shown in Table 6. Increases in GDP per capita and the real exchange rate increase 'openness', but the current account deficit has no significant effect here. If simply included as a dummy variable (column 2), trade liberalisation has a small significant positive effect on the trade share. When we estimate thresholds (columns 9 to 11 in Table A2) we find two significant thresholds at 4 and 7 years since liberalisation, respectively. The aggregate results in column (3) of Table 6 show no significant effect of trade liberalisation on the trade share in the first four years and a positive and significant effect after it, increasing again after the seventh year. So it seems that trade liberalisation does increase openness, but only some time after it has been initiated (four years is our estimate).

Table 6. The trade share channel.

	(1) Trade	(2) Trade	(3) Trade
Gpc	0.145***	0.158***	0.152***
	(0.0384)	(0.0376)	(0.0380)
LnPop	0.113	0.113	0.102
	(0.0776)	(0.0770)	(0.0768)
CAD	−0.000230	−0.000176	−0.000349
	(0.00122)	(0.00122)	(0.00121)
lnRer	0.0774***	0.0778***	0.0790***
	(0.0116)	(0.0116)	(0.0117)
LIB		0.0225*	
		(0.0133)	
LIB (YSL < 4)			0.00600
			(0.0128)
LIB (4 < YSL < 7)			0.0393**
			(0.0197)
LIB (7 < YSL)			0.0865***
			(0.0204)
F-stat	73.71***	73.06***	73.06***
R-squared	0.861	0.861	0.864
Observations	1,227	1,227	1,227

Notes: See Table 1.

4. System results

In this section we present the results of estimating the above equations as a system using SUR, where the thresholds estimated above are imposed on the liberalisation dummy in the relevant equations. We then use these estimates to calculate the effects of trade liberalisation on growth for our full sample and for the five regions. The estimation results, which are very close to those for the individual equations above, are shown, including the regional effects in Tables 7 and Appendix Table A3, where the latter excludes the liberalisation variable from the growth equation. We do not report the estimated coefficients on the control variables in the channel equations, as these are not of primary concern and differ only in minor ways from the corresponding estimates in Section 3.[14]

We have grouped the regional coefficients by regime. In the growth equation, column (1) of Table 7, we find that the direct effect of liberalisation is positive and significant in each region, with strongest effects for the OECD, other and Latin America, Africa then Asia. The regional effects for the investment equation are shown in column (4) of Table 7. Some diversity is revealed. Only in Latin America does trade liberalisation have a significant (positive) effect on the investment share in the first two years after liberalisation. Latin America and Asia have significant positive effects in years 2 through 7 and all regions have significant and positive effects once seven years have elapsed. These results confirm Wacziarg's conclusion that trade liberalisation results in a significant increase in the investment share, but also indicate regional diversity in the time taken for this increase to appear.

When we allow for region-specific liberalisation coefficients in the BMP channel in column (5) of Table 7, we find significant reductions in the BMP from the date of liberalisation for Africa, OECD and Other, All countries have significant reductions in the BMP after 5 years, except our OECD sample which exhibits a puzzling increase in the BMP

Table 7. SUR results including liberalisation in growth equation.

	(1) Grow	(2) Govt	(3) Trade	(4) Invest	(5) BMP
Invest	0.234*** (0.0248)				
Govt	−0.134*** (0.0371)				
Trade	−0.0109 (0.00783)				
ΔPop	−0.549** (0.256)				
BMP	−0.000472 (0.000371)				
LIB					
Low Regime		YSL<7	YSL<4	YSL<2	YSL<5
ASIA	0.0148* (0.00837)	0.00295 (0.00677)	0.103*** (0.0362)	0.00326 (0.0125)	−0.307 (0.712)
AFRICA	0.0162*** (0.00538)	−0.0311*** (0.00430)	−0.0738*** (0.0228)	−0.0130 (0.00796)	−1.360*** (0.455)
LAT AM.	0.0194*** (0.00434)	−0.0188*** (0.00347)	0.0349* (0.0184)	0.0163** (0.00639)	0.561 (0.375)
OECD	0.0218* (0.0129)	−0.0134 (0.0111)	−0.0185 (0.0660)	0.00413 (0.0241)	−2.332* (1.281)
OTHER	0.0194*** (0.00434)	−0.0266*** (0.00716)	−0.0621 (0.0393)	−0.00642 (0.0144)	−2.374*** (0.762)
Middle Regime			4<YSL<7	2<YSL<7	
ASIA			0.140*** (0.0424)	0.0355*** (0.0112)	
AFRICA			−0.0550** (0.0277)	0.00884 (0.00731)	
LAT AM.			0.0591*** (0.0228)	0.0390*** (0.00611)	
OECD			−0.0340 (0.0694)	0.00643 (0.0189)	
OTHER			−0.00363 (0.0475)	0.00268 (0.0122)	
High Regime		7<YSL	7<YSL	7<YSL	5<YSL
ASIA		0.0164** (0.00816)	0.226*** (0.0399)	0.0228* (0.0122)	−2.508*** (0.723)
AFRICA		−0.0183*** (0.00580)	−0.0305 (0.0291)	0.0463*** (0.00875)	−3.224*** (0.531)
LAT AM.		0.00112 (0.00428)	0.114*** (0.0215)	0.0425*** (0.00664)	−1.679*** (0.414)
OECD		−0.0280** (0.0110)	−0.00541 (0.0540)	0.0335** (0.0165)	3.854*** (1.088)
OTHER		−0.0409*** (0.00737)	0.0489 (0.0365)	0.0246** (0.0112)	−3.382*** (0.725)
Chi Squared	571.0***	5127.6***	39339.7***	40583.4***	7297.2***
R-squared	0.319	0.813	0.868	0.646	0.843
Observations	1,227	1,227	1,227	1,227	1,227

Notes: See Table 1.

Table 8. Effects of trade liberalisation on growth (%) aggregate sample.

Years Since Liberalisation	Direct effect	Investment Channel	Govt share Channel	Trade share Channel	BMP Channel	Total (*)
			Liberalisation in the growth equation			
0–1	1.68*	0.06	0.22*	0.00	0.02	1.98 (1.90)
2–3	1.68*	0.56*	0.22*	0.00	0.02	2.48 (2.46)
4	1.68*	0.56*	0.22*	−0.03	0.02	2.45 (2.46)
5–6	1.68*	0.56*	0.22*	−0.03	0.11	2.54 (2.46)
7+	1.68*	0.94*	0.08*	−0.08	0.11	2.73 (2.70)
			Liberalisation not in the growth equation			
0–1	NA	0.06	0.32*	0.00	0.04	0.42 (0.32)
2–3	NA	0.55*	0.32*	0.00	0.04	0.91 (0.87)
4	NA	0.55*	0.32*	−0.03	0.04	0.88 (0.87)
5–6	NA	0.55*	0.32*	−0.03	0.17*	1.01 (1.04)
7+	NA	0.93*	0.12*	−0.09	0.17*	1.13 (1.22)

Notes: *Indicates that the relevant coefficients are significant.

five years after liberalisation.[15] The estimates for regional differences in the government share channel appear in column (2) of Table 7. In Africa, the OECD and Other, trade liberalisation brings significant reductions in the government share in both regimes, although the effects are larger after seven years for the OECD and Other. An initial decline fades away after seven years in Latin America. Asia is unusual in that trade liberalisation leads to a significant *increase* in the share of government after seven years. The corresponding results for the trade channel are in column (3) of Table 7. In Asia trade liberalisation leads to a sustained expansion of the trade share from the outset. It has a positive effect in all regimes in Latin America, with the strongest effects between the fourth and seventh years post-liberalisation. In Africa the effects are initially negative and significant, but this effect disappears and the trade share returns to its pre-liberalisation value after four years. Trade liberalisation has no effect on the openness of our Other and OECD subsamples.

We now use the estimates in Tables 7 and A3, and Tables A4 and A5 for the aggregate sample, to calculate the growth effects of trade liberalisation. We begin with the aggregate sample. When we collect the separate thresholds estimated for the liberalisation variable in each equation together, we get the time pattern of adjustment shown in the first column of Table 8. Which channels come into play in each year since liberalisation can be read from the patterns of coefficient changes in the Table. The direct effect of liberalisation on growth is shown in column 2. The numbers in the cells in the other (channel) columns correspond to the coefficient on that channel in the growth equation multiplied by the coefficient on the liberalisation variable in that channel equation, taking into account the threshold effects. The derived growth effects are shown for the system estimated with and without the liberalisation variable in the growth equation. We include both for two reasons. First, because the results without liberalisation in the growth equation are comparable to those of Wacziarg (2001). Second, because a comparison of the estimated effects indicates which channels are robust to the inclusion of a direct effect of liberalisation on growth. The results are quite consistent. Excluding the liberalisation variable from the growth equation increases the estimated effect through the government share channel by about 30% and marginally increases the BMP channel effect in some cases.[16] The investment and trade channels are unaffected.

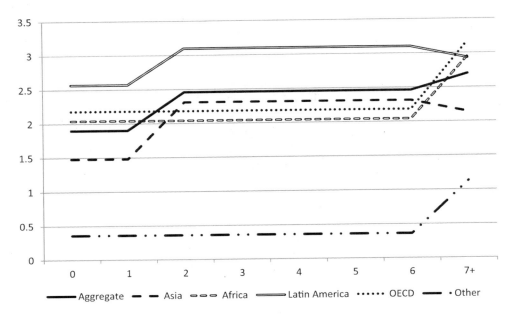

Figure 1. Estimated growth effects: statistically significant channels only.

Table 8 indicates that the effects in descending order of magnitude are the direct effect, then the channel effects through investment, government and the BMP. The trade channel has no significant effect on growth. The direct effect dominates. It is at least 65 per cent of the total, suggesting the presence of important omitted channels. Of the channel effects, the

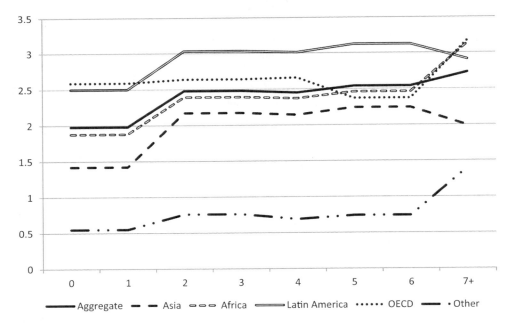

Figure 2. Estimated growth effects: all channels.

Table 9. Effects of trade liberalisation on growth (%).

Years Since Liberalisation	Direct effect	Investment Channel	Govt share Channel	Trade share Channel	BMP Channel	Total (*)
(A) Asia						
		Liberalisation in the growth equation				
0–1	1.48*	0.08	−0.04	−0.11	0.01	1.42 (1.48)
2–3	1.48*	0.83*	−0.04	−0.11	0.01	2.17 (2.31)
4	1.48*	0.83*	−0.04	−0.15	0.01	2.14 (2.31)
5–6	1.48*	0.83*	−0.04	−0.15	0.12	2.24 (2.31)
7+	1.48*	0.53*	−0.22*	−0.24	0.12	1.99 (2.14)
		Liberalisation not in the growth equation				
0–1	NA	0.08	−0.05	−0.11	0.02	0.04 (0.00)
2–3	NA	0.84*	−0.05	−0.11	0.02	0.70 (0.84)
4	NA	0.84*	−0.05	−0.15	0.02	0.66 (0.84)
5–6	NA	0.84*	−0.05	−0.15	0.14	0.78 (0.84)
7+	NA	0.54*	−0.28*	−0.25	0.14	0.15 (0.26)
(B) Africa						
		Liberalisation in the growth equation				
0–1	1.62*	−0.30	0.42*	0.08	0.06	1.88 (2.04)
2–3	1.62*	0.21	0.42*	0.08	0.06	2.39 (2.04)
4	1.62*	0.21	0.42*	0.06	0.06	2.37 (2.04)
5–6	1.62*	0.21	0.42*	0.06	0.15	2.46 (2.04)
7+	1.62*	1.08*	0.25*	0.03	0.15	3.13 (2.95)
		Liberalisation not in the growth equation				
0–1	NA	−0.30	0.54*	0.08	0.07	0.39 (0.54)
2–3	NA	0.21	0.54*	0.08	0.07	0.90 (0.54)
4	NA	0.21	0.54*	0.06	0.07	0.88 (0.54)
5–6	NA	0.21	0.54*	0.06	0.17	0.98 (0.54)
7+	NA	1.10*	0.32*	0.04	0.17	1.63 (1.42)
(C) Latin America						
		Liberalisation in the growth equation				
0–1	1.94*	0.38*	0.25*	−0.04	−0.03	2.50 (2.57)
2–3	1.94*	0.91*	0.25*	−0.04	−0.03	3.03 (3.10)
4	1.94*	0.91*	0.25*	−0.06	−0.03	3.01 (3.10)
5–6	1.94*	0.91*	0.25*	−0.06	0.08	3.12 (3.10)
7+	1.94*	0.99*	0.02	−0.12	0.08	2.91 (2.93)
		Liberalisation not in the growth equation				
0–1	NA	0.39*	0.33*	−0.04	−0.03	0.65 (0.72)
2–3	NA	0.92*	0.33*	−0.04	−0.03	1.18 (1.25)
4	NA	0.92*	0.33*	−0.06	−0.03	1.16 (1.25)
5–6	NA	0.92*	0.33*	−0.06	0.09	1.28 (1.25)
7+	NA	1.01*	0.02	−0.12	0.09	1.00 (1.01)
(D) OECD						
		Liberalisation in the growth equation				
0–1	2.18*	0.10	0.18	0.02	0.11	2.59 (2.18)
2–3	2.18*	0.15	0.18	0.02	0.11	2.64 (2.18)
4	2.18*	0.15	0.18	0.04	0.11	2.66 (2.18)
5–6	2.18*	0.15	0.18	0.04	−0.18	2.37 (2.18)
7+	2.18*	0.78*	0.38*	0.01	−0.18	3.17 (3.34)

Table 9. Effects of trade liberalisation on growth (%). *(Continued)*

Years Since Liberalisation	Direct effect	Investment Channel	Govt share Channel	Trade share Channel	BMP Channel	Total (*)
		Liberalisation not in the growth equation				
0–1	NA	0.10	0.23	0.02	0.13	0.48 (0.00)
2–3	NA	0.15	0.23	0.02	0.13	0.53 (0.00)
4	NA	0.15	0.23	0.04	0.13	0.55 (0.00)
5–6	NA	0.15	0.23	0.04	−0.21	0.21 (0.00)
7+	NA	0.80*	0.49*	0.01	−0.21	1.09 (1.29)
(E) Other						
		Liberalisation in the growth equation				
0–1	0.16	−0.15	0.36*	0.07	0.11	0.55 (0.36)
2–3	0.16	0.06	0.36*	0.07	0.11	0.76 (0.36)
4	0.16	0.06	0.36*	0.00	0.11	0.69 (0.36)
5–6	0.16	0.06	0.36*	0.00	0.16	0.74 (0.36)
7+	0.16	0.58*	0.55*	−0.05	0.16	1.40 (1.13)
		Liberalisation not in the growth equation				
0–1	NA	−0.15	0.46*	0.07	0.13	0.51 (0.46)
2–3	NA	0.06	0.46*	0.07	0.13	0.72 (0.46)
4	NA	0.06	0.46*	0.00	0.13	0.65 (0.46)
5–6	NA	0.06	0.46*	0.00	0.18	0.70 (0.46)
7+	NA	0.58*	0.71*	−0.05	0.18	1.42 (1.29)

Notes: *Indicates that the relevant coefficients are significant.

investment effect is the largest, except in the two years immediately following liberalisation. We can see from the lower part of Table 8 that the investment channel ranges from upwards of fifty per cent of the total channel effects, which is consistent with Wacziarg's conclusions. The size of the growth effect through the government channel is reduced to nearly a third in the long run.

The corresponding calculations for the regions are given in Table 9A–E, and a comparison of the implied effects of trade liberalisation on growth are provided in Figures 1 and 2. While the Tables report the full range of effects, we limit our discussion to those found to be statistically significant. Unspecified channels (the direct effect) are significant in all regions except Other, and capture the bulk of the effects of trade liberalisation on growth. Focussing on the specified channels, only the investment and government share channels are ever statistically significant for the regions. In the longer term (after seven years) the investment channel dominates in every region except Other. In Latin America, growth increases through both the investment and government share channels from the outset, though the gain from a reduced government share has passed after seven years. In the OECD there are no significant channel effects until seven years have elapsed. In Africa and Other the government share is the only channel operating in the first seven years. In Asia the investment channel is significant after two years, though its contribution declines, but remains significant, after seven years. The unusual feature of the Asian region is the significant but negative contribution of trade liberalisation to growth through the expansion of the government share. This seems unlikely to be explained by governments expanding social safety nets. Figure 1 illustrates the outcomes when only the statistically significant channels are included, and Figure 2 when all channels are included.

In summary, in no region does trade liberalisation have a negative effect on growth. The investment share is the most important channel, but may take some time to exert its influence. Reductions in the government share have a positive and significant effect on growth in Africa, Latin America, Other and, in the longer term, the OECD. But this same channel has a negative and significant effect in Asia, in the longer term.

5. Conclusions

Our objective in this paper has been to use threshold regression techniques to investigate the channels through which trade liberalisation affects growth and the timing of those effects. We considered four channels – the share of investment in GDP, the share of government in GDP, the trade share in GDP and macroeconomic policy through the black market premium. When considering our full sample, the evidence suggested that the share of investment was positively related to growth, the share of government and sometimes the BMP were negatively related to growth, but that the trade share had no significant effect on growth. Significant thresholds emerged in all channel equations. Trade liberalisation has a positive direct effect on growth. It also has a positive effect through the investment share, though this effect is negligible in the first two years and becomes strongest after seven years. Trade liberalisation eventually has a positive effect on the trade share, but not until the economy has had four years to adjust. Its effect is strongest after seven years. Liberalisation has a negative effect on the share of government, and this is its strongest growth-channel effect in the short run, though this effect is reduced by two-thirds after seven years. Trade liberalisation appears to have no significant effects on the black market premium in the first five years after liberalisation, but from then on the premium is significantly reduced indicating a reduction in price distortions. These aggregate results appear to amalgamate a diversity of regional effects. While the investment channel is important in all regions in the longer run (after seven years), in the short run (less than two years post-liberalisation) it is important in Latin America, and in both Latin America and Asia in the medium run. The government share channel is significant for Africa, Latin America and 'other' in the short and medium terms (up to seven years), but is only a significant contributor to growth in the longer term in the OECD. Because trade liberalisation increases the government share in Asia, its effects on growth through this channel are negative in the longer term.

In terms of the relative importance of the channels, we confirm Wacziarg's finding of the importance of the investment channel. There is also a smaller, but sizable, positive effect through a reduced share of government in economic activity. The magnitude and significance of the estimated coefficients when the liberalisation variable is included directly in the growth equation along with the channels, indicates that these latter channels only capture a part of the effects of trade liberalisation on growth. The missing channels are a topic for future research. Clearly our panel approach is very limited in its ability to expose the full dynamics of adjustment to trade liberalisation. What we have sought to provide through our threshold analysis, is evidence that a dynamic adjustment process does take place, through a range of channels which differ in the timing of their effects. We have done this while imposing a common structure of channels and thresholds on our diverse sample of trade liberators. The extent to which this common structure survives the idiosyncrasies of individual country adjustment awaits analysis at the country level. But the diversity shown by our 'regional' results and consideration of the diversity of the countries grouped into these regional subsamples, strongly suggest that regional thresholds should be estimated when data permits.

Acknowledgements

We thank the editor, referees and participants in the First Annual NTU/GDC Workshop on Economic and Policy Developments in East Asia for comments.

Notes

1. For the period 1980–1989 for example, 79% of all loans had conditions in the trade policy area, in excess of those which attached to any other policy (Greenaway, 1998).
2. See Singh (2010) for a survey.
3. However, their liberalisation dates are generally consistent with those of Wacziarg and Welch (2008).
4. Indirect evidence is provided by the recent literature on exporting and productivity (for a review see Greenaway and Kneller 2007).
5. The trade share regression includes the growth of per capita income, land area, population and the three trade policy indicators – the import duty share, NTB coverage and the Sachs-Warner indicator of liberalisation status.
6. The estimated indicators are: including all three variables $TP1 = -34.73$ (Import Duty share) $- 0.22$ (NTBs) $+ 11.26$ SW; and dropping the SW indicator of liberalisation status $TP2 = -60.91$(Import Duty share) $- 0.24$ (NTBs).
7. This has its origins in the Sachs and Warner (1995) openness indicator which is a dummy variable, with a country being classified as *closed* if it displayed at least one of five criteria, namely; (i) average tariff rates of 40% or more, (ii) non-tariff barriers covering 40% or more of trade, (iii) a Black Market exchange rate (BMP) that has depreciated by 20% or more relative to the official exchange rate, on average, (iv) a state monopoly on major exports, (v) a socialist economic system. The *liberalisation date* is then defined as the year in which none of these criteria are met. The openness measure was heavily criticised by Rodríguez and Rodrik (2000), who argued that the information on the BMP and the state monopoly on major exports played the major role in its classification of countries as open or closed. They went on to argue that a high BMP is likely to reflect factors other than trade policy, including macroeconomic mismanagement, weak enforcement of the rule of law and high levels of corruption, while the information on the state monopoly of exports works like an Africa dummy. In updating this indicator, Wacziarg and Welch (2008) note that the liberalisation date is less subject to criticism, and are careful to cross-check their dates against case studies of reforms in developing countries.
8. There is some econometric analysis of the dynamics of trade liberalisation and income levels or growth. Greenaway, Leybourne, and Sapsford (1997) use a smooth transition model to test for a transition in the level and trend of real GDP per capita for 13 countries and relate these to liberalisation. While all displayed a transition in level or trend, the majority were negative, and the positive transformations generally could not be related to liberalisation episodes. Greenaway, Morgan, and Wright (1998, 2002) (GMW) use a dynamic panel model to examine both the short- and long-run impact of liberalisation on growth in a large sample of countries. Results using three measures of liberalisation suggest a J-curve effect, growth at first falls but then increases after liberalisation.
9. SUR allows for correlation in error terms across equations and should be more efficient than OLS.
10. Our choices of variables and hence channels is constrained in two ways. First, there are the usual data constraints. The unavailability of data on many variables of interest for developing countries is well known. Using thresholds based on years-since-liberalisation also benefits from the inclusion of early liberalisation episodes. Second, it is best to view our equations, like Wacziarg's, as reduced form equations where many endogenous influences have been eliminated. We are not attempting to estimate a structural model of an economy. While the inclusion of country and time fixed effects in all equations captures idiosyncratic country and time (e.g. international business cycle) influences, there remain many variables which might be included. We have concentrated on a parsimonious set of 'exogenous' variables, similar to those chosen by Wacziarg. Some variables (e.g. political variables) which were not found to be significant in any equation have been dropped from the analysis, and are not reported.

11. To ensure that the threshold is related to the effects of trade liberalisation and not to other shocks and that the estimated threshold does not depend on the experience of a few early liberalisers, we only consider thresholds at 15 years or less since liberalisation.
12. These include geographical variables and other fixed characteristics (such as colonial status, ethnic diversity and resource endowments).
13. These coefficients are largely unaffected by the inclusion of thresholds, except that FDev becomes insignificant once the regional effects are included.
14. The exceptions are that CAD and RER are now statistically significant in the trade channel, and FDev is statistically significant in the investment channel.
15. This may reflect the small number of countries in this group and the lack of variation in their black market premia.
16. Indeed the BMP channel becomes significant in the high regime in the aggregate results.

References

Anderson, J. E., and J. P. Neary. 2005. *Measuring the Restrictiveness of International Trade Policy*. Cambridge, MA: MIT Press.

Bond, S. R., and A. Malik. 2007. *Explaining Cross-country Variation in Investment: The Role of Endowments, Institutions and Finance*. Oxford: Oxford University.

Chan, K. 1993. "Consistency and Limiting Distribution of the Least Squares Estimator of a Threshold Autoregressive Model." *The Annals of Statistics* 21: 520–33.

Dollar, D. 1992. "Outward-oriented Developing Economies Really do Grow More Rapidly." *Economic Development and Cultural Change* 40: 523–44.

Edwards, S. 1998. "Openness, Productivity and Growth: What Do We Really Know?" *Economic Journal* 108: 383–398.

Gemmell, N., R. Kneller, and I. Sanz. 2008. "Foreign Investment, International Trade and the Size and Structure of Public Expenditures." *European Journal of Political Economy* 24: 151–71.

Greenaway, D. 1998. "Does Trade Liberalisation Promote Economic Development?" *Scottish Journal of Political Economy* 45: 491–511.

Greenaway, D., and R. Kneller. 2007. "Firm Heterogeneity, Exporting and FDI." *Economic Journal* 117: F134–61.

Greenaway, D., S. Leybourne, and D. Sapsford. 1997. "Modelling Growth (and Liberalisation) Using Smooth Transitions Analysis." *Economic Inquiry* 35: 798–814.

Greenaway, D., C. W. Morgan, and P. Wright. 1998. "Trade Reform, Adjustment and Growth: What Does the Evidence Tell Us?" *Economic Journal* 108: 1547–61.

Greenaway, D., C. W. Morgan, and P. Wright. 2002. "Trade Liberalisation and Growth in Developing Countries." *Journal of Development Economics* 67: 229–44.

Hansen, B. E. 1996. "Inference When a Nuisance Parameter is not Identified Under the Null Hypothesis." *Econometrica* 64: 413–30.
Hansen, B. E. 2000. "Sample Splitting and Threshold Estimation." *Econometrica* 68: 575–603
Lee, J. W. 1995. "Capital Goods Imports and Long-run Growth." *Journal of Development Economics* 48: 19–110
Rodríguez, F., and D. Rodrik. 2000. "Trade Policy and Economic Growth: A Skeptic's Guide to the Cross-national Evidence." In *NBER Macroeconomics Annual 2000*, edited by B. Bernanke and K.S. Rogoff. Cambridge, MA: MIT Press.
Rodrik, D. 1992. "The Limits of Trade Policy Reform in Developing Countries." *Journal of Economic Perspectives* 6: 87–105.
Sachs, J., and A. Warner. 1995. "Economic Reform and the Process of Global Integration." *Brookings Papers on Economic Activity* 1: 1–118.
Salinas, G., and A. Aksoy. 2006. Growth Before and After Trade Liberalisation. *World bank policy research working paper* no. 4062, Washington, DC.
Singh, T. 2010. "Does International Trade Cause Economic Growth? A Survey." *The World Economy* 33: 1517–64.
Wacziarg, R. 2001. "Measuring the Dynamic Gains From Trade." *World Bank Economic Review* 15: 393–429.
Wacziarg, R., and K. Welch. 2008. "Trade Liberalisation and Growth: New Evidence." *World Bank Economic Review* 22: 187–231.

Appendix 1. Supplementary tables

Table A1.   Liberalising countries and episodes by region.

Asia: Bangladesh 1996, Republic of Korea 1968, Indonesia 1970, Malaysia 1963, Nepal 1991, Pakistan 2001, Philippines 1988, Sri Lanka 1977, 1996.
Africa: Botswana 1979, Burundi 1999, Cameroon 1993, Cote d'Ivoire 1994, Egypt 1995, Gambia 1985, Ghana 1985, Kenya 1963, 1993, Mali 1988, Mauritania 1995, Mauritius (N/A), Morocco 1984, Niger 1994, South Africa 1991, Tanzania 1995, Tunisia 1989, Uganda 1988.
Latin America: Argentina 1991, Barbados 1996, Bolivia 1995, Brazil 1991, Colombia 1986, Costa Rica 1986, Dominican Republic 1992, Ecuador 1991, El Salvador 1991, Guatemala 1988, Honduras 1991, Jamaica 1962, 1989, Mexico 1986, Panama 1996, Paraguay 1989, Peru 1991, Trinidad and Tobago 1992, Uruguay 1990, Venezuela 1989, 1996.
OECD: Australia 1964, Japan 1964, New Zealand 1986.
Other: Armenia 1995, Bulgaria 1991, Czech Republic 1991, Hungary 1990, Israel 1985, Jordan 1965, Latvia 1993, Lithuania 1993, Poland 1992, Slovak Republic 1991, Slovenia 1991, Turkey 1989.

Table A2. Threshold regressions.

	(1) Growth	(2) Invest	(3) Invest	(4) Invest	(5) BMP	(6) BMP	(7) Govt	(8) Govt	(9) Trade	(10) Trade	(11) Trade
LIB1	0.0169*** (0.00353)	0.00264 (0.00475)	0.00286 (0.00480)	0.00283 (0.00479)	−0.413 (0.286)	−0.423 (0.286)	−0.0197*** (0.00303)	−0.0209*** (0.00346)	0.0149 (0.0133)	0.00600 (0.0128)	0.00617 (0.0128)
LIB2	0.0219*** (0.00530)		0.0240*** (0.00508)	0.0238*** (0.00509)		−1.901*** (0.404)		−0.0190*** (0.00333)		0.0393** (0.0197)	0.0406** (0.0197)
LIB3				0.0406*** (0.00607)	−2.051*** (0.410)	−2.422*** (0.521)	−0.00733* (0.00420)	−0.00690 (0.00433)			0.0794*** (0.0211)
LIB4		0.0278*** (0.00500)	0.0404*** (0.00613)	0.0374*** (0.00838)					0.0770*** (0.0195)	0.0865*** (0.0204)	0.0984*** (0.0241)
Threshold	12.0	**2.0**	**7.0**	13.0	**5.0**	9.0	**7.0**	1.0	**7.0**	**4.0**	10.0
P-value	0.196	0.000***	0.000***	0.576	0.000***	0.11	0.000***	0.648	0.000***	0.042**	0.292
F-stat	5.33***	19.77***	19.72***	19.70***	58.05***	57.56***	47.23***	46.72***	73.57***	74.28***	74.77***
R-squared	0.317	0.632	0.636	0.636	0.833	0.833	0.802	0.802	0.863	0.864	0.864
Observations	1,227	1,227	1,227	1,227	1,227	1,227	1,227	1,227	1,227	1,227	1,227

Notes: Coefficients on control variables have been omitted to save space. Significant thresholds are in Bold.

Table A3. SUR results excluding liberalisation from the growth equation.

	(1) Grow	(2) Govt	(3) Trade	(4) Invest	(5) BMP
Invest	0.237***				
	(0.0248)				
Govt	−0.173***				
	(0.0362)				
Trade	−0.0110				
	(0.00781)				
ΔPop	−0.543**				
	(0.254)				
BMP	−0.000539				
	(0.000367)				
Liberalisation					
Low Regime					
ASIA		0.00281	0.102***	0.00328	−0.303
		(0.00677)	(0.0362)	(0.0125)	(0.712)
AFRICA		−0.0314***	−0.0754***	−0.0130	−1.357***
		(0.00430)	(0.0228)	(0.00796)	(0.455)
LAT AM.		−0.0190***	0.0329*	0.0163**	0.564
		(0.00347)	(0.0184)	(0.00639)	(0.375)
OECD		−0.0133	−0.0209	0.00409	−2.324*
		(0.0111)	(0.0660)	(0.0241)	(1.281)
OTHER		−0.0264***	−0.0619	−0.00644	−2.373***
		(0.00716)	(0.0393)	(0.0144)	(0.762)
Middle Regime					
ASIA			0.138***	0.0355***	
			(0.0424)	(0.0112)	
AFRICA			−0.0566**	0.00885	
			(0.0277)	(0.00731)	
LAT AM.			0.0571**	0.0390***	
			(0.0228)	(0.00611)	
OECD			−0.0364	0.00643	
			(0.0694)	(0.0189)	
OTHER			−0.00332	0.00267	
			(0.0475)	(0.0122)	
High Regime					
ASIA		0.0162**	0.225***	0.0228*	−2.506***
		(0.00816)	(0.0399)	(0.0122)	(0.723)
AFRICA		−0.0185***	−0.0322	0.0463***	−3.221***
		(0.00580)	(0.0291)	(0.00875)	(0.531)
LAT AM.		0.000986	0.112***	0.0425***	−1.674***
		(0.00428)	(0.0214)	(0.00664)	(0.414)
OECD		−0.0283**	−0.00768	0.0336**	3.854***
		(0.0110)	(0.0540)	(0.0165)	(1.088)
OTHER		−0.0410***	0.0493	0.0246**	−3.384***
		(0.00737)	(0.0365)	(0.0112)	(0.725)
Chi Squared	538.3***	40043.2***	39339.5***	40583.4***	6577.9***
R-squared	0.303	0.813	0.868	0.646	0.843
Observations	1,227	1,227	1,227	1,227	1,227

Notes: See Table 1.

Table A4. SUR results including liberalisation in growth equation: Aggregate sample.

	(1) Grow	(2) Govt	(3) Trade	(4) Invest	(5) BMP
Invest	0.236*** (0.0246)				
Govt	−0.110*** (0.0364)				
Trade	−0.00979 (0.00774)				
ΔPop	−0.608** (0.252)				
BMP	−0.000525 (0.000366)				
LIB1	0.0168*** (0.00359)	−0.0196*** (0.00281)	0.00421 (0.0143)	0.00273 (0.00479)	−0.406 (0.294)
LIB2			0.0342* (0.0177)	0.0238*** (0.00478)	
LIB3		−0.00746** (0.00378)	0.0849*** (0.0189)	0.0399*** (0.00576)	−2.041*** (0.360)
lnGpc		−0.0189*** (0.00612)	0.148*** (0.0288)	0.130*** (0.00892)	−2.695*** (0.572)
LnPop		−0.122*** (0.0144)	0.0806 (0.0584)		
P15-64		−0.149** (0.0607)		0.0686 (0.0846)	
P65+		−0.615*** (0.171)		−0.603*** (0.213)	
lnRer			0.0738*** (0.00814)		−0.0159 (0.172)
CAD			−0.00436*** (0.000857)		0.0293 (0.0183)
RPCap				0.0192*** (0.00439)	
FDev				−0.000332*** (0.000126)	0.0490*** (0.00860)
F-Test	563.56***	4978.22***	39121.73***	41113.83***	6121.01***
R-squared	0.315	0.802	0.862	0.636	0.833
Observations	1,227	1,227	1,227	1,227	1,227

Notes: See Table 1.

Table A5. SUR results excluding liberalisation from the growth equation: Aggregate sample.

	(1) Grow	(2) Govt	(3) Trade	(4) Invest	(5) BMP
Invest	0.233*** (0.0248)				
Govt	−0.164*** (0.0362)				
Trade	−0.0106 (0.00781)				
ΔPop	−0.537** (0.254)				
BMP	−0.000827** (0.000367)				
LIB1		−0.0197*** (0.00281)	0.00262 (0.0143)	0.00268 (0.00479)	−0.430 (0.294)
LIB2			0.0326* (0.0177)	0.0238*** (0.00478)	
LIB3		−0.00751** (0.00378)	0.0833*** (0.0189)	0.0399*** (0.00576)	−2.063*** (0.360)
lnGpc		−0.0188*** (0.00612)	0.148*** (0.0288)	0.130*** (0.00892)	−2.702*** (0.572)
LnPop		−0.121*** (0.0144)	0.0813 (0.0584)		
P15-64		−0.150** (0.0607)		0.0685 (0.0846)	
P65+		−0.616*** (0.171)		−0.604*** (0.213)	
lnRer			0.0738*** (0.00814)		−0.0111 (0.172)
CAD			−0.00436*** (0.000856)		0.0289 (0.0183)
RPCap				0.0192*** (0.00439)	
FDev				−0.000332*** (0.000126)	0.0492*** (0.00860)
F-Test	539.82***	4978.14***	39120.55***	41110.80***	6018.21***
R-squared	0.303	0.802	0.862	0.636	0.831
Observations	1,227	1,227	1,227	1,227	1,227

Notes: See Table 1.

Trade, finance, specialization and synchronization in the Asia-Pacific

Shihan Xie,[a,b] Tianyin Cheng[a,c] and Wai-Mun Chia[a]

[a]*Division of Economics, School of Humanities and Social Sciences, Nanyang Technological University, Singapore;* [b]*Division of Mathematics, School of Physical and Mathematical Sciences, Nanyang Technological University, Singapore;* [c]*Daiwa Capital Markets Singapore Limited, Singapore*

In this paper, we examine the relationship between trade, finance, specialization and output synchronization of 12 Asia-Pacific economies by studying the direct and indirect effects of increasing trade and financial integration on output synchronization. Using cross-sectional data for the periods of 1984–1996 and 1999–2007, we estimate a system of equations accounting for both endogeneity and simultaneity. Our main findings suggest that: (1) trade and financial integration has direct positive effects, while specialization has direct negative effects on output correlations. An increase in the coefficient of trade intensity and the significance of financial integration is observed in the post-Crisis period. (2) Most estimated coefficients have signs consistent with the existing literature and the results remain robust under different measures of output correlation, but a notable difference is that trade and finance have sizable positive effects on specialization; however, specialization is not a driving force of trade. (3) Countries with more variance in exchange rates have less synchronized cycles.

1. Introduction

Asia-Pacific countries are making an effort on seeking economic integration mainly through trade and financial integration. A wave of bilateral and regional trade agreements has swept the Asia-Pacific region (Petri, Plummer, and Zhai 2011). Prior to 2000, there were only four major trade agreements among Asia-Pacific Economic Cooperation (APEC) economies. Today, there are 39 trade agreements, with others in negotiation. These trade agreements have promoted free trade and economic cooperation throughout the Asia-Pacific region. Besides trade agreements, the launching of regional cooperative initiatives such as the Chiang Mai Initiative Multilateralization (CMIM) and the Asian Bond Market Initiative are designed to enhance monetary cooperation and integrate regional financial markets. The efforts at enhancing both trade and financial integration are consistent with the observed increasing bilateral business cycle correlations within the Asia-Pacific region.

Theoretically, many variables can explain why some countries are more synchronized than others. The first is bilateral trade. The impact of trade integration on business cycle correlations could go either way. The direct effect shows that if the demand channel is the dominant driving force and intra-industry trade prevails, positive output shocks in a country can generate an increase in its demand for foreign goods, boosting economies abroad

(Frankel and Rose 1998). The indirect effect, however, suggests that if industry-specific shocks are the dominant driving force and inter-industry trade prevails, trade integration leads to greater specialization in different industries, which in turn leads to asymmetric effects of industry-specific shocks (Kenen 1969; Krugman 1993). Given the theoretical ambiguity, empirical investigation is essential. Many empirical studies, such as those by Frankel and Rose (1998), Clark and van Wincoop (2001) and Baxter and Koupiratsas (2005) show direct positive effect of bilateral trade on business cycle synchronization.

The second is financial integration. The link between financial integration and business cycles, however, is ambiguous for two reasons. First, the direct link is theoretically uncertain. On the one hand, limited ability to borrow and lend internationally for investors in financially less-integrated countries hampers the transfer of resources across countries, forcing investors to invest domestically and thereby increasing output correlations. However, on the other hand, imperfect information, liquidity constraints or regulatory limits to capital flows in financially less-integrated countries may lead investors to withdraw capital simultaneously from many destinations, reducing investment, output and output correlations of these countries with other countries. Second, the indirect specialization effect could either strengthen or lessen the direct link. Kalemli-Ozcan, Sorensen, and Yosha (2001) empirically document a significantly positive relationship between specialization and risk sharing. Thus, financial integration should negatively affect business cycle synchronization indirectly through its effect on specialization.

Both openness to goods trade and liberalization in financial markets are likely to induce specialization. Therefore, given the importance of industrial structure and specialization, these variables are also used in the literature. The empirical evidence on industrial structure and specialization on business cycle synchronization are rather mixed. While Imbs (2004, 2006) shows that countries with more similar industrial structures and less specialization tend to be more synchronized in terms of their business cycles, Baxter and Koupiratsas (2005) and Clark and van Wincoop (2001) find that this relationship is either not robust or not significant.

Finally, other variables such as membership of a currency union or a trade agreement, distance between two countries, common border, common language, and so on have also been used to explain why some countries are more synchronized than the others.

The complex direct and indirect linkages between trade in goods, financial openness, specialization and business cycle synchronization as shown in Figure 1 is the motivation for the investigation of the determinants of business cycle synchronization in the context of a system of simultaneous equations. Following Imbs (2004), we investigate the relations

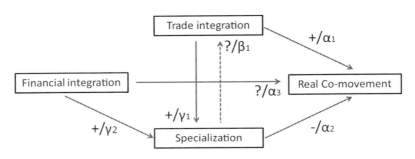

Figure 1. Direct and indirect channels (adopted from Imbs 2004).

between trade integration, financial integration, specialization and the correlation of business cycles in the Asia-Pacific region for the period 1984–2007. In particular, we consider the evolution of such interactions over time, with focus on sub-periods divided by the Asian Financial Crisis (AFC). As we primarily focus on the East Asian economies and their major trading partners, we have included in our paper the five co-founding members of ASEAN (Indonesia, Malaysia, Philippines, Singapore and Thailand), two Asian newly industrialized economies (Korea and Hong Kong), the two largest economies in the region (Japan and China) and three major trading partners of East Asian economies (the United States, Australia and New Zealand).

Our paper extends the literature on business cycle synchronization of the Asia-Pacific region in several ways. First, our work on the Asia-Pacific region builds on the simultaneous-equations framework used by Imbs (2004). Such an approach accounts for both the direct and the indirect channels linking business cycle correlations, trade integration, financial integration and specialization. Some of the links we consider have been investigated empirically but not simultaneously. Second, financial market regulations after the AFC indicate a possible structural break after the Crisis. Using the AFC as a breakpoint, we identify possible changes in the roles of trade integration, financial integration and specialization in business cycle synchronization. Third, we perform robustness checks using different measures of business cycle correlations. We also take into account possible omission of variables by controlling for exchange rate volatility.

The paper is organized as follows. Section 2 presents our econometric methodology. Section 3 describes the data. Section 4 analyses the estimation results and discusses the economic relevance of our findings. Section 5 concludes.

2. Methodology

2.1. *The system of simultaneous equations*

In order to unravel the complexity of interactions between trade, finance, specialization and output correlations in Asia-Pacific economies, we need to model both the direct and the indirect channels to business cycle synchronizations. As single-equation estimation mostly accounts for the direct channels only, we employ a simultaneous-equations model to account for the possible endogeneity of trade, finance and specialization. The system of equations estimated follows the model used by Imbs (2004):

$$\rho_{i,j} = \alpha_0 + \alpha_1 T_{i,j} + \alpha_2 S_{i,j} + \alpha_3 F_{i,j} + \alpha_4 \mathbf{X}_{1,i,j} + \varepsilon_{1,i,j}, \tag{1}$$

$$T_{i,j} = \beta_0 + \beta_1 S_{i,j} + \beta_2 \mathbf{X}_{2,i,j} + \varepsilon_{2,i,j}, \tag{2}$$

$$S_{i,j} = \gamma_0 + \gamma_1 T_{i,j} + \gamma_2 F_{i,j} + \gamma_3 \mathbf{X}_{3,i,j} + \varepsilon_{3,i,j}, \tag{3}$$

$$F_{i,j} = \delta_0 + \delta_1 \mathbf{X}_{4,i,j} + \varepsilon_{4,i,j}, \tag{4}$$

where $\rho_{i,j}$ refers to the bilateral business cycle correlation between country i and j, and $T_{i,j}$ and $F_{i,j}$ are measures of trade and financial integration, respectively, $S_{i,j}$ is a specialization index indicating the industrial structure similarities between country i and country j. In this system, bilateral business cycle correlations, trade and financial integration as well as specialization are endogenous. The interactions between them are summarized in Figure 1.

The direct effect of trade on business cycle correlations is measured by α_1 and, as documented by Frankel and Rose (1998), is expected to be positive. However, the intensity of intra- and inter-industry trade may have different roles to play. The effect of intra-industry trade depends on the extent to which bilateral trade is accounted by similarities in the two countries' economic structures, as captured by β_1, while the effect of inter-industry trade works indirectly through the effect of trade-induced specialization, as captured by γ_1. Therefore, $\alpha_1\beta_1$ and $\alpha_2\gamma_1$ measure the effect of intra-industry and inter-industry trade, respectively. Similarly, the direct effect of financial integration is represented by α_3 but has an indeterminate sign. The indirect effect works via specialization as captured by $\alpha_2\gamma_2$. According to Kalemli-Ozcan, Sorensen, and Yosha (2001, 2003), financially integrated regions tend to be more specialized (positive γ_2), but deepening specialization results in less synchronized business cycles (negative α_2).

The exogenous variables are included in the four vectors: X_1, X_2, X_3, and X_4. In the literature on single-equation estimations of output correlations, the focus is usually on only one of the three variables. Hence, we have included more variables in our model compared with the existing literature. Consistent with Imbs (2004) model, we leave X_1 empty for our baseline model of estimation and put the later specified policy coordination measures into X_1 for robustness testing. The specification of X_2 variables is standard following the classical gravity model. Accordingly, we include measures of both countries' GDP, the geographic distance between two countries, binary variables indicating the presence of a common border and common language, as well as an indicator for ASEAN membership. X_3 summarizes the exogenous determinants of specialization. As discovered by Imbs and Wacziarg (2003), countries initially tend to diversify into various industries but will respecialize once a certain income per capita level is reached. This provides us insights into the components for X_3. Like Imbs (2004), we include GDP per capita levels in both economies as well as the gap in their GDP levels in our model. Last, institutional variable measuring financial development, as introduced by La Porta, Lopez-de-Silanes, and Shleifer (1998), is one available choice for X_4. This is suggested by Kalemli-Ozcan, Sorensen, and Yosha (2003) to account for the possible endogeneity of F. However, its compatibility to our model is subject to empirical testing.

2.2. *Policy coordination*

Although we have included more variables in explaining output correlations than most other previous work, the possibilities of omission due to convergence in policy still exist. Imbs (2004) does not take the role of fiscal and monetary policies into consideration. However, in a study by Inklaar, Jong-A-Pin, and de Haan (2008) on re-examining the relationship between trade and business cycle correlations among OECD countries, the effect of exchange rate variability, monetary and fiscal policies are found to be significant. In this paper, as we are focusing on the Asia-Pacific region, we shall not omit the possibility that policy changes after the AFC have a role to play in reinforcing output correlations. Thus, in the robustness test, we include in X_1 two exogenous variables to capture the similarities in monetary and fiscal policies between countries. To capture the increase in exchange rate coordination emerging since the 1997–1998 AFC, we consider a third exogenous variables in X_1 to capture the volatility of the bilateral exchange rate.

2.3. *Econometric issues*

The choice of regression method for our model is important. In this subsection, we briefly discuss three econometric methods that are relevant to our model estimation: two-stage least squares (2SLS), seemingly unrelated regressions (SUR) and three-stage least squares (3SLS).

The 2SLS method is the simplest and the most common estimation method for the simultaneous-equations model. It is an equation-by-equation technique, where the endogenous regressors on the right-hand side are instrumented with all the exogenous variables in the system. 2SLS estimation is consistent, but generally not efficient. The SUR method is an estimation method for a linear regression model that consists of several seemingly unrelated regression equations. Although each individual equation can be estimated by ordinary least squares (OLS) consistently, the estimates are generally not as efficient as the SUR method, which amounts to feasible generalized least squares with a specific form of the variance–covariance matrix. The 3SLS estimator combines 2SLS with SUR and hence is a consistent and more efficient estimator than 2SLS.

In summary, for a simultaneous-equations model with correlated cross-equation error terms, the estimation properties are as follows. For equation-by-equation estimations, OLS reports inconsistent estimation, while 2SLS achieves consistency but not efficiency. For system estimations, SUR is efficient compared with OLS but inconsistent due to the endogeneity bias. In contrast, 3SLS provides consistent and efficient estimation, and hence, it is our choice of estimation method.

3. Data and measurement

Data were collected to measure business cycle correlations, bilateral trade intensity, bilateral financial integration and the similarity in industrial structures.

3.1. *Business cycle correlations*

We examine GDP correlations in 12 Asia-Pacific economies over two periods: 1984–1996 and 1999–2007.[1] The sample includes the original five members of ASEAN (Indonesia, Malaysia, Philippines, Singapore and Thailand), the two Asian newly industrialized economies (Korea and Hong Kong), the two largest economies in the region (Japan and China) and the three major trading partners of East Asian economies (the United States, Australia and New Zealand). The dependent variable in Equation (1) is the bivariate correlation between filtered annual GDP at constant 2000 US dollars. All the GDP data are drawn from the primary World Bank database – World Development Indicators (WDI). Three different filtering methods are employed in our study. In the first step, to avoid complexity, the simple unconditional correlation coefficient of the first difference of the natural logarithm of real GDP series is used as our measure of bilateral business cycle synchronization. To perform robustness tests on our model, correlation coefficients of the logarithm of real GDP series filtered by a quadratic trend[2] and the Hodrick–Prescott filter[3] are used as proxies for output correlations. Nonetheless, since the unconditional correlation coefficient is bounded at −1 and 1, the error terms in the regression model are unlikely to be normally distributed. Furthermore, the relationship between trade and output correlation is unlikely to be linear, since when ρ is close to 1, increase in trade intensity could have little effect, but the effect could be much larger when ρ is around 0. This issue, however, with very few exceptions, has not been seriously treated in many previous studies and hence complicates reliable inference. In our model, following Inklaar, Jong-A-Pin, and de Haan (2008), Fisher's z-transformations of the correlation coefficients are employed as the dependent variable instead. The transformed correlation coefficients are calculated based

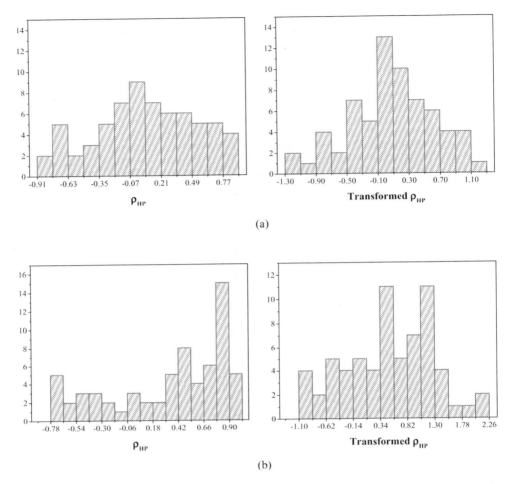

Figure 2. (a). Estimated density plots for untransformed ρ_{HP} and transformed ρ_{HP} (1984–1996). (b). Estimated density plots for untransformed ρ_{HP} and transformed ρ_{HP} (1999–2007).

on the following:

$$\text{trans}\_\rho = \frac{1}{2}\ln\left(\frac{1+\rho}{1-\rho}\right),$$

where ρ is the pair-wise correlation coefficient for each country pair. The one-to-one correspondence between ρ and trans_ρ implies that for each value of ρ, there is a one-to-one correspondence between partial differentiation of ρ and trans_ρ with respect to other variables of our interest. Such relationship can be shown as follows:

$$\frac{\partial \rho_{\text{untransformed}}}{\partial K} = \frac{\partial \rho_{\text{transformed}}}{\partial K}\left(1 - \rho_{\text{untransformed}}^2\right), \tag{5}$$

where K represents T, S, F or variables controlling for policy coordination.

Figure 2(a) and (b) shows the density plots of the untransformed and transformed HP-filter correlation coefficients for the two periods, which suggest that it is necessary to transform the dependent variables.[4]

3.2. Bilateral trade intensity

To measure bilateral trade intensity, the data on bilateral trade volume and each country's total global trade volume are collected from the United Nations Commodity Trade Statistics Database (UN Comtrade) and the IMF International Financial Statistics online. Following the method of Calderón, Chong, and Stein (2007), we develop the proxy for bilateral trade integration using both import and export data as follows:

$$T_{ijt} = \frac{1}{\tau} \sum_t \frac{x_{ijt} + m_{ijt}}{X_{it} + M_{it} + X_{jt} + M_{jt}},$$

where x_{ijt} denotes total nominal exports from country i to country j during year t, m_{ijt} denotes the total nominal imports from country i to country j during year t; X_{it}, X_{jt}, M_{it} and M_{it} denote total global exports and imports for the corresponding country; and τ is the length of the each period. It is noted that for each country pair, the trade data reported by the country with the larger GDP is used. Under such measurement, larger values of T imply closer trade ties between two countries.

3.3. Similarity in industry specialization

The measure of similarity in industry specialization follows Imbs (2004) by aggregating the absolute sectorial difference between the two countries and averaging over time:

$$S_{i,j} = \frac{1}{\tau} \sum_t \sum_n |s_{n,i} - s_{n,j}|,$$

where $s_{n,i}$ denotes the GDP share of industry n in country i. Therefore, S would reach its maximum value if two countries share no sector in common. We compute S using data on industrial GDP shares taken from the UN Statistics Division. One of the defects with data is that the industrial sectorial data are aggregate data with seven broad categories.[5]

3.4. Bilateral financial integration

There are broad ways of measuring bilateral financial integration but none are well established. From the point of view that restrictions on capital flows impede financial integration, indices capturing capital account restrictions could be one reasonable proxy. An alternative approach relies on the variables reflecting effective financial flows. In our paper, we adopt the latter approach, as increased capital market openness does not necessarily result in deeper financial integration. Using data from an updated and extended version of the External Wealth of Nations Mark II database developed by Lane and Milesi-Ferretti (2007), we develop the following measure as our proxy for F:

$$\text{LMF} = \frac{1}{\tau} \sum_t \left| (\text{NFA/GDP})_i - (\text{NFA/GDP})_j \right|_t,$$

Table 1. Summary statistics.

Variable	Mean	Min.	Max.	Std. dev.	No. of obs.
1984–1996					
ρ_{FD}	0.112	−0.931	1.233	0.439	66
ρ_{HP}	0.084	−1.166	1.245	0.544	66
$\rho_{quadratic}$	0.146	−1.384	1.835	0.691	66
T	0.017	0.002	0.170	0.025	66
S	0.434	0.164	0.921	0.175	66
F	0.577	0.033	1.834	0.446	66
1999–2007					
ρ_{FD}	0.490	−0.774	1.893	0.563	66
ρ_{HP}	0.504	−1.022	2.245	0.784	66
$\rho_{quadratic}$	0.442	−0.774	1.949	0.639	66
T	0.019	0.001	0.153	0.023	66
S	0.484	0.183	1.035	0.205	66
F	0.973	0.085	2.925	0.872	66

where NFA denotes the net foreign assets positions in country i measured in current US dollars, a composition of net position in foreign direct investment, equities and debt. LMF will take high values for countries that are divergent in their external positions, which are more likely to lend and borrow from each other, implying deeper financial integration.

3.5. Summary

Table 1 summarizes several key statistics of the four endogenous variables in our model. It is interesting to note that the means of all variables increased from Period 1 (1984–1996) to Period 2 (1999–2007). The cross-sectional business cycle correlations are similar for both periods, irrespective of the filtering methods. A significant increase in the means is observed for all three different proxies of output correlations, evidencing the deeper economic integration among the Asia-Pacific economies. The effect of intensive financial regulations on Asian countries after the AFC is reflected in this table by a notable increase in the mean of F, implying deeper financial integration in the region.

Table 2 reports the corresponding unconditional correlation with a few interesting features. First, proxies for output correlations are highly correlated with one another. Second, trade integration is positively correlated with all measures of business cycle correlations in both periods. Third, specialization is negatively correlated with output correlations in the first period, but the correlation is weakly positive in the second period. Fourth, there is evidence of a positive correlation of finance with business cycle synchronization in the second period we study. However, the reported unconditional correlations are informative only, a more rigorous examinations using econometric methods are necessary.

3.6. Exogenous variables

As discussed earlier, we leave X_1 empty in our baseline model. X_2 contains the following set of gravity variables[6]: the (log) product of both countries' GDP, the (log mile) distance between two countries, dummies for the presence of common border and common language as well as ASEAN membership. The set of X_3 variables are different from those of X_2: the (log) product of each country's GDP per capita and the (log) GDP gap, defined as $\max[(Y_i/Y_j), (Y_j/Y_i)]$. Finally, as suggested by Imbs (2004), the X_4 contains the following:

Table 2. Unconditional correlations.

Correlation	ρ_{FD}	ρ_{HP}	$\rho_{quadratic}$	T	S	F
1984–1996						
ρ_{FD}	1.000					
ρ_{HP}	0.778	1.000				
$\rho_{quadratic}$	0.766	0.764	1.000			
T	0.014	0.005	0.086	1.000		
S	−0.175	−0.143	−0.185	0.200	1.000	
F	0.018	−0.011	0.057	−0.013	0.142	1.000
1999–2007						
ρ_{FD}	1.000					
ρ_{HP}	0.940	1.000				
$\rho_{quadratic}$	0.808	0.722	1.000			
T	0.069	0.130	0.057	1.000		
S	0.069	0.161	0.019	0.224	1.000	
F	0.089	0.108	0.052	−0.035	0.208	1.000

measures of shareholder rights (with variables capturing the percentage of capital necessary to call an extraordinary shareholders' meeting, whether one share carries one vote, whether the distribution of dividends is mandatory and whether proxy vote by mail is allowed), an aggregate index of creditor rights, and an assessment of accounting standards and the rule of law, developed by La Porta et al. (1998). Measures for China are not included but can be retrieved from the work of Allen, Qian, and Qian (2005) on the development of the legal and financial system in China.

There are three sets of proxies used to control for policy coordination. First, we measure similarities in fiscal policy by using the bilateral correlations of the government balance as a percentage of GDP. All countries data on government balance as a percentage of GDP except for China[7] are from the Economic Intelligence Unit's Database.[8] Second, Inklaar, Jong-A-Pin, and de Haan (2008) uses the correlation of short-term interest rates as a proxy for similarities in monetary policy. In a similar manner, we use the correlations of real interest rates obtained from the WDI database operated by the World Bank. Third, in view of emerging exchange rate cooperation between Asian countries since the AFC, a measure of bilateral exchange rate volatility is needed to ensure a reliable control of convergence in policy. However, due to the fact that exchange rate is defined in a twofold manner, the construction of a variable to measure exchange rate variation remains controversial. In our paper, we adopt the coefficients of variation in the exchange rate between country i and country j during period τ as the proxy. It is crucial to determine which country's currency is to be quoted in another when deciding which exchange rate is to be used for each country pair. The criteria adopted is based on currency distribution of global foreign exchange market turnover reported by the Bank of International Settlement, meaning that we use the more frequently traded currency as the base currency for exchange rate quoting between any country pair.[9]

4. Results

This section reports the paper's main results. Regression results using 3SLS methods for both periods are reported for our baseline model estimation. We perform robustness analysis by evaluating the sensitivity to alternative measures of output correlations as well as by

Table 3. Three-stage least-square regression results.

	1984–1996	1999–2007
Correlation ρ		
T	8.738 (2.17)**	15.995 (3.02)***
S	−3.316 (4.87)***	−2.615 (3.47)***
F	0.200 (1.36)	0.168 (1.81)*
Trade T		
S	0.010 (0.33)	0.024 (1.12)
GDP product	0.005 (4.17)***	0.006 (5.70)***
Distance	−0.011 (2.70)***	−0.013 (3.85)***
Border	0.042 (3.61)***	0.030 (3.23)***
Language	0.010 (1.89)*	0.007 (1.78)*
ASEAN	−0.013 (1.24)	−0.005 (0.65)
R^2	0.396	0.461
Specialization S		
T	2.496 (2.02)**	2.791 (1.90)*
F	0.092 (1.94)*	0.068 (2.34)**
GDP per capita	−0.021 (1.91)*	−0.023 (1.76)*
GDP gap	0.024 (1.88)*	0.006 (0.38)
R^2	0.128	0.166

controlling for policy coordination. Regression results based on other different econometric methods are reported as final sensitivity tests.

4.1. Three-stage least-square results

To begin with, we perform 3SLS to our simultaneous-equations model. We exclude Equation (4) in our estimation since no appropriate instruments for F exist. There is little documentation of $\mathbf{X}_4$ variables in the existing literature. In Imbs (2004), instrumenting F using the institutional variables introduced by La Porta, Lopez-de-Silanes, and Shleifer (1998) resolves the endogeneity of F and thus results in increased significance of the coefficient of F. However, when we instrumented F using the same set of instrumental variables proposed by Imbs (2004), low R-square value of Equation (4) results (about 0.05). Moreover, the significance as well as the magnitude of coefficients of F did not change much after instrumentation. Due to the principle of parsimony, we choose to drop Equation (4) in our study. The specification of the first three equations in our model is as discussed in the methodology regarding the baseline model. The estimates are presented in Table 3.

In our baseline model, $\mathbf{X}_1$ is empty. According to the results in Table 3, the estimates of α_1 and α_2 are significant at the 5% level in both periods, with signs consistent with the existing literature. Trade integration exerts strong positive direct effects on output correlations among Asia-Pacific economies and the effect is found to be stronger in the post-Crisis period, denoted by the higher α_1 in Period 2. As α_1 characterizes the effect of trade on transformed ρ only, we can apply Equation (5) to obtain the effect of trade intensity on ρ at different levels. Since $\partial \rho / \partial T$ is a function of output correlation, it varies across country pairs. Figure 3 presents the scatter plot of $\partial \rho / \partial T$ in Period 2 versus Period 1. Each point in the figure represents one country pair, and any point above the 45-degree line indicates an increase in $\partial \rho / \partial T$ between the two countries. The scatter plot is denser at the upper left panel, indicating that the direct effect of trade integration is indeed stronger in the post-Crisis period. Conversely, specialization has a direct negative effect on business cycle

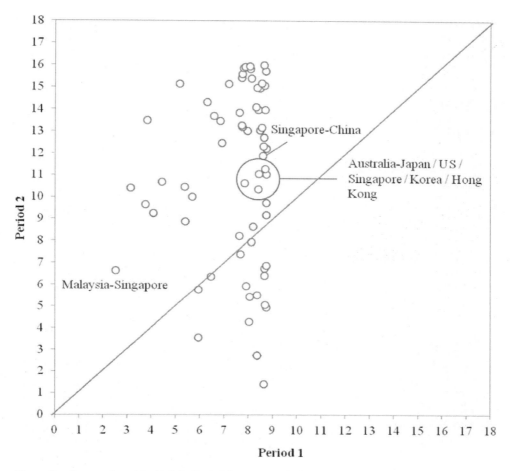

Figure 3. Scatter plot of $\partial\rho/\partial T$ for Period 2 versus Period 1.

correlations, which means that the business cycles of countries with more similar industrial structures are more synchronized. The direct effect of financial integration is found to be weak, but positive and significant on ρ, especially in the post-Crisis period. The observed increase in significance of α_3 is consistent with the greater post-Crisis financial regulation within the region.

The coefficients for the product of both countries' GDP, distance between two countries and the dummy for common border are significant at the 1% level, with signs consistent with what is predicted by the gravity model. However, the coefficient of S is insignificant in both periods. Hence, specialization appears not to be a driving force of trade integration for Asia-Pacific economies based on our finding.

According to the estimation results of Equation (3), financial integration has the predicted specialization effects, as documented by Kalemli-Ozcan, Sorensen, and Yosha (2003). High LMFs are associated with high S, i.e., financially integrated countries tend to have dissimilar industrial sectorial patterns. Different from Imbs (2004), the effect of trade integration on specialization is found to be significant. Closer trade partners are observed to share more differences in specialization patterns.

Besides addressing the issue of non-linear effect of trade on output correlation, the adoption of transformed ρ shows another advantage by solving the problem of non-normality in the residuals. Figure 4 checks the normality of residuals obtained from 3SLS by using either transformed ρ or untransformed ρ as the dependent variable. Q–Q plot shows that the error process of the equations using transformed ρ is indeed Gaussian (Figure 4(a)). However, the curve with residuals from untransformed ρ does not converge to normal distribution since it is bowl shaped (Figure 4(b)).

4.2. *Robustness check*

In the previous subsection, simple unconditional correlation coefficient of the first difference of logarithm of real GDP series are used as the measure of business cycle synchronizations. In this subsection, we present the results using two different measures of business cycle correlations obtained by different filtering methods: quadratic trend filter and Hodrick–Prescott filter.

The regression results are reported in Table 4. Similar conclusions can be drawn with our new sets of proxies. The magnitude and significance of the exogenous and endogenous variables are very similar with all different measures of output correlations, reinforcing our baseline findings.

4.3. *Control for policy and exchange rate coordination*

As mentioned earlier, one of the possible omissions of variables in our baseline model of estimation is convergence in policy. Therefore, we add three exogenous variables to control for policy coordination to X_1 in our model. Measures of similarities in policy include correlations of bilateral fiscal and monetary policy as well as bilateral exchange rate fluctuation.

As reported in Table 5, there are no significant changes in coefficients of most exogenous and endogenous variables in Period 1 except that the indirect effect of specialization turns out to be positively significant. None of the policy variables appear to exert significant effects on ρ.

As for the period after financial crisis, the signs of all coefficients are the same, but the direct effect of trade and financial integration on ρ is weakened. The direct effect of specialization remains robust. As expected, the significance of the policy variables increased in the post-Crisis period. Convergence in fiscal policy reinforces the correlations in output correlation, but country pairs with more variance in exchange rates have less synchronized cycles, as seen from the negative coefficient of exchange rate policy coordination. Such results indicate that stability in exchange rates between two countries contributes to the convergence in their business cycle synchronization. Strong exchange rate coordination is beneficial to countries or regions seeking economic integration.

4.4. *Comparison of estimation methods*

In this part, we compare and contrast the regression results obtained from OLS, SUR, 2SLS and 3SLS estimations. Tables 6(a) and (b) reports the estimation results. Although estimations of Equations (2) and (3) appear to be very close in the signs and significance of variables, the coefficients of endogenous variables in Equation (1) differ greatly among different estimation methods. As we compare the regression results between OLS and 2SLS or between SUR and 3SLS, an apparent increase in the coefficients of T, S and F can be

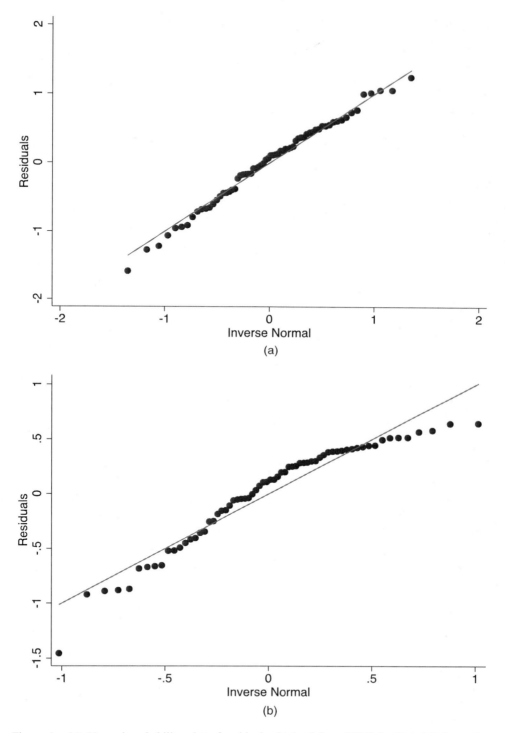

Figure 4. (a). Normal probability plot of residuals obtained from 3SLS for Period 2 data using transformed ρ. (b). Normal probability plot of residuals obtained from 3SLS for Period 2 data using untransformed ρ.

Table 4. Robustness check using different measures of output correlation.

	1984–1996		1999–2007	
	$\rho_{\text{quadratic}}$	ρ_{HP}	$\rho_{\text{quadratic}}$	ρ_{HP}
Correlation ρ				
T	17.593 (2.78)***	13.287 (2.72)***	19.785 (3.12)***	18.318 (2.68)**
S	−5.502 (5.19)***	−3.435 (4.15)***	−3.964 (4.64)***	−2.03 (2.00)**
F	0.385 (1.69)*	0.156 (0.91)	0.214 (1.92)*	0.173 (1.43)
Trade T				
S	0.014 (0.45)	0.013 (0.42)	0.021 (0.98)	0.026 (1.19)
GDP product	0.006 (4.34)***	0.006 (4.50)***	0.006 (5.51)***	0.006 (5.80)***
Distance	−0.011 (2.65)***	−0.011 (2.77)***	−0.012 (3.57)***	−0.013 (3.71)***
Border	0.044 (3.75)***	0.043 (3.76)***	0.032 (3.41)***	0.030 (3.21)***
Language	0.010 (1.97)**	0.012 (2.46)**	0.009 (2.01)**	0.008 (1.95)*
ASEAN	−0.010 (1.00)	−0.010 (0.99)	−0.007 (0.90)	−0.004 (0.46)
R^2	0.395	0.393	0.467	0.459
Specialization S				
T	2.434 (1.98)**	2.670 (2.17)**	2.882 (1.97)**	2.779 (1.89)*
F	0.086 (1.83)*	0.097 (2.05)**	0.071 (2.49)**	0.068 (2.31)**
GDP per capita product	−0.020 (1.81)*	−0.027 (2.49)**	−0.027 (2.15)**	−0.024 (1.75)*
GDP gap	0.011 (0.84)	0.011 (0.88)	0.008 (0.59)	0.003 (0.16)
R^2	0.148	0.164	0.170	0.168

Table 5. Control for policy and exchange rate coordination.

	1984–1996	1999–2007
Correlation ρ		
T	10.621 (2.76)***	6.463 (1.38)
S	−3.567 (4.13)***	−2.447 (4.43)***
F	0.334 (2.10)**	0.094 (1.25)
Fiscal policy	0.151 (1.18)	0.418 (3.15)***
Monetary policy	0.222 (1.62)	−0.093 (0.53)
EX coordination	0.855 (1.33)	−6.078 (5.05)***
Trade T		
S	0.066 (2.78)***	0.032 (1.63)
GDP product	0.005 (3.69)***	0.006 (5.33)***
Distance	−0.008 (2.21)***	−0.011 (3.15)***
Border	0.034 (3.18)***	0.030 (3.30)***
Language	0.009 (1.75)*	0.008 (1.87)*
ASEAN	−0.006 (0.68)	−0.007 (0.87)
R^2	0.270	0.449
Specialization S		
T	3.772 (3.23)***	3.351 (2.32)**
F	0.073 (1.62)	0.070 (2.44)**
GDP per capita product	−0.018 (1.71)*	−0.029 (2.23)**
GDP gap	0.018 (1.47)	0.007 (0.48)
R^2	0.052	0.166

observed, indicating that the endogeneity may cause inconsistency. Though the change in the magnitudes of the coefficients is relatively small if we compare the results of OLS and SUR or 2SLS and 3SLS, careful scrutiny suggests that the increase in significance level is noteworthy. Therefore, the use of 3SLS is crucial to study business cycle co-movements in

Table 6A. Simultaneous equations: Period 1984–1996.

	OLS	SUR	2SLS
Correlation ρ			
T	0.934 (0.41)	1.572 (0.72)	6.23 (1.49)
S	−0.483 (1.49)	−0.475 (1.51)	−2.123 (2.82)***
F	0.045 (0.37)	0.042 (0.35)	0.141 (0.91)
Trade T			
S	0.014 (0.92)	0.030 (2.11)**	−0.005 (0.14)
GDP product	0.006 (4.16)***	0.006 (4.37)***	0.006 (4.10)***
Distance	−0.011 (2.57)**	−0.010 (2.55)**	−0.012 (2.62)***
Border	0.041 (3.44)***	0.040 (3.58)***	0.043 (3.44)***
Language	0.010 (1.76)*	0.010 (1.91)*	0.010 (1.76)*
ASEAN	−0.012 (1.28)	−0.010 (1.15)	−0.015 (1.42)
R^2	0.398	0.386	0.382
Specialization S			
T	1.915 (2.31)**	2.621 (3.31)***	2.900 (2.25)**
F	0.112 (2.28)**	0.105 (2.25)**	0.117 (2.34)**
GDP per capita product	−0.036 (3.03)***	−0.034 (3.03)***	−0.039 (3.15)***
GDP gap	0.014 (0.94)	0.009 (0.67)	0.016 (1.03)
R^2	0.186	0.174	0.168

Table 6B. Simultaneous equations: Period 1999–2007.

	OLS	SUR	2SLS
Correlation ρ			
T	1.574 (0.49)	5.791 (1.88)*	12.102 (2.18)**
S	0.103 (0.28)	−0.016 (0.05)	−1.432 (1.69)*
F	0.054 (0.64)	0.048 (0.61)	0.139 (1.32)
Trade T			
S	0.016 (1.46)	0.029 (2.80)***	0.011 (0.45)
GDP product	0.006 (4.98)***	0.006 (5.77)***	0.006 (4.91)***
Distance	−0.012 (3.15)***	−0.012 (3.54)***	−0.012 (3.07)***
Border	0.035 (3.47)***	0.032 (3.42)***	0.036 (3.43)***
Language	0.008 (1.67)*	0.008 (1.80)*	0.008 (1.68)*
ASEAN	−0.008 (1.07)	−0.005 (0.74)	−0.010 (1.05)
R^2	0.471	0.458	0.468
Specialization S			
T	2.458 (2.31)**	3.333 (3.28)***	2.939 (1.92)*
F	0.081 (2.65)***	0.076 (2.60)***	0.083 (2.68)***
GDP per capita product	−0.036 (2.41)**	−0.034 (2.39)**	−0.037 (2.45)**
GDP gap	0.010 (0.54)	0.005 (0.31)	0.011 (0.58)
R^2	0.178	0.167	0.176

Asia-Pacific. The comparison between different regression methods serves as a justification of the simultaneous relation between ρ, T, S and F. By resolving the problem of endogeneity and simultaneity, our model provides consistent and efficient estimation for the relevant channels.

5. Conclusions

The essential issue this paper sought to resolve is the complex relationship between trade, finance, specialization and business cycle synchronization of Asia-Pacific economies. To achieve this, we employ the simultaneous-equations framework introduced by Imbs (2004) and applied it to 12 Asia-Pacific economies for the periods 1984–1996 and 1999–2007, respectively. That is, we investigate business cycle synchronization before and after the AFC. 3SLS regression is used to account for the presence of endogeneity and simultaneity in the model. We perform robustness tests using different measures of output correlation and controls for policy coordination in the sample of countries.

Our main findings suggest that: (1) trade and financial integration has direct positive effects, while specialization has direct negative effects on output correlations. An increase in the coefficient of trade intensity and the significance of financial integration is observed in the post-Crisis period. (2) Most estimated coefficients have signs consistent with the existing literature and the results remain robust under different measures of output correlation, but a notable difference is that trade and finance have sizable positive effects on specialization; however, specialization is not a driving force of trade. (3) Countries with more variance in exchange rates have less synchronized cycles, implying that the post-Crisis exchange rate policy coordination may have been effective.

Our findings suggest that stronger trade and financial integration among the Asia-Pacific economies as well as deeper exchange rate cooperation should be effective in promoting regional economic integration.

Acknowledgements

The authors would like to thank Professor Noel Gaston and the anonymous referee for very helpful comments that greatly improved the paper. The authors also thank participants at Bond-NTU first annual workshop for useful comments. The authors are grateful for Mr Liyu Dou's assistance in the collection of data.

Notes

1. Inclusion of the Crisis year tends to distort the estimation for both periods. The time series graph with 9-year moving output correlations excluding AFC displays considerable increase in the post-Crisis period, indicating a clear structure break at the AFC.
2. We fit each country's log (GDP) series over a quadratic trend and compute the pairwise correlation of residuals as proxies for business cycle synchronization.
3. The Hodrick–Prescott filter decomposes a series into a trend series and its corresponding cyclical component. The cyclical components are filtered by finding a trend that satisfies: min $\sum_{t=1}^{T}(y_t - \tau_t)^2 + \lambda \sum_{t=2}^{T-1}[(\tau_{t+1} - \tau_t) - (\tau_t - \tau_{t-1})]^2$, where in our case, y_t is the log (GDP). Since our data are annual series, we set $\lambda = 100$. The pairwise correlations of cyclical components are used as the proxy for business cycle synchronization.
4. The density plots for first-difference correlations and quadratic correlations show similar patterns and the plots are available upon request from the authors.
5. The categorization of seven sectors is as follows: (1) Agriculture, hunting, forestry, fishing (ISIC A and B); (2) Mining, Utilities (ISIC C and E); (3) Manufacturing (ISIC D); (4) Construction (ISIC D); (5) Wholesale, retail trade, restaurants and hotels (ISIC G, H); (6) Transport, storage and communication (ISIC I); and (7) Other Activities (ISIC J-P).
6. Some of the gravity variables are taken from Andrew Rose's website: http://faculty.haas.berkeley.edu/arose/
7. China's data on government budget balance expressed in RMB are available on the CEIC database. We normalized it by GDP at current price in RMB collected from WDI to obtain the percentage of government balance in GDP for China.
8. Data for all countries except Hong Kong and Thailand are available since 1984. For Hong Kong and Thailand, we use data for shorter periods as 1988–2007 and 1989–2007, respectively.
9. The ranking of currencies-based currency distribution of global foreign exchange market turnover is as following (descending): for the period 1984–1996: US dollar, Japanese yen, Australian dollar, Singapore dollar, Hong Kong dollar, Korean Won, New Zealand dollar, Indonesian Rupiah, Thai Baht, Chinese Renminbi, Philippine Peso and Malaysian Ringgit; for the period 1999–2007: US dollar, Japanese Yen, Australian dollar, Hong Kong dollar, New Zealand dollar, Korean Won, Singapore dollar, Chinese Renminbi, Malaysian Ringgit, Indonesian Rupiah, Thai Baht and Philippine Peso.

References

Allen, F., J. Qian, and M. Qian. 2005. "Law, Finance, and Economic Growth in China." *Journal of Financial Economics* 77: 57–116.

Baxter, M., and M.A. Kouparitsas. 2005. "Determinants of Business Cycle Co-Movement: A Robust Analysis." *Journal of Monetary Economics* 52: 113–57.

Calderón, C., A. Chong, and E. Stein. 2007. "Trade Intensity and Business Cycle Synchronization: Are Developing Countries Any Different?" *Journal of International Economics* 71: 2–21.

Clark, T.E., and E. van Wincoop. 2001. "Borders and Business Cycles." *Journal of International Economics* 55: 59–85.

Frankel, J.A., and A.K. Rose. 1998. "The Endogeneity of the Optimum Currency Area Criteria." *Economic Journal* 108: 1009–25.

Imbs, J. 2004. "Trade, Finance, Specialization and Synchronization." *Review of Economics and Statistics* 86: 723–34.

Imbs, J. 2006. "The Real Effect of Financial Integration." *Journal of International Economics* 68: 296–324.

Imbs, J., and R. Wacziarg 2003. "Stages of Diversification." *American Economic Review* 93 (1): 63–86.

Inklaar, R., R. Jong-A-Pin, and J. de Haan. 2008. "Trade and Business Cycle Synchronization in OECD Countries, a Re-Examination." *European Economic Review* 52: 646–66.

Kalemli-Ozcan, B., B.E. Sorensen, and O. Yosha. 2001. "Economic Integration, Industrial Specialization, and the Asymmetry of Macroeconomic Fluctuations." *Journal of International Economics* 55: 107–37.

Kalemli-Ozcan, B., B.E. Sorensen, and O. Yosha. 2003. "Risk Sharing and Industrial Specialization: Regional and International Evidence." *American Economic Review* 93 (1): 903–18.

Kenen, P.B. 1969. "The Optimum Currency Area: An Eclectic View." In *Monetary Problems of the International Economy*, edited by Mundell, A. Robert, Swoboda, and K. Alexandar, 41–60. Chicago, IL: University of Chicago Press.

Krugman, P. 1993. "Lesson of Massachusetts for EMU." In *The Transition to Economic and Monetary Union in Europe*, edited by F. Giavazzi and F. Torres, 241–61. New York: Cambridge University Press.

La Porta, R., F. Lopez-de-Silanes, and A. Shleifer. 1998. "Law and Finance." *Journal of Political Economy* 106 (6): 1113–55.

Lane, P., and G.M. Milesi-Ferretti 2007. "The External Wealth of Nations Mark II: Revised and Extended Estimates of Foreign Assets and Liabilities, 1970–2004." *Journal of International Economics* 73: 223–50.

Petri, A.P., M. Plummer, and F. Zhai, 2011. *The Trans-Pacific Partnership and Asia Pacific Integration: A Quantitative Assessment.* East-West Center Working Paper, Economic Series, No. 119. Honolulu, HI: East-West Center.

International migration and the welfare state: Asian perspectives

Noel Gaston[a] and Gulasekaran Rajaguru[b]

[a]*Productivity Commission Melbourne, Victoria 3000, Australia;* [b]*Globalisation and Development Centre and School of Business, Bond University, Gold Coast, Queensland 4229, Australia*

Immigration is a controversial topic in Australia and some of its Asian neighbours. Given the potential impact on native welfare, such as effects on relative wages and unemployment, there has been political mobilisation on the immigration question. The presence of a redistributive welfare state in all major immigrant host countries creates yet another margin on which immigration affects native welfare. The focus of the paper is whether a large intake of immigrants leads to a reduction in welfare state effort. It is often argued that steady increases in immigration lead to public pressure for stricter immigration controls or for less generous publicly funded social expenditures. In terms of immigrants with similar employability and claims on the public purse to natives, it is hypothesised that the impact on welfare spending is neutral. These ideas are tested using detailed data for migration to developed countries.

1. Introduction

A notable development in the last century was the steady rise of national policies to control immigration – legal and illegal. As Sassen (1999) points out, the development of democracy, nationalism and welfare states have made migration a politically more difficult, and potentially more explosive, issue in contemporary times compared with earlier times. The policies to affect the levels and patterns of international migration are now quite widespread. In developed countries, policies are motivated by issues such as low fertility and demographic ageing, unemployment or skilled worker shortages, brain drain and brain gain, social integration, and national security.

According to United Nations Population Division (UNPOP) (2009), in 2010, the number of international migrants in the world was almost 214 million, which represents 3.1% of the world population. In the two decades between 1990 and 2010, the world had 59 million more international migrants (see Table 1). While 3% seems a trifling amount, there are considerable differences across regions and individual countries. Developed countries have absorbed about three-quarters of the increase in the number of international migrants in the past two decades. The proportion of migrants in the total population between 1990 and 2010 increased in all the more developed regions and declined in the less developed regions. Lowell (2007) notes that these trends actually extend back to at least 1975. In fact, a relatively small number of countries host the majority of the world's international migrants (UNPOP 2009).

The impact of immigration on the traditional immigrant-receiving countries – Australia, Canada and the United States – has been integral to the economic and social development of

Table 1. Estimated number of international migrants, 1990–2010.

Development group and major area	Number of international migrants (millions)		Percentage of total population		Percentage distribution of international migrants	
	1990	2010	1990	2010	1990	2010
World	154.8	213.9	2.9	3.1	100.0	100.0
More developed regions	82.4	127.7	7.2	10.3	53.2	59.7
Less developed regions	72.5	86.2	1.8	1.5	46.8	40.3
Africa	16.4	19.3	2.5	1.9	10.6	9.0
Asia	49.8	61.3	1.6	1.5	32.2	28.7
Latin America and the Caribbean	7.0	7.5	1.6	1.3	4.5	3.5
North America	27.6	50.0	9.8	14.2	17.8	23.4
Europe	49.4	69.8	6.9	9.5	31.9	32.6
Oceania	4.8	6.0	16.2	16.8	3.1	2.8

Source: United Nations, Department of Economic and Social Affairs, Population Division. *Trends in the International Migration Stock: The 2008 Revision* (UNPOP 2009).
Notes: 2010 figures are estimates. More developed regions comprise all regions of Europe plus North America, Australia/New Zealand and Japan. Less developed regions are Africa, Asia (excluding Japan), Latin America, the Caribbean, plus Melanesia, Micronesia and Polynesia. International migrant stock: Mid-year estimate of the number of people living in a country or area other than that in which they were born. If the number of foreign-born was not available, the estimate is the number of people living in a country other than that of their citizenship.

those countries. For example, Australia has experienced a steady population increase since the end of World War II, as a result of both high post-war fertility and rising levels of immigration. While only 10% of Australia's population was foreign-born in 1947, the post-war establishment of a national government immigration portfolio led to the gradual increase in migration levels over the following decades. Today, people born overseas are approximately one-quarter of the country's total population. These immigrants have been crucial to Australian prosperity during the years of its mining boom (Bond and Gaston 2011).

During most of the 1990s, while there was no significant increase in legal immigration flows, illegal migration increased steadily. On the one hand, these facts point to the effectiveness of policies aimed at restricting immigration. On the other hand, the difficulty in controlling illegal flows has elevated immigration to an important place on the political stage in many developed countries. Migration and population policies are driven by different considerations in source, transit and eventual host countries. However, migration policies have changed most notably in many developed countries: from an almost open policy (for whites, at least) to much more targeted programmes favouring migrants with higher levels of education, skills and human capital. According to Borjas (1999), all migration policies address two questions: 'How many immigrants should the country allow in?' and 'Who should those immigrants be?' Australia and Canada have a 'points system' for the admission of new residents with a 'desirable' set of characteristics.[1]

Table 2 shows that more than two-thirds of the immigrants in OECD countries come from the low-income regions of the world. While this does suggest that the gains from migration are greatest for those with relatively low incomes, this also suggests that, on average, people migrate from regions with low levels of human capital and labour productivity to regions with labour markets with higher average levels of human capital and labour productivity.

Table 2. Share of OECD immigrants by sending region, 2000.

Low-income sending region	
Mexico, Central America, the Caribbean	0.2
South and Southeast Asia	0.15
Eastern Europe	0.13
Africa	0.080
Middle East	0.06
South America	0.04
Pacific Islands	0
Total	0.67
High-income sending region	
Western Europe	0.24
Asia, Oceania	0.06
North America	0.03
Total	0.33

Source: Adapted from Hanson (2009), table 2.
Notes: High-income North America includes Canada and the United States, and high-income Asia and Oceania includes Australia, Hong Kong, Japan, Korea, New Zealand, Singapore and Taiwan.

Lowell (2007) shows that there was a net increase of just less than 7.5 million non-tertiary-educated migrants from less developed and into more developed nations during the 1990s (an increase of 64%). In fact, in 2000, almost 96% of all adult migrants with less than a tertiary education settled in North America, Europe or Oceania.[2]

More skilled workers usually find legal entry into a new country easier (and less costly) than their unskilled counterparts do. Temporary workers have become increasingly important in Western European countries. Such workers are thought to enhance labour market flexibility (particularly, when immigration restrictions are in place) and to help meet temporary sectoral shortfalls of particular types of labour. However, the most heated debates are undoubtedly concerned with the immigration of unskilled labour, particularly from developing countries, and the impact on the labour market performance of native workers.

As is well known, the 1980s and 1990s were associated with growing wage and income inequality in many wealthy countries. The flow of migrants from developing to developed countries is suggestive of a link between this immigration and inequality. Kahanec and Zimmermann (2009) argue that drawing such a link may be misleading due to the fact that the 'New World' countries with a high share of foreign-born population, such as the United States or Australia, also have higher income inequality. Post-transition OECD countries tend to have very low shares of foreign population and low Gini coefficients. Western European countries are in between the two extremes. However, they do find that for Northern and Western European countries, which share similar histories of immigration and economic institutions, there is a distinct negative relationship between the Gini coefficient and the share of foreigners in the labour force.

While immigration is generally thought to have had a relatively minor impact on national wage levels, there may be unwanted effects on the wages of certain occupations or skill groups. As with trade liberalisation, these distributional issues are prominent in the debate about the desirability of immigration.

This paper studies the relationship between international migration and spending on the welfare state. The latter is shaped by distributional concerns. In particular, we address whether an increase in immigration leads to a reduction in spending on the welfare state. In the next section, we review the relevant literature. In particular, we discuss the welfare economics and the political economy of immigration. In Section 3, a simple model is then presented, which attempts to capture the main forces motivating expenditures on the welfare state and how these will respond to immigration. Two effects are identified: an 'exposure effect,' according to which an increase in unemployment risk due to an inflow of immigrants motivates a positive relationship between immigration and unemployment, and a 'redistribution effect', whereby increased inflows of migrants lead to a reduction in taxation as domestic residents resist any resultant redistribution. We then turn to the empirical work in Section 4. To preview the results, we find a weak positive relationship between immigration and spending on the welfare state. This can be explained in terms of the exposure effect dominating the redistribution effect. Another focus of the empirical investigation in the paper is on Asian immigration and the impact on countries in the Asia-Pacific region. Section 5 concludes.

2. The political economy of migration[3]

Immigrants generally differ on a number of dimensions from natives. Most economic research focuses on economically relevant differences (i.e. individual factor endowments, usually taken to be some measure of skill). However, even the most cursory reading of the history of immigration should make it clear that other dimensions of difference can also matter a great deal. Similarly, the emergence of radical right parties in Europe has been strongly associated with anti-immigrant politics that can only very partially be explained by any economic effects of that immigration. 'Foreigners' make a particularly attractive target for more-or-less unfocused anger in the context of general economic difficulties. Thus, while it is surely true that attitudes toward immigrants are affected by an understanding of labour market effects, recent research suggests that such effects are dwarfed by social concerns. Card, Dustmann, and Preston (2009) refer to these social concerns as 'compositional amenities'. Given the overall conclusion of empirical research on labour market effects of migration, and the increasingly heated public politics of immigration, the centrality of such compositional amenities should not surprise us.

All industrial countries, the major host countries for migration, maintain more-or-less extensive welfare states that provide some combination of income support and direct provision of goods (e.g. housing, health care, education). These policies were created, and are generally justified, as a right of citizenship, i.e. a necessary component of a good community. Some such justification is necessary since welfare state provision is inherently redistributive. The level of such provision is controversial even in the context of a relatively homogeneous community, but it is dramatically more controversial in the face of large immigration flows. Part of the difficulty stems from the rights of non-citizens, or 'foreigners' (on some politically relevant dimension) even if a citizen, to these community goods. This is an extension of the 'compositional amenity' issue mentioned above. The literature on the fiscal effects of immigrants focuses on the fact that immigrants have implications for both the expenditure and revenue sides of the welfare state. If, as much of the theoretical literature presumes, immigrants are younger, poorer, and have more children than natives, their pattern of consumption of services and contribution to the welfare state will differ from those of natives. In particular, the usual presumption is that welfare states in most relatively wealthy countries involve net transfers from natives to immigrants. This presumption is undermined, to some extent, by two factors: the actual pattern of immigration and the valuation of lifetime effects. Most countries are not characterised simply by a large shock of young, poor immigrants. Studies that attempt to evaluate the current fiscal effect of immigrants deal with this problem explicitly (MaCurdy, Nechyba, and Bhattacharaya 1998;

Nannestad 2007). The overall result of these studies is that immigrants receive net transfers from natives via the welfare system.[4]

The workhorse model for analysing both the distributive effects and the overall national welfare effects of migration is the m-factor $\times$ 1-sector model, commonly in the 2×1 form. Borjas (1993) provides a detailed development of welfare analysis using this model. Consistent with Kemp (1993), Borjas does not count migrant welfare in his evaluation of the national welfare effects in the destination country. The key here is that, as with the analysis of tariffs, the net of redistributive effect of restriction on immigration is a deadweight loss triangle (called the *immigration surplus* from relaxing restrictions). Also, as with tariffs, for plausible levels of liberalisation, these triangles are quite small relative to total national income. Borjas also makes the point that the size of the immigration surplus is increasing in the magnitude of redistribution. More importantly, for Borjas, this small net gain needs to be placed in the context of native losses via the actually existing welfare system. That is, to the extent that immigrants are fiscally a net drain on native income, that loss must be set against the small immigration surplus. Thus, the small size of the immigration surplus becomes part of the argument for illiberal policy.

Political economy research generally proceeds relative to some 'good' policy outcome, deviations from which are explained by 'political economy' forces. For economists, this 'good' outcome is the welfare optimum; for political scientists, it is the democratic optimum. The, usual villain, for both, is 'special interests' (though the early pluralist theory saw lobbying as a way of conveying information about preference intensity rather than distorting outcomes from the democratic optimum). For the case of immigration, what these optima are is so fraught that most work leaves them implicit. While nothing like as extensive as research on the political economy of trade, there is a very lively literature on the political economy of immigration. Much, perhaps most, of the recent work has focused on identifying the preferences of citizens, a small amount has sought to model equilibrium outcomes as a function of factor price effects, and a larger sub-literature has focused on the political economic link between immigration and welfare state provision. We comment briefly on each of these.

It is a straightforward task to derive the effects of immigration on relative wages. Under otherwise standard assumptions, the essential assumption for generating certain redistributive effects is that the number of factors of production should exceed the number of sectors. Among others, this will be the case in one-sector models with many types of labour and in specific-factor models. Since factor market effects play a large role in political economy modelling, it is not surprising that a substantial amount of effort has gone into finding evidence of such effects. A novel approach to doing this is to use individual responses in public opinion polls on questions relating to immigration policy, along with information on individual skill endowments, to 'test' for consistency between model predictions and individual evaluations. For this purpose, endowments are usually considered as more and less skilled labour, and measured by education. In this approach, it is common to find that individual preferences on immigration policy are determined, at least in part, by endowment (Scheve and Slaughter 2001; O'Rourke and Sinnott 2006). While this seems sensible, there are at least two problems: first, if the findings of research on the labour market effect of immigration are correct (i.e. that the labour market effects are small to zero, even on unskilled natives), it is not clear what we should make of the results from opinion polls; and, second, it seems likely that, in addition to its relationship to labour market status, education is related to things like cosmopolitanism that affect tolerance, or to training in economics that predisposes people to more liberal attitudes on globalisation in general and immigration in particular (Hainmueller and Hiscox, 2007).

As the previous section noted, another channel via which immigration affects native economic interests is the welfare state/fiscal redistribution channel. Recent research on individual attitudes that seeks to take such considerations into account is characterised by mixed results. For example, Facchini and Mayda (2008) find that while both labour market and redistributive effects are significant, the latter are stronger; but Hainmueller and Hiscox (2010) find that neither of these channels is unambiguously supported. Finally, as we noted above, while labour market effects (to the extent that they can be effectively identified with education-based endowments) and redistributive effects surely matter, there is evidence that compositional amenities may be even more important.

While the findings of research on both labour market effects and citizen attitudes are such as to lead us to doubt that such effects are the primary causal factor in determining immigration policy, there is still a significant literature seeking to analyse immigration policy in precisely this way. As in the literature on the political economy of international trade, there are two broad classes of political institution that are considered in solving for political economic equilibrium: referendum models and lobbying models. It is probably most useful to think of the single issue referendum model as a reduced form for considering the general effect of public preferences on immigration policy. The median voter theorem, combined with the auxiliary assumptions that the immigration issue is one-dimensional (e.g. size of quota) and the preferences identified by factor ownership are single-peaked over that dimension, yields a simple prediction about the link between preferences and political outcomes. A small number of studies have attempted to frame accounts of contemporary immigration policy outcomes in these terms (Facchini and Mayda 2008). It is also possible to rationalise policy via lobbying models and systematic empirical work is presented, suggesting consistency between immigration policy outcomes and the predictions of these models (Facchini and Mayda 2008). The latter paper is particularly interesting in its presentation of both referendum and lobbying models and is an attempt to provide a link between these two modes of policy determination. A fundamental problem with the lobbying models is that, unlike lobbying on trade policy, the actual patterns of lobbying are not particularly consistent with the predictions of the model. While there certainly are influential economic interests involved in lobbying (e.g. Western agricultural interests), these groups do not reflect the broad, economy-wide interests implied by claims about national-level labour market effects. Instead, national-level groups tend to be religious and environmental (Gimpel and Edwards 1999).

The presence of a redistributive welfare state can change both the welfare optimum and the individual political economic calculation (Wildasin 1994; Wellisch and Walz 1998). The basic question addressed by this body of research is clear: does admitting immigrants (especially unskilled immigrants) lead to a reduction in welfare state effort? The overwhelming majority of papers on this topic use some version of a referendum as the political economic mechanism and assume that immigrants receive immediate access to full welfare state benefits. In addition, most work on this topic also assumes that immigrants receive immediate access to the franchise. Given the well-known problems with spatial voting models in higher dimensions, these models all rely on relatively special assumptions about the sequencing of votes on issues and admission. Partly as a result of such structure, and partly given the mix of static and dynamic structures, the theoretical models yield a large range of results (Mazza and van Winden 1996; Scholten and Thum 1996; Haupt and Peters 1998; Razin, Sadka, and Swagel 2002; Hansen 2003; Dolmas and Huffman 2004; Mayr 2007). What little systematic empirical research exists on this topic tends to find that increased immigration from relatively poor countries is associated with lower public support for the welfare state and lower welfare state effort. For example, Hanson, Scheve, and

Slaughter (2007) find that high exposure to immigrant fiscal pressures reduces support for freer immigration among natives. In a consistent fashion, Razin, Sadka, and Swagel (2002), using data on 11 European countries over the period 1974–1992, find that a higher share of low-education immigrants in the population leads to a lower tax rate on labour income and less generous social transfers.[5] In the next section, we outline a simple model of how welfare state spending is affected by immigration.

3. A simple model of welfare state spending

To begin with, assume a population of n workers. Workers are heterogeneous and may be either employed or unemployed. In particular, let the probability of being employed be denoted by e. Hires and layoffs are independent across agents and time. On average, high-e workers spend more time employed. The distribution of types (abilities) is public knowledge. The aggregate steady state rate of employment is denoted by $\bar{e}$.

Workers each supply one efficiency unit of labour. The wage for employed workers is w. The tax rate on earned income is $\tau \in [0, 1]$. As in the literature, e.g. Razin, Sadka, and Swagel (2002), we assume that the best egalitarian income tax is approximated by a linear tax. Labour is inelastically supplied, so the tax is non-distortionary. The tax revenues are used to fund the provision of 'free' public services, such as health and education. These services are distributed to *all* residents – immigrant or native – as a lump-sum, g.

The expected utility of worker i, not conditioned on their current employment status, is given by

$$V = e_i U(w(1-\tau) + g) + (1 - e_i)U(g), \qquad (1)$$

where $U(.)$ is a concave utility function. In a steady state, the policy-maker's balanced budget constraint is $\tau \bar{e} w = g$. The government is assumed to maximise the welfare of the median worker (voter); we summarise the key findings in the following.

Proposition 1 (Autarchy)

Let $\rho = \tilde{e}/\bar{e}$, where $\tilde{e}$ is the probability of being employed for the median worker.[6]

(i) If $\rho \leq 1$, then there is perfect insurance across employed and unemployed states, i.e. $g_a = \bar{e}w$.
(ii) If $\rho > 1$, then $g_a < \bar{e}w$.
(iii) A worker of type i with $e_i > \tilde{e}$ would choose fewer government services, $g_i < g_a$.
(iv) Conditional on being employed, worker i prefers $g_i = 0$ (i.e. $\tau_i = 0$); conversely, conditional on being unemployed, worker i prefers $g_{\max} = \bar{e}w$ (i.e. $\tau = 1$).

Proof: g is chosen to maximise Equation (1), subject to the balanced budget condition. Inada conditions on $U(.)$ ensure an interior solution. The first-order condition is $(1 - \tilde{e})[U'_u - U'_e] + (1 - \rho)U'_e = 0$ (subscripts e and u, respectively denote employed and unemployed states), which establishes parts (i) and (ii). Parts (iii) and (iv) are trivial.

What parts (i) and (iv) of the proposition show is that workers exposed to unemployment risk always prefer positive taxation and welfare state expenditures. This has been termed an *exposure* or *insurance effect*. Parts (ii) and (iii) show that workers with a higher probability of working always prefer lower taxes and fewer services. This has been termed a *redistribution* or *tax effect* (Saint-Paul 1996). In this model, an exposure to unemployment creates a demand for welfare state spending. The balanced budget constraint is also important as higher welfare state expenditures necessitate higher taxes on earned incomes.

Now, consider the effects of immigration. Assume that the population consists of natives and immigrants, i.e. $n + n_m = N$. The subscript m denotes immigrant workers. As noted above, there is evidence that, for some period at least, immigrants in developed economies are a net drain on the public purse. For transparency, we make the extreme assumption that immigrants are not taxed, so that $\tau \bar{e}nw = Ng$ or $\tau \bar{e}w = (1+m)g$, where $m = n_m/n$ is the proportion of immigrants to natives. The first-order condition is now

$$\frac{\tilde{e}((\bar{e}-1)-m)U'_e}{\bar{e}} + (1-\tilde{e})U'_u = 0. \qquad (2)$$

We now have the following results.

Proposition 2 (Immigration)

(i) When $m > 0$, the level of government services is lower, i.e. $g_m < g_a$.
(ii) If $e_m = \bar{e}$, then $g_m = g_a$.

Proof: Part (i) follows immediately from Equation (2); part (ii) is trivial.

Hence, all native workers, regardless of their underlying labour productivity, would vote to reduce government benefits *if* immigrants are a fiscal drag. Similarly, part (ii) shows that if immigrant workers have the same probability of finding work as the mean native worker, then there is no impact on welfare state spending. While the conclusion is that more open immigration places downward pressure on welfare state spending, this very much depends on who it is that immigrates.

The exposure effect and redistribution effect work in opposite directions. What the simple model illustrates is that if, at least for some period, immigrants in developed economies are a net drain on the public purse, the latter effect will likely dominate when immigration is increasing. Also, recall that there is scant evidence for a significant deleterious effect of immigration on native labour market outcomes, which suggests that the redistribution effect may well dominate. During a severe economic downturn, there is increased pressure for a tighter immigration policy to help support the existing level of welfare state spending. Failing this, unabated increases in levels of immigration are likely to place further stress on the welfare state.

4. Some evidence
4.1. *Visual evidence*

Visual evidence of the relationship between immigration and welfare state spending can be presented using recent data from the Organisation for Economic Co-operation and Development (OECD). Table 3 presents the descriptive statistics of the data used here. As a measure of welfare state spending, we use data on government social expenditures (expressed as a percentage of GDP). Public social expenditures probably come closest to what we normally think of as welfare state spending.[7] Based on this measure, South Korea has the relatively smallest welfare state and Sweden the largest. (Australia's social expenditures – 16.72% – rank below the mean and median.)

Table 3. Descriptive statistics for 25 OECD countries.

		TM/pop		Non-OECD/TM		SOCX/GDP	
Mean		0.49		62.65		20.68	
Standard deviation		0.28		19.59		5.57	
Median		0.38		68.50		20.65	
Minimum		0.07	(Poland)	12.71	(Switzerland)	6.00	(S. Korea)
Maximum		1.12	(Spain)	87.27	(France)	29.08	(Sweden)

Notes: TM/pop = total migration/total population and Non-OECD/TM = migration from non-OECD countries/total migration (*Source*: OECD International Migration Statistics (SOPEMI database); available at http://www.oecd-ilibrary/content/datacollection/mig-data-en). SOCX/GDP = public social expenditures/GDP (*Source*: OECD Social Expenditure Statistics; available at http://www.oecd-ilibrary/content/datacollection/socx-data-en). Data for each period are averaged for the period 1998–2007.

Data on migration are from the OECD's SOPEMI database. The data are for the stock of foreign-born population by country of birth (or failing that, the stock of foreign population by nationality). Total migration in Spain has been a sizable 1.12% on *average* – given a population of nearly 45 million in 2007; this is a substantial absolute and relative inflow. (Australia's total migration of 0.67% ranks above the mean and median.) Immigration from non-OECD countries is largest in France. (Australia's figure of 56.58% ranks below the mean and median.)

Now consider the cross-country evidence for 25 OECD economies.[8] In Figure 1, the data are averages of the yearly figures for each country for the 10-year period 1998 to 2007. There is evidence of a weak positive relationship between immigration and the amount of a country's income spent on social expenditures ($\rho = 0.09$). Outwardly, this provides some evidence that the exposure effect may dominate the redistribution effect. Next, we consider these relationships in a multivariate setting.

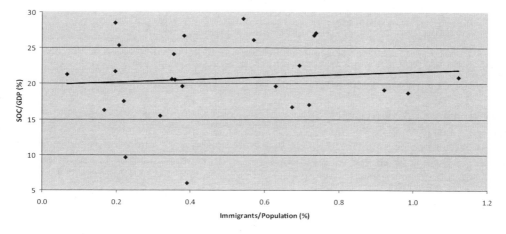

Figure 1. Immigration and social expenditures. Note: See notes to Table 3 for definitions and data sources.

4.2. Econometric evidence

In order to analyse the impact of immigration and other key variables on social expenditure, we estimate the following dynamic panel data model[9]:

$$g_{it} = \beta_0 g_{it-1} + \sum_{k=1}^{K} \beta_k x_{ikt-1} + \theta_i + \mu_t + u_{it}, \qquad (3)$$

where for country i and time period t, g_{it} is our measure of social welfare expenditure, θ_i and μ_t are country-specific and time-specific fixed effects, and $u_{it} \sim IID(0, \sigma_u^2)$. The lagged value of the dependent variable appears as government social welfare expenditures are likely to be highly persistent due to their quasi-contractual nature. A fixed-effects model, rather than a random-effects model, is estimated, as the θ_i's represent omitted time-invariant, country-specific characteristics. The variables, x_{ik}, included as determinants of welfare expenditures (other than the immigration variables) follow the literature, e.g. Dreher (2006), Gemmell, Kneller, and Sanz (2008) and Gaston and Rajaguru (2008). Since g_{it} is a function of θ_i, then so too is g_{it-1}. Therefore, g_{it-1} is correlated with u_{it} and ordinary least square (OLS) results in biased and inconsistent estimates, even if the u_{it}'s are serially uncorrelated. Accordingly, we first difference Equation (3) to eliminate the country-specific fixed effects, i.e.

$$\Delta g_{it} = \beta_0 \Delta g_{it-1} + \sum_{k=1}^{K} \beta_k \Delta x_{ikt-1} + \Delta \mu_t + \Delta u_{it}. \qquad (4)$$

We estimate the parameters of Equation (4) by the generalised methods of moments (GMM) technique proposed by Arellano and Bond (1991). The technique uses the predetermined lags of the variables as instruments to exploit a potentially large set of over-identifying restrictions and provides consistent coefficient estimates.

The validity of the assumptions used to obtain Equation (4) can be tested using the standard test of over-identifying restrictions, viz., a Sargan test. Note that Δu_{it} is MA(1) with a unit root. Hence, the key identifying assumption that there is no serial correlation in the disturbances can be tested by testing for no *second*-order serial correlation in the first-differenced residuals, while negative first-order serial correlation is expected in the first-differenced residuals.

In Table 4, we present the GMM estimates for the determinants of social expenditures. Total social expenditures are normalised by GDP rather than by government expenditures, as the latter measure would focus on the composition of expenditures independently of the size of a welfare state. First, note that the AR(1) and AR(2) test statistics indicate that the residuals in Equation (3) are serially uncorrelated and that the Sargan test confirms the validity of the instruments.

Next, as anticipated, there is a high degree of persistence in social expenditures. In terms of controls, we group the variables in a similar fashion to Gaston and Rajaguru (2008).

Tax/budget effects: These effects are central elements of political economy theories of government spending. While each country's budget should act as a hard constraint on government spending, as the latest financial crisis in Europe reminds us, higher *debt* tends to be associated with higher social expenditures. This may reflect the quasi-contractual and political nature of social expenditure programmes for many countries. Overall, the countries that are more indebted have larger welfare states; a correlation noted by Garrett (1998). (As we show below, the statistical significance of this finding is sensitive to the

Table 4. Determinants of social expenditures, GMM estimates.

	(i)	(ii)	(iii)	(iv)	(v)
SOCX/GDP (−1)	0.844*** (0.065)	0.850*** (0.057)	0.833*** (0.059)	0.862*** (0.056)	0.856*** (0.056)
Tax/budget effects					
UR (−1)	−0.244** (0.109)	−0.233** (0.093)	−0.250** (0.102)	−0.243** (0.096)	−0.231** (0.095)
Debt (−1)	0.019** (0.009)	0.017** (0.008)	0.019** (0.009)	0.017** (0.008)	0.016** (0.008)
Dependency ratio (−1)	0.227 (0.144)	0.157 (0.115)	0.150 (0.121)	0.147 (0.115)	0.172 (0.114)
Political/institutional effects					
Union (−1)	−0.353** (0.169)	−0.296** (0.136)	−0.323** (0.149)	−0.291** (0.140)	−0.281** (0.134)
Left (−1)	0.304 (0.195)	0.245 (0.160)	0.257 (0.171)	0.236 (0.159)	0.213 (0.159)
Globalisation					
KOF-economic (−1)	−0.319** (0.143)	−0.256** (0.112)	−0.282** (0.124)	−0.259** (0.113)	−0.253** (0.112)
Immigration/population (−1)	0.820* (0.488)				
OECD/total migration (−1)		−0.594 (0.669)			
Educated/total migration (−1)			−1.740** (0.871)		
Asian/total migration (−1)				0.005 (0.009)	
HIAO/total migration (−1)					−0.021 (0.016)
Diagnostics					
R2	0.959	0.969	0.966	0.968	0.969
AR(1)	−2.46**	−2.43**	−2.42**	−2.38**	−2.38**
AR(2)	0.25	0.17	0.15	0.17	0.29
Sargan probability	1.00	1.00	1.00	1.00	1.00

Note: Standard errors are in the parentheses. ***, ** and * denote rejection of null of zero restriction at 1%, 5% and 10% levels of significance, respectively.

inclusion of Japan in the sample.) We find that the unemployment rate, UR, is always statistically significant. The negative sign was anticipated in that those economies with higher steady-state unemployment rates 'cannot afford' to have generous social programmes. (In particular, note that there is no lock-step relationship of higher unemployment leading to higher welfare payments.)

The findings for DR, the dependency ratio, may appear to be somewhat surprising, in that they are statistically insignificant. However, as we show below in the sensitivity analysis, this finding varies with sample composition. DR is measured as the percentage of the population aged younger than 15 years and older than 65 years. It is included to explicitly control for demographic influences. In the political economy literature (Burgoon 2001, e.g.), a higher DR is expected to be positively correlated with spending on policies directed at the elderly or the young (such as retirement benefits or family benefits, respectively).

Political/institutional effects: To the extent that *Union* is positively correlated with insulating some workers from the rigours of competitive labour markets, the *Union* effect should *lower* the support for social spending. There appears to be some support for this notion.[10] We find that the political variable generally had no statistically significant effect on social spending. In some sense, this was an unexpected result because *Left* is normally thought to be associated with policies that are more favourable to the welfare state. However, the coefficient always has the 'correct' sign.

Globalisation effects: There are two competing perspectives on the relationship between the welfare state and globalisation. The first is that globalisation places considerable stress on the welfare state, so social policies will display tendencies of a 'race to the bottom'. For instance, Garrett (1998) has argued that by forcing welfare states to turn increasingly to borrowing to fund programmes, the international capital market ends up imposing an increasing premium on large welfare states. It has also been argued that globalisation increases the general credibility of orthodox (i.e. market-oriented) policy advice, thus reducing the plausibility of arguments supporting welfare state expansion and enhancing the credibility of arguments in favour of welfare state retrenchment (Krugman 1999). This has been termed the efficiency or disciplining hypothesis.

The opposing view is that social policies respond in ways such as to minimise any adverse consequences of globalisation for vulnerable workers. A plausible story advanced by some authors is that more generous unemployment benefits and changes to cash transfer and income tax systems have arisen to ensure the acquiescence of the potential losers from globalisation and associated microeconomic reforms (e.g. Rodrik 1998). That is, greater 'progressive' redistribution may be 'the price to pay' for political or social compliance with the structural changes driven by globalisation, including increased immigration. This has been termed the compensation hypothesis.

In terms of the empirical work, Burgoon (2001) finds that various measures of openness have a small effect on welfare outcomes and that openness is far from being the most important determinant of welfare efforts in OECD countries. This is also in line with Gaston and Rajaguru (2008), who find no statistically significant effect of trade openness on labour market expenditures.[11] In contrast, Rodrik (1997) finds a significant positive correlation among cross-sectional measures of openness and welfare for OECD countries, while panel data for the same set of countries suggest the opposite. Rodrik argues that globalisation has created strains by making it more difficult for nation states to finance social support systems and safety nets. Likewise, we find that the KOF index has a statistically significant negative effect on social expenditures. That is, evidence of the disciplining effect of economic globalisation.

A closer look at immigration effects: More interestingly, in line with the cross-sectional evidence in Figure 1, the estimates in column (i) indicate that increased immigration results in higher social spending. While immigration engenders both an exposure effect and a redistribution effect on social expenditures, the former effect dominates. However, we show below that this finding is sensitive to which countries are included in the sample.

Next, consider the results of immigration from OECD countries in column (ii). We find no statistically significant effect for the proportion of immigration from OECD countries. (Once again, this changes when the composition of countries in the sample is changed; see below.) When countries are instead classified according to educational level, we find that immigration from one of the 20 countries with the highest levels of education is associated with smaller welfare state effort.[12] Outwardly, the estimates in columns (ii) and (iii) suggest support for the exposure effect.

On the other hand, it needs to be noted that the findings may indicate the importance of immigrant self-selection. High social welfare expenditures imply higher (current or future) taxes. Simple Tiebout logic provides another explanation for the result. The highest-skilled and well-educated individuals are usually the highest-income earners; it follows that they generally have higher tax burdens. Mobile individuals with high-income earning capacity are, all else equal, likely to choose jurisdictions with lower tax obligations. This is a hitherto little researched topic in the recent literature on the formation of policies to target more highly skilled immigrants (see Ruhs 2008 for example).

Finally, we look at immigration from Asian countries in the last two columns. Column (iv) contains estimates for total Asian immigration and column (v) for migration from high-income Asia and Oceania (HIAO), as defined in the footnote to Table 2. The results in both cases indicate essentially zero effects on welfare state expenditures in OECD countries. This may reflect the fact that while Asia has become the world's predominant source of international labour migrants, the Middle East and other Asian nations are the main destinations (Hugo 2006). Moreover, to the extent that Asians migrate to the OECD, they do so to essentially four countries – Australia, Canada, the United Kingdom and the United States. Indeed, the HIAO countries tend to have net immigration rather than emigration (Hugo 2005). According to Hugo (2005), Asian immigrants are predominantly skilled, not more likely to be unemployed or to claim welfare benefits compared with natives.[13] Since they come to work, they are not a fiscal drag. As hypothesised, we expect that Asian immigrants have a neutral effect on welfare state expenditures – see part (ii) of Proposition 2.

4.3. *Sensitivity analysis*

In this sub-section, we discuss the results of tests that were performed to check the robustness of our results. To see how sensitive our results are to pooling the OECD countries, we first delete each country one at a time and compare the resulting model with the results reported in Table 4. In large part, this procedure did not affect any of the signs of the coefficients reported in the tables. Unsurprisingly, however, due to the smaller sample sizes, the GMM results are somewhat sensitive to country exclusions. Depending on the country, the coefficients of some variables became statistically significant, while others became statistically insignificant. However, it is important to stress that there were only three minor sign reversals – none statistically significant. These results are summarised in Table 5.

To illustrate how to interpret Table 5, consider deleting Japan (JA) from the sample. Doing so makes the coefficient for *DR* statistically significant in three of the five specifications. Moreover, the coefficient for *debt* becomes statistically insignificant in four of five

Table 5. Sensitivity analysis.

	(i)			(ii)			(iii)			(iv)			(v)		
	Min.	Max.		Min.	Max.		Min.	Max.		Min.	Max.		Min.	Max.	
SOCX/GDP (−1)	0.676	0.964		0.713	0.953		0.682	0.977		0.708	0.966		0.702	0.961	
Tax/budget effects															
UR (−1)	−0.56	−0.19		−0.51	−0.19		−0.64	−0.21		−0.53	−0.2		−0.52	−0.19	
Debt (−1)	0.01	0.03	AL, JA‡	0.01	0.03	JA‡	0.01	0.03	AL, JA‡	0.01	0.03	JA‡	0.01	0.02	
Dependency ratio (−1)	0.07	0.49	IT, JA, NL, PT, US†	0.02	0.34	JA, NL, PT†	−0.01	0.36	b)	0.02	0.34	PT†	0.04	0.37	IT, JA, NL, PT†
Political/institutional effects															
Union (−1)	−0.78	−0.27		−0.67	−0.22		−0.85	−0.25		−0.67	−0.22		−0.66	−0.21	
Left (−1)	0.2	0.49		0.14	0.41	BE†	0.18	0.39		0.17	0.4		0.12	0.37	
Globalisation															
KOF-economic (−1)	−0.53	−0.24		−0.46	−0.19		−0.59	−0.22		−0.47	−0.19		−0.46	−0.19	
Immigration/population (−1)	0.57	1.33	AL, BE, CA, GE, HN, PL, PT‡												
OECD/total migration (−1)				−1.17	0.9	a)	−2.46	−1.09							
Educated/total migration (−1)									AL, GE‡	0	0.01	c)			
Asian/total migration (−1)															
HIAO/total migration (−1)													−0.03	−0.01	

Notes: † denotes that the coefficient became statistically significant when one of the countries listed was deleted from the sample.
‡ denotes that the coefficient became statistically insignificant when one of the countries listed was deleted from the sample.
a)The coefficient is always negative, unless PT is deleted from the sample; the coefficient is statistically insignificant in all cases.
b)The coefficient is always positive, unless GE is deleted from the sample; the coefficient is statistically insignificant in all cases.
c)The coefficient is always positive, unless AU or DK is deleted from the sample; the coefficient is statistically insignificant in all cases.

specifications. Given Japan's enormously high level of public debt, this is unsurprising. That is, one can conclude that public debt is a particularly important determinant of welfare spending for Japan. Using a similar argument, the dependency ratio is an insignificant factor driving changes in welfare spending for Japan – this occurs because in Japan's static population, the rising proportion of aged population is matched by the growing 'shortage' of people aged less than 15 years. Overall, what is immediately obvious from Table 5 is that the signs of the coefficients reported in Table 4 are remarkably robust. Sign reversals occur in just three cases; the most 'severe' case for the purposes of this paper occurs when Portugal is excluded from the sample; doing so reverses the sign on the *Educated* migrant coefficient in column (ii); as noted above, the coefficient is still statistically insignificant.

Finally, we replicated the sample of countries used by Razin, Sadka, and Swagel (2002). Recall that they use data on 11 European countries over the period 1974–1992 and find that a higher share of low-education immigrants in the population leads to a lower tax rate on labour income and less generous social transfers.[14] Superficially, this seems to cast some doubt over column (ii) estimates in Table 4. However, when we restrict the sample to the Razin, Sadka, and Swagel (2002) sample of 11 countries, we also find a negative effect on the non-OECD migration variable. Clearly, their particular finding is restricted to just those particular 11 European countries. As Gemmell, Kneller, and Sanz (2008) caution, results testing the impact of globalisation on government expenditures or the composition of those expenditures are sensitive not only to choice of estimation method, but also to which countries are included in their sample.

5. Concluding comments: post-GFC challenges for the welfare state

The global financial crisis (GFC), commonly thought to have been triggered by the collapse of Lehman Brothers in September 2008, is viewed as the most significant economic downturn post-World War II. In many countries, its effects are ongoing. The GFC has reduced economic migration to the major immigrant-receiving countries. In part, this is due to the fact that the GFC was primarily a developed country malaise. The welfare of intending migrants is sensitive to high unemployment and the lack of jobs in destination countries. Obviously, low-skilled workers are the most economically sensitive: poor local language skills and low educational attainment are more of a drawback in times of recession. Some of the countries worst hit by the GFC, such as Ireland and Greece, went from having net immigration to having net *emigration* (MPI 2010).

Immigrant workers, including the less-skilled, were increasingly welcomed during the pre-GFC boom years. As we argue above, immigrants are easy targets for populists and xenophobes when economic conditions deteriorate. Faced with anaemic domestic economies and persistent unemployment, many national governments increased the stringency of policies to suppress the inflow of migrants, encourage the departure of immigrants and to protect labour markets for native-born workers. Some countries, including Australia, reduced the number of work permits and visas for foreigners. Other countries, such as the United Kingdom, tightened admission requirements. Italy and France cracked down on illegal immigrants by stepping up enforcement and curbing access to public services. An interesting development was the 'pay-to-go' schemes designed to repatriate migrants. Spain, the Czech Republic and Japan offered incentives such as paid one-way tickets 'home' and lump-sum payments to migrants willing to leave the country (MPI 2009). These developments have been linked with a concern about immigrants consuming too many publicly funded benefits and with competing with natives for jobs in tight labour markets (MPI 2010).

While nothing like as extensive as research on the political economy of liberalising international trade, there is a very lively literature on the political economy of immigration. Much, perhaps most, of the recent work has focused on identifying the preferences of citizens, a small amount has sought to model equilibrium outcomes as a function of factor price effects and a larger sub-literature has focused on the political economic link between immigration and welfare state provision. The basic question addressed by this latter body of research is clear: Does admitting immigrants (especially poor immigrants) lead to a reduction in welfare state effort? This paper focused on this issue.

More importantly, for the purpose of this paper at least, our findings provide support to the view that globalisation, and immigration in particular, has had at best only a very modest effect on the formation of, and relationship between, welfare state spending. There is some support for the view that the welfare state responds to the increased flows of immigrants and the increased sense of vulnerability of native workers. However, other effects appear to be more important; in particular, government indebtedness and the rate of unemployment. These factors are indicative of the central role played by the burden of taxation and the redistributive consequences associated with the welfare state.

Acknowledgements

The authors thank Sukai Farrell-Yamamoto and Jay Majtyka for assistance with data collection. Rod Falvey and Shravan Luckraz were generous with their comments.

Notes

1. In Australia, for example, since the mid-1990s, there has been a significant shift toward skilled migrants (and away from migrants entering under the family migration programme). This has been justified in the context of alleviating skill shortages in the labour market. Politically, it was also seen as necessary to 'restore public confidence' in Australia's migration programme (Khoo, 2002).
2. The fact that most migrants flow to a relatively small number of wealthy OECD countries is in stark contrast to the effects of liberalised trade, which are not so geographically concentrated.
3. Some of the material in this section is drawn from Gaston and Nelson (2011, 2012).
4. The issue is really whether, controlling for observable characteristics, immigrants' rate of use of the welfare state is higher than that of natives. It is likely that immigrants from developing countries have traits that involve greater current transfers, i.e. they are young, poor, less-skilled and have relatively more children than natives. A different issue is whether immigrants are attracted to locations as a result of generosity of welfare systems, i.e. the 'welfare magnet' hypothesis. The link between welfare provision and immigration is a mainstay of open economy public finance theory (e.g. Wildasin, 1994). The empirical results here are quite mixed, clustering around a finding of no effect to small positive effects (Barrett and McCarthy, 2008).
5. Goto (2010) reports similar findings for Japan.
6. In general, if $F(.)$ is unimodal and negatively skewed, then $\rho > 1$.
7. The social spending component of public expenditures is on the following benefits: old age, survivors, incapacity-related benefits, health, sickness, family, active labour market programmes, unemployment, housing and other social policy areas. The data are from the OECD SOCX database.
8. The 25 countries are Australia, Austria, Belgium, Canada, Czech Republic, Denmark, Finland, France, Germany, Hungary, Italy, Japan, South Korea, the Netherlands, Norway, New Zealand, Poland, Portugal, Slovakia, Spain, Sweden, Switzerland, Turkey, the United Kingdom and the United States.
9. Standard panel unit root tests confirm that all variables in the model are stationary. Hence, we estimate the short-run relationships between the variables of interest. (Estimating an error correction model, which captures both short-run and long-run effects, would be inappropriate, *cf*., Gemmell, Kneller, and Sanz (2008)).

10. An alternative explanation is provided by Aghion, Algan, and Cahuc (2008), who show that there is a negative correlation between union density and the quality of labour relations as well as state regulation of the minimum wage. They argue that this is explained, on the one hand, by a 'good' equilibrium characterised by high union density and low state regulation, and a 'bad' equilibrium, characterised by distrustful labour relations, low union density and strong state regulation of the minimum wage (and impliedly, a stronger government intervention, in the form of welfare).
11. See also Dreher (2006) and Gemmell, Kneller, and Sanz (2008) for similar findings.
12. The data for average years of schooling are for the years of formal schooling received by adults over age 15. The data are from the Barro–Lee data set: www.worldbank.org/html/prdmg/grthweb/ddbarle2.htm.
13. Smith (2006) finds that legal migrants to the United States are 'keeping up' with native-born Americans in terms of educational attainment and wage outcomes.
14. The Razin, Sadka, and Swagel (2002) sample comprises Austria, Belgium, Denmark, Finland, France, Germany, Italy, the Netherlands, Spain, Sweden and the United Kingdom.

References

Aghion, P., Y. Algan, and P. Cahuc. 2008. *Can policy Interact with Culture? Minimum Wage and the Quality of Labor Relation* (NBER Working Paper no.14327). Cambridge, MA: NBER.

Arellano, M., and S. Bond. 1991. "Some Tests of Specification for Panel Data: Monte Carlo Evidence and an Application to Employment Equations." *Review of Economic Studies* 58: 277–97.

Barrett, A., and Y. McCarthy. 2008. "Immigrants and Welfare Programmes: Exploring the Interactions Between Immigrant Characteristics, Immigrant Welfare Dependence, and Welfare Policy." *Oxford Review of Economic Policy* 24 (3): 543–60.

Bond, M., and N. Gaston. 2011. "The Impact of Immigration on Australian-Born Workers: An Assessment Using the National Labour Market Approach." *Economic Papers* 30 (3): 400–13.

Borjas, G. J. 1993. "The Intergenerational Mobility of Immigrants." *Journal of Labor Economics* 11 (1): 113–35.

Borjas, G. J. 1999. *Heaven's Door: Immigration Policy and the American Economy*. Princeton, NJ: Princeton University Press.

Burgoon, B. 2001. "Globalization and Welfare Compensation: Disentangling the Ties That Bind." *International Organization* 55 (3): 509–51.

Card, D., C. Dustmann, and I. Preston. 2009. *Immigration, Wages, and Compositional Amenities (NBER Working Paper no. 15521)*. Cambridge, MA: NBER.

Dolmas, J., and G. W. Huffman. 2004. "On the Political Economy of Immigration and Income Redistribution." *International Economic Review* 45 (4): 1129–68.

Dreher, A. 2006. "The Influence of Globalization on Taxes and Social Policy: An Empirical Analysis for OECD Countries." *European Journal of Political Economy* 22: 179–201.

Dreher, A., N. Gaston, and P. Martens. 2008. *Measuring Globalisation – Gauging Its Consequences*. New York: Springer.

Facchini, G., and A. M. Mayda. 2008. "From Individual Attitudes Towards Migrants to Migration Policy Outcomes: Theory and Evidence." *Economic Policy* 23 (56): 651–713.

Gaston, N., and D. Nelson. 2000. "Immigration and Labour Market Outcomes in the United States: A Political-Economy Puzzle." *Oxford Review of Economic Policy* 16 (3): 104–14.

Gaston, N., and D. Nelson. 2011. "International Migration." In *Palgrave Handbook of International Trade*, edited by D. M. Bernhofen, R. Falvey, D. Greenaway, and U. Kreickemeier, 657–694. Basingstoke: Palgrave Macmillan.

Gaston, N., and D. Nelson. 2012. "Bridging Trade Theory and Labour Econometrics: The Effects of International Migration." *Journal of Economic Surveys*, 27 (1), 98–139.

Gaston, N., and G. Rajaguru. 2008. "The Rise (and Fall) of Labour Market Programmes: Domestic vs. Global Factors." *Oxford Economic Papers*, 60(4), 619–48.

Garrett, G. 1998. *Partisan Politics in the Global Economy*. Cambridge: Cambridge University Press.

Gemmell, N., R. Kneller, and I. Sanz. 2008. "Foreign Investment, International Trade and the Size and Structure of Public Expenditures." *European Journal of Political Economy* 24 (1): 151–71.

Gimpel, J. G., and J. R. Edwards. 1999. *The Congressional Politics of Immigration Reform*. Boston, MA: Allyn & Bacon.

Goto, J. 2010. "Aging and Migration in Japan." In *Globalization and Economic Integration: Winners and Losers in the Asia-Pacific*, edited by N. Gaston and A. Khalid, 205–222. Cheltenham: Edward Elgar.

Hainmueller, J., and M. J. Hiscox. 2007. "Educated Preferences: Explaining Attitudes Toward Immigration in Europe." *Industrial Organization* 61 (2): 399–442.

Hainmueller, J., and M. J. Hiscox. 2010. "Attitudes Toward Highly Skilled and Low Skilled Immigration: Evidence from a Survey Experiment." *American Political Science Review* 104 (1): 61–84.

Hansen, J. D. 2003. "Immigration and Income Distribution in Welfare States." *European Journal of Political Economy* 19 (4): 735–46.

Hanson, G. 2009. "The Economic Consequences of International Migration." *Annual Review of Economics*, 1: 179–208.

Hanson, G. H., K. Scheve, and M. J. Slaughter. 2007. "Public Finance and Individual Preferences over Globalization Strategies." *Economics and Politics* 19 (1): 1–33.

Haupt, A., and W. Peters. 1998. "Public Pensions and Voting on Immigration." *Public Choice* 95 (3–4): 403–13.

Hugo, G. 2005. *Migration in the Asia-Pacific region*. Geneva: Global Commission on International Migration.

Hugo, G. 2006. "Immigration Responses to Global Change in Asia: A Review." *Geographical Research* 44 (2): 155–72.

Kahanec, M., and K. F. Zimmermann. 2009. "International Migration, Ethnicity and Economic Inequality." In *Oxford Handbook on Economic Inequality*, edited by W. Salverda, B. Nolan and T. Smeeding, 455–490. Oxford: Oxford University Press.

Kemp, M. C. 1993. "The Welfare Gains from International Migration." *Keio Economic Studies* 30 (1): 1–5.

Khoo, S.-E. 2002. "Immigration Issues in Australia." *Journal of Population Research*, Special Issue, 67–78.

Krugman, P. 1999. "Domestic Policies in a Global Economy." In *Brookings Trade Forum – 1999*. Washington, DC: Brookings Institution Press.

Lowell, B. L. 2007. *Trends in International Migration Flows and Stocks, 1975–2005* (OECD Social, Employment and Migration Working Paper no. 58). Paris: OECD Publishing.

MaCurdy, T., T. Nechyba, and J. Bhattacharaya. 1998. "An Economic Framework for Assessing the Fiscal Impacts of Immigration." In *The Immigration Debate: Studies on the Economic, Demographic, and Fiscal Effects of Immigration*, edited by J. P. Smith, and B. Edmonston, 13–65. Washington, DC: National Academies Press.

Mayr, K. 2007. "Immigration and Income Redistribution: A Political Economy Analysis." *Public Choice* 131 (1–2): 101–16.

Mazza, I., and F. van Winden. 1996. "A Political Economic Analysis of Labor Migration and Income Redistribution." *Public Choice* 88 (3–4): 333–63.

Migration Policy Institute (MPI). 2009. *Migration and the Global Recession*. Report Commissioned by the BBC World Service. Washington, DC: Migration Policy Institute.

Migration Policy Institute (MPI). 2010. *Migration and Immigrants Two Years After the Financial Collapse: Where Do We Stand?* Report Commissioned by the BBC World Service. Washington DC: Migration Policy Institute.

Nannestad, P. 2007. "Immigration and Welfare States: A Survey of 15 Years of Research." *European Journal of Political Economy* 23 (2): 512–32.

O'Rourke, K. H., and R. Sinnott. 2006. "The Determinants of Individual Attitudes Towards Immigration." *European Journal of Political Economy* 22 (4): 838–61.

Razin, A., E. Sadka, and P. Swagel. 2002. "Tax Burden and Migration: A Political Economy Theory and Evidence." *Journal of Public Economics* 85 (2): 167–90.

Rodrik, D. 1997. *Has Globalization Gone Too Far?* Washington, DC: Institute for International Economics.

Rodrik, D. 1998. "Why Do More Open Economies Have Bigger Governments?" *Journal of Political Economy* 106 (5): 997–1032.

Ruhs, M. 2008. "Economic Research and Labour Immigration Policy." *Oxford Review of Economic Policy* 24 (3): 403–26.

Saint-Paul, G. 1996. "Exploring the Political Economy of Labour Market Institutions." *Economic Policy* 23: 263–315.

Sassen, S. 1999. *Guests and Aliens*. New York: New Press/W.W. Norton.

Scheve, K. F., and M. J. Slaughter. 2001. "Labor Market Competition and Individual Preferences over Migration Policy." *Review of Economics and Statistics* 83 (1): 133–45.

Scholten, U., and M. Thum. 1996. "Public Pensions and Immigration Policy in a Democracy." *Public Choice* 87 (3–4): 347–61.

Smith, J. P. 2006. "Immigrants and the Labor Market." *Journal of Labor Economics* 24 (2): 203–33.

United Nations Population Division (UNPOP) 2009. *Trends in the International Migration Stock: The 2008 Revision*. Report by United Nations Population Division, Department of Economic and Social Affairs. New York: United Nations.

Wellisch, D., and U. Walz. 1998. "Why Do Rich Countries Prefer Free Trade over Free Migration? The Role of the Modern Welfare State." *European Economic Review* 42 (8): 1595–612.

Wildasin, D. E. 1994. "Income Redistribution and Migration." *Canadian Journal of Economics* 27 (3): 637–56.

Appendix 1. Variable description and data sources

Dependent variables: The data for social expenditure spending is from the OECD's *Social Expenditure Database, 1980–2007*. We use two measures of social expenditure: total social expenditure as a fraction of total government expenditure and total social expenditure as a fraction of GDP. (See also Notes 9 and 10.)

Independent variables: All data, unless otherwise stated, are from the OECD.

Tax and budget effects: *Debt* is measured as consolidated central government debt as a fraction of GDP. *UR* is unemployment as a percentage of total labour force. *DR* is the dependency ratio and is measured as (1 − the percentage of the population aged from 15 to 64 years of age). *Institutional and political effects* are captured by *Union*, which is measured by the total union membership as represented in OECD's *Union Members and Employees* tables. *Left* is based on the variable EXECRLC in the Database of Political Institutions concorded by Philip Keefer, the Development Research Group, World Bank, December 2010. Party orientation with respect to economic policy is coded based on the description of the party, using the following criteria. Right (1): for parties that are defined as conservative, Christian democratic or right-wing. Left (3): for parties that are defined as communist, socialist, social democratic or left-wing. Centre (2): for parties that are defined as centrist or when party position can best be described as centrist (e.g. party advocates strengthening private enterprise in a social-liberal context). *Globalisation*: The measure of globalisation that we employ is the KOF index of economic globalisation (Dreher, Gaston, and Martens 2008). This index is based on data for actual economic flows, i.e. trade, foreign direct investment (FDI) and portfolio investment, as well as restrictions on trade and capital, which uses data for hidden import barriers, mean tariff rates, taxes on international trade and capital controls. *Migration variables: Total migration* is measured as the total inflow of foreign population (by nationality). These data are from the OECD's *International Migration Database, 1980–2007 (SOPEMI)*. Migration data are further broken down into the following classifications: Migration from OECD countries, from Asian countries (comprising East, South-east and South Asia), from 'high-income Asia and Oceania' or HIAO (see Table 2) and migration from any one of the top 20 countries ranked by average years of education (see Note 11).

Corruption, democracy and Asia-Pacific countries

Neil Campbell[a] and Shrabani Saha[b]

[a]*Faculty of Business, Bond University, Gold Coast, Australia;* [b]*School of Accounting, Finance and Economics, Edith Cowan University, Perth, Australia*

This paper argues that the relationship between democracy and corruption is non-monotonic. When a country shifts from autocratic rule to highly imperfect democracy (an 'electoral democracy') it is frequently perceived that the level of corruption increases. Conversely, when the democracy level is already relatively high (approaching 'mature democracy') an increase in the level of democracy is typically expected to decrease the level of corruption. To assist with our discussion of these issues, before going on to the empirical part of the paper, we look specifically at the case of South Korea to illustrate how corruption responded to an increasing level of democracy. Using panel data, we find strong empirical support for the non-monotonic relationship. For Asia-Pacific countries, we find that the democracy-corruption relationship becomes negative, at a surprisingly high level of democracy. Moreover we also find that the South Asian region is the most corrupt.

1. Introduction

There is now a substantial literature that postulates that while there is a relationship between corruption and democracy, this relationship is complex and non-linear[1]. Countries that are mature democracies, with well-developed institutions such as an independent judiciary and media, have either relatively low, or very low, levels of corruption. However, when countries shift from authoritarian rule to electoral democracy[2], typically corruption does not fall, indeed, it is quite common to observe that it increases (Shleifer and Vishny 1993; Cohen 1995; Harris-White and White 1996). It follows from this that we might expect to observe a trend where, when countries transform from authoritarian government to electoral democracy to mature democracy, corruption only falls when countries approach fully mature democracy. In this paper, we explore the relationship between corruption and democracy with a particular focus on the regions within the Asia-Pacific.

We argue that if democracy can work effectively then it will have an inherent tendency to inhibit corruption. If corruption is unpopular then there is a political advantage associated with being seen to take action against it[3]. Obviously, this has close parallels with Sen's famous argument that those governments which have to face re-election will make sure that famines do not happen[4]. However, in electoral democracy this mechanism is blunted. Think of the situation where the media is mostly owned by government supporters, the judges are government appointees, the police are incompetent, and whistle-blowers and activists are in danger of being murdered[5]. In this situation corruption can thrive although a government may seek to gain popularity by prosecuting the occasional scapegoat. Obviously one way to eliminate critics and rivals is to charge such people with corruption offences[6]. Vague laws and regulations, that are so complex and vague, that almost everybody is not totally in compliance with, are useful weapons for governments that have hijacked the legal system and wish to intimidate potential critics.

If a country transforms from electoral democracy to mature democracy, the probability of getting caught acting corruptly increases substantially. With an official 'shaking down' an individual or firm for a bribe, the potential victim can feel confident to report this. Where the briber and the bribee (an official) are 'willing conspirators', there are a variety of possible mechanisms that make it likely that they will be caught. For example, the briber's rivals may complain about the briber getting special treatment or the victims of a building collapsing may complain that corruption amongst building inspectors is the most likely explanation. Overall, the argument is that if the institutions of a mature democracy work sufficiently well, the expected return from corrupt activity is negative and only a few individuals with very poor judgement choose to engage in it.

It is important here not to regard the maturing of democracy as being synonymous with the strengthening of the rule-of-law. The rule-of-law, through effectively operating institutions, is essential to the maturing of democracy, as is a free press. However, at the core of mature democracy is the holding of governments to account for their actions, or, lack of action. With mature democracy, government has both the motivation and the means to act against corruption. While mature democracy and the rule-of-law are associated with each other, we are not arguing that the maturing of democracy only reduces corruption because it is associated with rule-of-law. A country with limited democracy, but with a strong rule-of-law, would probably have a low level of illegal corrupt activity. However, if corruption is broadly defined, we argue that there is an inherent tendency for government ministers, in such a country, to favour themselves, their families and their associates. We argue this because where there is limited democracy, the probability of an electoral backlash as a reaction to bad behaviour (for example granting family members government contracts) is low.

With the shift from an authoritarian regime to an electoral democracy there are a number of reasons why we should not be surprised by corruption becoming a more serious problem. With electoral competition the demand for donations to the ruling political party and associated organisations increases. While making political donations obviously need not necessarily be a corrupt activity, it is so when a portion of the donation is taken by political leaders and their associates for personal gain. Another reason why the demand for payments may increase with electoral democracy is that leaders and officials may suspect that they will only have their jobs for a short period of time.

The most theoretically elegant explanation for an increase in corruption following the shift to electoral democracy is supplied by Shleifer and Vishny (1993). They refer to a situation where a dictator co-ordinates officials to maximise the total revenue from bribes as 'centralised corruption'. They contrast this with 'decentralised corruption' where there is no dictator and individual officials are free to set whatever bribe level they choose. With this latter situation each individual official, seeking to maximise his/her individual revenue, will set a higher bribe level than would have been the case when corruption was centralised. This is because with decentralised corruption the officials do not take into account the negative externalities that they inflict upon each other. Think of their analysis this way; to carry out a particular activity people need the permission of a number of officials. Different people have a differing willingness-to-pay (pay the total of the bribes necessary to carry out the activity). Thus the officials are facing a downward sloping demand curve. When each individual official increases his/her price (the size of the bribe) he/she will not take into account the cost in terms of reduced 'sales' inflicted upon other officials.

The remainder of the paper is structured as follows. In Section 2, we discuss how democratisation has affected corruption in South Korea. By selecting one particular country to discuss in detail – we are able to make our discussion of the relationship between corruption and democracy far more concrete. In Sections 3 and 4 we conduct a panel data analysis. Our explanatory variables for corruption are democracy, real per capita gross domestic product (GDP), rule-of-law, size of government, and openness. With the relationship between corruption and democracy we find that a cubic relationship fits the data better than a linear or a quadratic specification. Examining scatter plots shows that when democracy is very low, a small increase in democracy will be associated with slightly reduced corruption, however, at intermediate levels of democracy a small increase in democracy will be associated with increased corruption, and, at higher levels of democracy a small increase in democracy will be associated with a fall in corruption. The use of regional dummies delivers an interesting finding that South Asian countries are the most corrupt in the Asia-Pacific region. In Section 5 we make some concluding comments.

2. Case study: The Republic of Korea

The Republic of Korea, or South Korea, (henceforth simply referred to as Korea) is an interesting example of a country that has shifted from an authoritarian military regime to something approaching a mature democracy. Park Chung-Hee came to power as president via a coup in 1961 and was assassinated in 1979. For his entire presidency Korea was under authoritarian rule even though prior to 1972 there was a 'managed democracy' where President Park and his Democratic Republican Party (DRP) could face electoral reverses. However, this period of managed democracy should be regarded as authoritarian rule rather than electoral democracy because of President Park's military backing. He was in a position in 1971 to respond to the opposition party gaining most of the parliamentary seats by declaring a state of national emergency. With his new constitution he was in such a powerful position that he was elected unopposed in 1972 and 1978. President Park, like his predecessor, engaged in corruption, even though he followed a policy of prosecuting lower-ranked officials who acted corruptly. Making donations to the ruling DRP party, either covertly or openly, was simply a cost of doing business. Apart from personal gain, a strong motivation for soliciting donations was to build up the wealth and hence the political effectiveness of the DRP.

The widely used term 'money politics' is a very appropriate description of Korean political corruption. Under the Park regime, restrictions on political activity were such that, unless a party had large numbers of wealthy members, it needed secret illegal donations to operate effectively (see Kang [2002]). Obviously this situation favoured the DRP. Donations to, or toward, the DRP could give firms access to low-interest loans and import licences. The DRP was able to gain popularity at a local level by using its wealth to pay for festivities and the formation of community organisations. However, it would be inappropriate to jump to the conclusion that these donations ended up being used largely for philanthropic purposes. Kang (2002) makes mention of the New Village Movement, a government endorsed organisation started in 1970. Its stated aim was to improve the quality of rural life, but Kang refers to it as also being a home for embezzlement, nepotism and cronyism. Large Korean conglomerate firms (the chaebol) donated very substantial amounts to the New Village Movement. Such donations are frequently termed quasi-taxes, since, while these donations to 'good causes' were legal, there were adverse consequences for firms that did not pay the required amount.

Clearly the authoritarian nature of President Park's government facilitated the extraction of donations; there were no, or very limited opportunities, to challenge corruption at the very top of the regime. Park Chung-Hee was no kleptocrat; facilitating economic growth, via export-orientated industrialisation, was a key objective. He did not want pervasive decentralised corruption with numerous petty officials all with their hand out. His authority was sufficient to prevent this from occurring. Wedeman (1997) uses the term 'dividend collecting' to characterise the 'compulsory' donations. Moran (1998) argues that while there was favouritism based on regional origins and personal relationships, if firms did not perform they could not buy continued favours with further donations. You (2005) takes a far less sanguine view of Park's relationship with business interests, noting that he would bailout large firms facing insolvency.

Following the assassination of Park Chung-Hee in 1979, Chun Doo-Hwan became president in 1980. While he was another military autocrat, his presidential term was a single seven years. His government was seen as lacking legitimacy and was under pressure from a democracy movement which was able to bring large numbers of protesters out on the streets. In 1987 his nominated successor, Roh Tae-Woo, agreed to a new constitution and to allow direct presidential elections. Roh Tae-Woo was elected president with the opposition vote split between two candidates. His presidency from 1988 to 1993 can be viewed as a time when Korea was very much in an 'electoral democracy' transitional phase with a new democratic constitution, but having many of the old practices from authoritarian times. The President was a former army general who had been a key official in Chun Doo-Hwan's authoritarian government. Cho (2002) touches on how the authoritarian mindset, to some extent, stayed in place within the justice system following 1987. He states that prosecutors have come under pressure from their superiors to not prosecute influential senior officials and politicians. He also states that in criminal prosecutions judges are inclined to accept evidence that was illegally obtained. Cho points out that, while the new constitution introduced in 1987 contained a bill-of-rights, the Korean Criminal Code Procedure has been amended in 1988 and 1995 to improve procedural justice. Jury trials were only in 2008, see Lee (2009). Kang (2002) notes that the legal regulations associated with corporate governance were, particularly prior to the Asian Economic Crisis of 1997, numerous, but vague and frequently not enforced. Obviously in such a regulatory environment there is a strong incentive for firms to pay bribes to avoid regulators taking a special interest in their affairs.

Following 1987, press freedom was introduced. Kyu and Salwen (1990) give a neat example of how groups, not directly under state control, can take an aggressive attitude toward the press in a newly liberalised environment. In 1989, a group of disabled veterans forced their way into the premises of a provincial daily newspaper and injured 20 of its employees. The veterans were upset because the newspaper had reported that the Pusan Public Transportation Commission was improper in its awarding of contracts, and, their veteran's village had been awarded a contract by this corporation.

In 1993, Kim Young-Sam, a long-term opposition leader, was elected as president. While the election of a civilian president was historic, his former party 'Party for Unification and Democracy' had merged with Roh Tee-Woo's 'Democratic Justice Party' and thus he cannot be classed as a successful opposition candidate (see You [2005]). His anti-corruption drive was noted for the trials and convictions of the former leaders Chun Doo-Hwan and Roh Tae-Woo. The trials established that both Chun and Roh took a substantial slice of the donations for personal gain.

Kang (2002) eloquently argues that with democracy, following 1987, corruption became a more serious problem in Korea. He (p. 197) provides the following quote from an anonymous businessman to illustrate how corruption had become decentralised:

"By the late 1980s Roh and later YS [Kim Young-Sam] had established so much 'democracy' that I needed over 100 envelopes [bribes] in order to build a factory last year. That never occurred under Park or Chun – they eliminated the middleman, and while you had to pay for access, you could do it at the top levels, and not worry so much about the bureaucracy."

Kang also argues that with democracy the demand for political donations increased because of the extra costs associated with political competition. He (p. 197) quotes the founder of Hyundai, Chung Jo-Yung, speaking in 1992, as saying: "I personally handed over to the ruler about 1 billion won yearly during the 3rd Republic [Park], about 5 billion won yearly during the 5th Republic [Chun], and 10 billion won yearly in the 6th Republic [Roh]."

In 1998, in the wake of the Asian Economic Crisis, Kim Dae-Jung was elected President. He put in place anti-corruption procedural reforms leading to greater transparency in government dealings with big business. He also introduced an independent commission against corruption. As You (2005) points out, he was the first opposition candidate elected president in Korean history. Obviously, government changing hands via the democratic process is an important milepost in the journey towards mature democracy. While the personally highly moral Kim Dae-Jung suffered the humiliation of two sons being imprisoned for corruption, a trend had become established. That is, with an increasingly well-established democracy, corruption levels (perceived corruption levels) have declined. Consider the following corruption perception index (CPI) figures for Korea during the office of various past presidents. These are the raw figures with close to 0 being very corrupt and close to 10 being very clean. Chun Doo-Hwan and Roh Tae-Woo had CPIs of 3.9 and 3.5 respectively. Kim Young-Sam and Kim Dae-Jung had CPIs of 4.3 and 4.2, respectively[7]. Thus with these leaders there was a slight reduction in the perceived level of corruption. The 2010 CPI for Korea is 5.4. So while these figures show a story of declining corruption, the decline has hardly been spectacular. Nevertheless, the overall story that comes through with Korea is that of the corruption problem becoming more severe with the initial shift to democracy and then the corruption situation improving as democracy becomes more firmly established.

3. Empirical models, data and methodology

3.1. *Empirical model*

We are not in a position, because of data limitations, to test any one given theory as to how the level of corruption responds to democratisation. Also, we do not have sufficient data to conduct single-country studies. To do that we would need to have very long time series for the relevant variables. After all, in some cases it may take over 100 years for the transformation from dictatorship to mature democracy to take place. However, we have sufficient panel data to investigate whether the relationship between democracy and corruption is non-monotonic. The data supports the proposition that we should not expect a shift from authoritarian rule to electoral democracy to reduce corruption. Indeed we should not be surprised if such a shift is associated with an increase in corruption. However, the data also support the proposition that if democracy shifts from an intermediate level of democracy (electoral democracy) to a high level of democracy (mature democracy) then we should expect a reduction in corruption. Obviously, the length of time countries spend as intermediate democracies, where corruption can thrive, is going to differ from case to case. It is a somewhat fruitless debate as to whether a country, such as the Philippines e.g., is permanently stuck at this level of democracy or whether such a country is simply taking a long time to transform into a mature democracy. Any policy measures that can build the effectiveness of key institutions associated with mature democracy are clearly welcome from the view point of reducing corruption.

We begin the analysis by considering a linear relationship between democracy and corruption. The basic regression model is specified as:

$$\mathrm{CPI}_{i,t} = \beta_0 + \beta_1 \mathrm{DEMO}_{i,t} + \beta_2 \mathrm{RULE}_{i,t} + \beta_3 \log(\mathrm{GSIZE})_{i,t} + \beta_4 \log(\mathrm{RGDP})_{i,t} + \beta_5 \log(\mathrm{OPEN})_{i,t} + \varepsilon_{i,t}, \quad (1)$$

where DEMO is a composite democracy index, RULE is the rule-of-law, GSIZE is the size of government, RGDP is the real per capita GDP, OPEN is trade openness, ε is an error term, i is country, t is time. The sign and significance of β_1 is of primary interest, if β_1 is negative that would reflect that democratisation reduces corruption. A higher value of all other control variables i.e. RULE, GSIZE, RGDP and OPEN are expected to reduce corruption (Ades and Di Tella 1999; Treisman 2000; Rock 2007; Billger and Goel 2009).

In the next step we estimate the non-linearity of the democracy–corruption relationship by incorporating the second and third degree polynomials of the democracy index and examine which degree of polynomial best fits the data. The linear and higher degree polynomial effects of democracy on corruption are computed using the panel estimation methodologies for 101 countries for the period 1995 to 2008. Also, period fixed effects as well as regional dummies are included in the robustness checks. All estimation is carried out with White heteroscedasticity consistent standard errors. The democracy–corruption relationship is also examined for the Asia-Pacific countries separately.

3.2. *The data*

Major obstacles to the comparative study of corruption have been the lack of a general definition of corruption and the absence of objective cross-national data on corrupt behaviour. Fortunately, Transparency International's (TI) annual corruption perceptions index (CPI) has gained wide acceptance as the principal measure of corruption.[8] The CPI measures the degree of corruption as seen by business people, academics and risk analysts. This index has been the most commonly used corruption measure in the literature.[9] While clearly there are limitations associated with perceptions-based measures, potential alternatives, such as a count of media reports of corruption, seem far more problematic. For simplicity and ease of exposition, the original ranking of the CPI has been converted into a scale from 0 (least corrupt) to 10 (most corrupt). It should be noted that Transparency International first published the CPI as an annual series in 1995. Therefore, the study covers the period from 1995 to 2008.

Freedom House's political rights and civil liberties indices are utilised to construct our democracy index.[10] Political rights include electoral process, political pluralism and functioning-of-government. Civil liberties encompass freedom of expression and belief, as well as, associational and organisational rights. Some researchers use the Freedom House political rights index or the political rights and civil liberties indices to represent the democracy index.[11] We have scaled our democracy index from 0 to 10, where a higher score indicates a higher level of freedom. For the other control variables i.e., RULE, GSIZE,

RGDP and OPEN the data sources are set out in Table A1. Descriptive statistics and a list of the countries used in our estimation are reported in Table A2 and A3, respectively.

4. Empirical results

The scatter plots are fitted with local polynomial Kernel regressions of the democracy and corruption variables are shown in Figure 1. It is apparent that democracy and the level of corruption are highly correlated and the relationship is non-monotonic for both all countries and Asia-Pacific only countries. Specifically, the effects of democracy on corruption are negative at the early and mature stages of democratisation but positive at the intermediate range, i.e., the scatter plots are consistent with a cubic functional form best fitting the democracy-corruption relationship.

The panel estimation results are presented in Table 1. Columns (1), (2), and (3) show the results for the linear, quadratic and cubic specifications of the democracy index along with all control variables. The panel least squares result of column (1) indicates that the coefficient of democracy has the expected positive sign although it is not significant. The coefficients of the other control variables also demonstrate the expected signs, and, except for government size, all these coefficients are significant at the 1% level.[12] The result confirms that there is a possibility of a high level of corruption even after a transformation to democracy. The specification in column (1) explains more than three-fourths of the variation in the levels of corruption across countries. Column (2) reports the quadratic model. Here the democracy coefficients are not significant and their signs are not all consistent with theory. It shows a negative linear and a positive quadratic term suggesting that corruption decreases at the early stages of democratisation, but increases with an expansion of democracy, which is not consistent with the theory and evidence from across the world. However, the results for the cubic model (column [3]) give a negative linear, a positive squared and a negative cubed term; all of these terms are highly significant. The results indicate that the transformation towards democracy from extreme autocracy reduces corruption initially, but increases with further democratisation, and finally the matured and consolidated democratic state is able

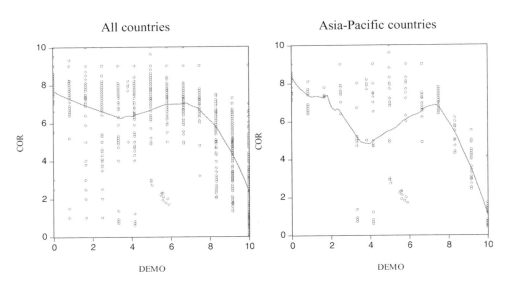

Figure 1. Democracy–corruption relationship.

Table 1. Impact of democracy on controlling corruption, 1995–2008: All countries.

	(1) PLS	(2) PLS	(3) PLS	(4) PFE	(5) PFE	(6) PEE
DEMO	0.002 (0.02)	−0.002 (0.04)	−0.99*** (0.06)	−0.03 (0.02)	−0.05* (0.03)	−0.97*** (0.09)
DEMO²		0.0004 (0.002)	0.24*** (0.02)		0.002 (0.002)	0.23*** (0.03)
DEMO³			−0.02*** (0.001)			−0.02*** (0.001)
RULE	−1.66*** (0.04)	−1.66*** (0.04)	−1.58*** (0.03)	−1.28*** (0.02)	−1.29*** (0.02)	−1.29*** (0.02)
Log (GSIZE)	−0.07 (0.06)	−0.07 (0.08)	−0.09 (0.05)	−0.41*** (0.04)	−0.42*** (0.04)	−0.47*** (0.04)
Log (RGDP)	−0.55*** (0.03)	−0.55*** (0.03)	−0.50*** (0.03)	−0.80*** (0.07)	−0.80*** (0.07)	−0.70*** (0.06)
Log (Open)	−0.21*** (0.02)	−0.21*** (0.02)	−0.12*** (0.01)	−0.49*** (0.02)	−0.48*** (0.03)	−0.43*** (0.02)
Asia-Pacific				0.41*** (0.08)	0.42*** (0.08)	0.12** (0.06)
Latin America				0.17* (0.09)	0.18* (0.09)	−0.34*** (0.08)
Africa				−0.26 (0.16)	−0.26 (0.16)	−0.33** (0.16)
Middle East				0.29*** (0.10)	0.30*** (0.10)	0.03 (0.17)
Eastern Europe				1.28*** (0.14)	1.28*** (0.14)	1.02*** (0.10)
Western Europe				0.24*** (0.14)	0.24*** (0.14)	0.25*** (0.14)
Constant	11.64*** (0.27)	11.66*** (0.24)	11.76*** (0.17)	15.44*** (0.54)	15.48*** (0.54)	15.67*** (0.66)
Wald test (p-value)	(0.00)	(0.00)	(0.00)	(0.00)	(0.00)	(0.00)
Maximum			7.08			7.33
Minimum			2.92			2.88
Observations	993	993	993	993	993	993
Countries	100	100	100	100	100	100
Adjusted R²	0.79	0.79	0.81	0.82	0.82	0.84

Note: Dependent variable is the CPI. PLS and PFE denote panel least squares and period fixed effects, respectively. White standard errors are in parentheses. ***, **, * indicate significance level at 1, 5 and 10 per cent, respectively.

Table 2. Impact of democracy on controlling corruption, 1995–2008: Asia-Pacific countries.

	(7) PLS	(8) PLS	(9) PLS	(10) PFE	(11) PFE	(12) PFE
DEMO	0.07** (0.03)	0.18*** (0.04)	−1.87*** (0.32)	0.11*** (0.02)	−0.90*** (0.18)	−2.48*** (0.49)
DEMO^2		−0.01*** (0.002)	0.46*** (0.07)		0.10*** (0.02)	0.49*** (0.09)
DEMO^3			−0.03*** (0.005)			−0.03*** (0.01)
RULE	−2.24*** (0.13)	−2.21*** (0.13)	−1.98*** (0.16)	−1.71*** (0.18)	−2.07*** (0.11)	−2.30*** (0.09)
Log (GSIZE)	−0.23 (0.09)	−0.15 (0.20)	−0.36* (0.21)	−0.15 (0.18)	−0.80*** (0.28)	−0.88*** (0.29)
Log (RGDP)	−0.33*** (0.12)	−0.31*** (0.12)	−0.19* (0.11)	−0.48*** (0.10)	−0.06 (0.14)	0.44*** (0.16)
Log (Open)	−0.27*** (0.09)	−0.32*** (0.09)	−0.51*** (0.15)	−0.50*** (0.13)	−0.23*** (0.07)	−0.42*** (0.16)
South Asia				−0.04*** (0.09)	0.76*** (0.19)	0.89*** (0.17)
East Asia				−0.20*** (0.05)	−0.95*** (0.15)	−1.21*** (0.18)
Pacific				−2.20*** (0.30)	−3.73*** (0.44)	−2.38*** (0.24)
Constant	10.14*** (1.40)	9.84*** (1.44)	12.13*** (1.57)	11.92*** (1.80)	10.53*** (0.96)	8.85*** (1.01)
Wald test (p-value)	(0.00)	(0.00)	(0.00)	(0.00)	(0.00)	(0.00)
Maximum			7.67			8.84
Minimum			2.56			3.49
Observations	179	179	179	179	179	179
Countries	18	18	18	18	18	18
Adjusted R^2	0.85	0.85	0.90	0.88	0.90	0.92

Note: Dependent variable is the CPUI. PLS and PFE denote panel least squares and period fixed effects, respectively. White standard errors are in parentheses. ***, **, * indicate significance level at the 1, 5 and 10 per cent, respectively.

to combat corruption with successful anti-corruption reforms. The best regression results are illustrated in the cubic model, as the adjusted R^2 increases from 0.79 to 0.8, along with the increased linear and quadratic term in comparison with quadratic equation. From this (and the scatter plots shown in Figure 1) we can conclude that the models containing just linear and/or quadratic terms are seriously mis-specified. This result is consistent with Sung (2004), however, our choice of explanatory variables (apart from democracy) is quite different. Also our democracy index is a combination of Freedom House's political rights and civil liberties indices, while Sung simply uses the political rights index.

Period fixed effects (PFE) after controlling for regional dummies in columns (4)–(6) also confirm the results shown in columns (1)–(3).[13] Other control variables such as strong rule-of-law, large government size, higher per capita income and openness combat corruption significantly.[14] It should be particularly noted that rule-of-law plays a strongly significant role in combating corruption.[15] Interestingly, Asia-Pacific countries are substantially more corrupt as the Asia-Pacific dummy in columns (4)–(6) is positive and significant.[16] Overall, the impact of our aggregated democracy indicator suggests that as democratisation progresses it acquires more power to control corruption only if the democratisation process transforms institutions to conform to democratic norms. Otherwise, there is a possibility of a higher level of corruption continuing indefinitely.

The relationship between democracy and corruption begins with a negative relationship (see Figure 1) until corruption reaches its (local) minimum at a democracy score of around 3 where it changes direction (i.e. negative to positive) and then achieves a maximum at around 7 and then starts to decrease again. In other words, the transformation towards democracy decreases corruption with a democratic score less than 3, followed by an increase in the corruption level with democracy between 3 and 7, and finally substantial corruption decreases occur at the democracy scores that are larger than 7.

The next step repeats the regression analysis only for the Asia-Pacific countries (Table 2). The findings are consistent with the all-country analysis discussed above.[17] That is, it is the cubic democracy-corruption relationship that best fits the data. These results support the hypothesis that a simple transformation towards democracy from autocracy does not necessarily confirm lower levels of corruption throughout. The increase in corruption levels is evident at the intermediate levels of democracy. However, the maximum critical point in the cubic model is between 8 to 9 which is quite high and worrisome for the Asia-Pacific countries. Furthermore, Asia-Pacific results interestingly reflect that the most corrupt countries in the region are South Asian countries whereas Pacific countries such as Australia and New Zealand are the least corrupt.

5. Conclusion

This paper investigated the role of democracy in controlling corruption with a special focus on the Asia-Pacific countries. Before entering into a formal analysis we gave considerable attention to the case of South Korea since here we have a country that has transformed from autocratic rule to something approaching mature democracy. From the available information it seems, in this case of recent South Korean history, that the democracy-corruption relationship was non-monotonic, as well as non-linear. The empirical work using multi-country panel data support this conjecture. That is, there is a cubic relationship between democracy and corruption, such that, a democratic transformation (starting at an extremely dictatorial level) initially reduces corruption, but at intermediate levels of democracy increases corruption, and finally, at mature stages of democracy, substantially reduces corruption.

Interestingly, we find that the turning point for democracy reducing corruption is relatively high for Asia-Pacific countries. A possible policy implication from this is that reforms to institutions and practices (such as promoting and protecting an independent media) need to be persisted with, and, we should not be disillusioned simply because past mature-democracy-enhancing reforms failed to impact upon the level of corruption. In general, the overall policy implication coming through from this paper is the importance of developing the appropriate institutions to facilitate the maturing of democracy.

We find that, using regional dummy variables, as a region, the Asia-Pacific is relatively corrupt. However, it needs to be kept in mind that the countries within the Asia-Pacific region are extremely diverse and include countries with a very low level of corruption such as New Zealand. We also find that within the Asia-Pacific, the South Asia region is the most corrupt. The South Asian countries have historical and cultural similarities. The obvious question for future research arises as to what are the reasons for the persistently high level of corruption in this group of countries.

Acknowledgements

The authors are grateful for comments both from the referees and from participants in the Globalisation and Development Centre workshop "Economic and Policy Developments in East Asia" held in October of 2011 at Bond University.

Notes

1. See Moran (2001), Montinola and Jackman (2002) and Sung (2004).
2. We define 'electoral democracy' as where elections are sufficiently free and fair that there is a realistic possibility that there can be a change in government, but where normal standards of due process do not hold and institutions that are fundamental to liberal democracy, such as an independent judiciary, are not functioning correctly. See Diamond (1996).
3. The degree to which corruption is unpopular is clearly going to differ between countries. Anti-corruption measures could be quite unpopular where a large proportion of the population are poorly paid petty officials. However, in general, petty corruption generates more ill-feeling amongst the population than high-level political corruption.
4. See Sen (1999).
5. A recent example of a murder, where there seems little prospect of those responsible being brought to justice, is the shooting of Indian anti-corruption activist Shehla Masood, see Chamberlain (2011).
6. In a report by the International Crisis Group (2008, p. 16) it is argued that the Bangladeshi military has attempted to extend its influence by using dubious corruption charges to remove officials and replace them with people who they have handpicked.
7. We obtained these historical Transparency International CPI figures from You (2005, p. 14). Transparency International only publishes CPI data going back to 1995.
8. For details see the Transparency International entries in Table A1. Here corruption is defined as the abuse of entrusted power (public sector power) for private gain.
9. See for example, Ades and Di Tella (1997); Johnson, Kaufmann, and Zoido-Lobaton (1998); Sandholtz and Koetzle (2000); Treisman (2000), Montinola and Jackman (2002); Gupta, Davoodi, and Alonso-Terme (2002); You and Khagram (2005); and Emerson (2006).
10. For details see the Freedom House entries in Table A1.
11. See Nelson and Singh (1998), Ades and Di Tella (1999), Sandholtz and Koetzle (2000), Bohara, Mitchell, and Mittendorff (2004) and Sung (2004) for details.
12. Following Montinola and Jackman (2002), we have utilised government share of GDP for government size. It is argued that higher government expenditure is due to the higher public sector wages which may in turn reduce corruption.
13. Two-way fixed effects estimate the effects inserting the dummies for each country and each period which reduces the degrees of freedom of estimation. Instead, period fixed effects with regional dummies incorporate dummies for each region and each period that increases the

degrees of freedom and improves the estimation results. A missing data problem prohibits performing random effects estimation.
14. Dynamic panel estimation results are also consistent with these results although not reported will be available upon request.
15. As is to be expected we find a highly significant negative relationship between corruption and the rule-of-law. It should be noted here that rule-of-law and our democracy indices are not as closely related as one might think. India is a prime example of a country that does well with regard to democracy, but does poorly with regard to the rule-of-law. In contrast, Singapore exhibits a strong rule-of-law with moderate democracy.
16. It is noted that the estimated coefficient of Africa is negative and significant in column (3). Examination of CPI scores confirms that Africa, Asia, Eastern Europe, Latin America and the Middle East countries are all perceived to be more corrupt than the Organisation for Economic Co-operation and Economic Development (OECD) countries. The estimation results of the regional dummies, excluding the control variables, show that African countries are perceived to be significantly more corrupt than Asia, Latin America, Middle East and the OECD countries (not reported here). However, after controlling for economic development, only Asia and East European countries remain more corrupt than OECD countries.
17. It is interesting to note that the coefficient of log (RGDP) is positive and significant which attracts special attention towards the Asia-Pacific countries. The result suggests that an increase in income per capita increases corruption which challenges the existing theory. We feel that it is something of a feature of this region that countries with fairly moderate to high levels of corruption also have experienced strong GDP growth.

References

Ades, A., and R. Di Tella. 1997. "The New Economics of Corruption: A Survey and Some New Results." *Political Studies* 45: 496–515.

Ades, A., and R. Di Tella. 1999. "Rents, Competition, and Corruption." *American Economic Review* 89: 982–993.

Billger, S. M., and R. K. Goel. 2009. "Do Existing Corruption Levels Matter in Controlling Corruption? Cross-country Quantile Regression Estimates." *Journal of Development Economics* 90: 299–305.

Bohara, A. K., N. J. Mitchell, and C. F. Mittendorff. 2004. "Compound Democracy and the Control of Corruption: A Cross-Country Investigation." *The Policy Studies Journal* 32: 481–499.

Chamberlain, G. 2011. "Shehla Masood Battled Corruption in India." Was That Why She Was Killed? [online]. *The Guardian*, 24 September, Accessed November 10, 2011. http://www.guardian.co.uk/world/2011/sep/24/shehla-masood-corruption-india-killed.

Cho, K. 2002. "The Unfinished "Criminal Procedure Revolution" of Post-democratization South Korea." *Denver Journal of International Law and Policy* 30: 377–394.

Cohen, A. 1995. *Crime and Corruption in Eurasia: A Threat to Democracy and International Security*. Washington, DC: The Heritage Foundation.

Diamond, L. 1996. "Is The Third Wave Over?" *Journal of Democracy* 7: 20–37.

Emerson, P. M. 2006. "Corruption, Competition and Democracy." *Journal of Development Economics* 81: 193–212.

Gupta, S., H. Davoodi, and R. Alonso-Terme. 2002. "Does Corruption Affect Income Inequality and Poverty?" *Economics of Governance* 3: 23–45.

Harris-White, B., and G. White. 1996. *Liberalization and New Forms of Corruption.* Brighton: Institute of Development Studies.

International Crisis Group. 2008. *Restoring Democracy in Bangladesh* [online]. Asia Report N° 151, 28 April. Accessed November 10, 2011. http://www.ecoi.net/file_upload/2107_1307092484_neu.pdf.

Johnson, S., D. Kaufmann, and P. Zoido-Lobaton. 1998. "Regulatory Discretion and the Unofficial Economy." *American Economic Review* 88: 387–392.

Kang, D. C. 2002. "Bad Loans to Good Friends: Money Politics and the Developmental State in South Korea." *International Organization* 56: 177–207.

Kyu, H. Y., and M. B. Salwen. 1990. "A Free Press in South Korea: Temporary Phenomenon or Permanent Fixture?" *Asia Survey* 30: 312–325.

Lee, J.-H. 2009. "Getting Citizens Involved: Civil Participation in Judicial Decision-Making in Korea." *East Asia Law Review* 4: 177–207.

Montinola, G. R., and R. W. Jackman. 2002. "Sources of Corruption: A Cross-Country Study." *British Journal of Political Science* 32: 147–170.

Moran, J. 1998. "Corruption and NIC Development: A Case Study of South Korea." *Crime, Law & Social Change* 29: 161–177.

Moran, J. 2001. "Democratic Transitions and Forms of Corruption." *Crime, Law and Social Change* 36: 379–393.

Nelson, M. A., and R. D. Singh. 1998. "Democracy, Economic Freedom, Fiscal Policy, and Growth in LDCs: A Fresh Look." *Economic Development and Cultural Change* 46: 677–696.

Rock, M. T. 2007. "Corruption and Democracy." DESA Working paper No 55.

Sandholtz, W., and W. Koetzle. 2000. "Accounting for Corruption: Economic Structure, Democracy, and Trade." *International Studies Quarterly* 44: 31–50.

Sen, A. 1999. "Democracy as a Universal Value." *Journal of Democracy* 10: 3–17.

Shleifer, A., and R. W. Vishny. 1993. "Corruption." *Quarterly Journal of Economics* 108: 599–617.

Sung, H.-E. 2004. "Democracy and Political Corruption: A Cross-National Comparison." *Crime, Law and Social Change* 41: 179–194.

Treisman, D. 2000. "The Causes of Corruption: A Cross-National Study." *Journal of Public Economics* 76: 399–457.

Wedeman, A. 1997. "Looters, Rent-scrapers, and Dividend Collectors: Corruption and Growth in Zaire, South Korea, and the Philippines." *Journal of Development Areas* 31: 457–478.

You, J.-S. 2005. "Embedded Autonomy or Crony Capitalism?" Conference paper prepared for delivery at the Annual Meeting of the American Political Science Association, Washington, DC, September 1–5.

You, J.-S., and S. Khagram. 2005. "A Comparative Study of Inequality and Corruption." *American Sociological Review* 70: 136–157.

Table A1. Data sources.

Variables	Data source
Corruption Perceptions Index (CPI)	CPI ranges from 0 (least corrupt) to 10 (most corrupt). Transparency International http://www.transparency.org/policy_research/surveys_indices/cpi http://www.transparency.org/policy_research/surveys_indices/cpi/2010/in_detail.
Democracy Index (DEMO)	Democracy index is an arithmetic mean of political rights and civil liberties and it ranges from 0 (no freedom) to 10 (maximum freedom). Freedom House http://www.freedomhouse.org/uploads/fiw/FIWAllScores.xls http://freedomhouse.org/template.cfm?page=351&ana_page=363&year=2010.
Real GDP Per Capita (RGDP)	RGDP with PPP adjusted is expressed in terms of 1990 US dollars. Groningen Growth and Development Centre http://www.ggdc.net/databases/ted.htm.
Rule of Law (RULE)	RULE ranges from −2.5(no rule of law) to 2.5 (good governance) World Bank Governance indicators 1996–2009 www.govindicators.org
Government Size (GSIZE)	Government Consumption Share of PPP Converted GDP Per Capita at 2005 constant prices. Penn World Table 7.0 http://pwt.econ.upenn.edu/
Open	Openness at 2005 constant prices (%). Penn World Table 7.0 http://pwt.econ.upenn.edu/

Table A2. Descriptive statistics.

	CPI	DEMO	LGSIZE	LOPEN	LRGDP	RULE
Mean	5.503	6.161	2.120	4.311	8.719	0.199
Median	6.300	6.667	2.152	4.294	8.846	0.074
Maximum	10.000	10.000	3.334	6.094	10.598	2.116
Minimum	0.000	0.000	−0.105	2.677	5.323	−2.110
Std. Dev.	2.588	3.345	0.403	0.540	1.061	1.081
Observations	1412	1414	1390	1390	1414	1010

Table A3. List of countries included in the analysis with Asia-Pacific countries asterisked.

Albania, Algeria, Argentina, Armenia, Australia*, Austria, Azerbaijan, Bangladesh*, Belarus, Belgium, Bosnia, Brazil, Bulgaria, Cambodia*, Canada, Chile, China*, Colombia, Congo Democratic Republic, Cote d' Ivore, Croatia, Cyprus, Czech Republic, Denmark, Ecuador, Egypt, Estonia, Ethiopia, Finland, France, Georgia, Germany, Ghana, Greece, Guatemala, Hong Kong*, Hungary, Iceland, India*, Indonesia*, Iran, Iraq, Ireland, Israel, Italy, Japan*, Jordon, Kazakhstan, Kenya, Kuwait, Kyrgyzstan, Latvia, Lithuania, Luxemburg, Macedonia, Malaysia*, Malta, Mexico, Moldova, Morocco, Myanmar*, Netherlands, New Zealand*, Nigeria, Norway, Oman, Pakistan*, Peru, Philippines*, Poland, Portugal, Qatar, Romania, Russia, Saudi Arabia, Serbia, Singapore*, Slovakia, Slovenia, South Africa, South Korea*, Spain, Sri Lanka*, Sudan, Sweden, Switzerland, Syria, Taiwan*, Tajikistan, Tanzania, Thailand*, Turkey Turkmenistan, Ukraine, United Arab Emirates, United Kingdom, United States, Uzbekistan, Venezuela, Vietnam* and Yemen.

Trends in income inequality in China: the effects of various sources of income

Pundarik Mukhopadhaya

Department of Economics, Macquarie University, Sydney, NSW, Australia

Using data from the *China Statistical Yearbook*, trends in income inequality for urban and rural China are studied. According to our estimates, the overall Gini for China increased from 1980/81 to 2008. The rural Gini increased at an exponential rate of 1.2% while the urban Gini rose at a rate of 2.7%. To overcome weaknesses in the existing Gini decomposition methodology, we use the method developed by Podder and Mukhopadhaya (2002. The Changing Pattern of Sources of Income and Its Impact on Inequality: The Method and Its Application to Australia, 1975–94. *Economic Record* 77 (238): 242–51). In rural China, the results show that household operations are the major component of rural disposable income, while the share of wage income is also high. Income from household operations is inequality reducing, as is the case with transfers. The dominant contributors to inequality are wages and property income. Arguably, the optimal way to reduce inequality is policy-induced increases in transfers and the household operations that help the poor. In the urban sector, wage and salary income have the maximum share in total disposable income. The results show that further increases in the wage share in urban sector will increase total inequality in China.

Introduction

The Chinese economy has grown rapidly since 1949. Economic growth was much faster during the reform period (from 1978) than in the pre-reform period. Economic success (especially during the reform period) has attracted increased interest among academic researchers and policy-makers. Along with its remarkable growth performance, China has experienced steadily increasing income inequality. The literature has identified that the coastal–inland development gap and the rural–urban divide are the main ingredients of overall inequality in China. According to Huang and Lao (2009), the urban to rural household per capita income ratio increased from 2.2 times in late 1980s to 3.2 times in 2004.

When people move out of poverty, particularly because of the employment opportunities created by the massive injection of domestic and foreign investment, a rise in inequality may be inevitable. This may not be problematic if people appreciate that rising income inequality is just an offshoot of changes that will ultimately provide the opportunity to escape unemployment and poverty. If people in the country feel that the state is acting to redress (by policy measures such as progressive income/asset tax) what is felt to be unacceptable inequality then the rising income inequality may not have much significance. However, if citizens consider that the state is in active (or encouraging) income inequality, then that could become a social as well as an economic problem. The recent spate of factory strikes, social unrest in various locations inside the country (as featured in many news outlets recently), have highlighted the clamour for higher wages by the people at the lower echelons of the income ladder. Whyte (2009) observed that anger and alienation from the system and its leaders by a significant portion of the Chinese population have become widespread. This is often hidden beneath the surface of official coercion. Thus, if the coercive diligence of the state is weakened then China may experience social unrest.

China, however, is still engaged in the transition to a market economy and the situation regarding disaffected groups suggests that markets diffuse some of these tendencies. The recent social apprehension emanating from rising income inequality is the motivation for investigating the changing pattern of income inequality in China in this paper. The method that we use evaluates the contribution of various factor incomes on total income inequality from a hitherto different perspective than used in the existing literature.

The next section discusses the methodology on Gini decomposition into factor incomes. The following section measures the trend of income inequality and discusses various causes of the trend. The fourth section employs the methodology of Gini decomposition into factor components and examines the trends. The last section summarises the findings.

The method

The Gini coefficient is measured as

$$G = \frac{1}{2n^2\bar{x}} \sum_{i=1}^{n} \sum_{j=1}^{n} |x_i - x_j|, \qquad (1)$$

where x_i and x_j are incomes of individuals i and j respectively, n is the total number of people in the community and $\bar{x}$ is their average income. Sen (1973, 33) interprets this formula: *'In any pair-wise comparison the man with the lower income can be thought to be suffering from some depression on finding his income to be lower. Let this depression be proportional to the difference of income. The sum total of such depressions in all possible pair-wise comparisons takes us to the Gini coefficient'*.

The visual counterpart of the Gini coefficient is captured by the Lorenz curve:[1]

$$\text{Gini coefficient} = \frac{\text{Area between Lorenz curve and diagonal}}{\text{Total area under diagonal}} \qquad (2)$$

The Gini coefficient is one of the most widely used inequality indices. From the relationship between the Gini coefficient and the Lorenz curve, it follows that the Gini coefficient can be expressed as a measure of individual discontent relative to the absolute egalitarian state where everyone's income is the same (i.e. equal to the average income).

Decomposition of the Gini into factors of income

In the literature, the decomposition of an inequality index into factor components is important as it allows identification of the components through which specific economic policies can be developed. The problem of decomposing total inequality into the contribution of each of the factor components consists in finding a way to add the contributions of each source of income. Let us denote x_{hi} as the income of income recipient i from source h such that: $x_i = \sum_h x_{hi}$. Then the natural decomposition of the Gini coefficient into factor components, due to Rao (1967), can be given by:

$$G = \sum_h S_h C_h, \qquad (3)$$

where S_h is the incomes' share of factor h, $S_h = \frac{\bar{x}_h}{\bar{x}}$, and C_h is called concentration coefficient of the factor h, defined as:

$$C_h = \frac{2}{n\bar{x}_h} Cov(i, x_{hi}). \qquad (4)$$

It is similar to the Gini coefficient[2] except for the fact that individuals' incomes are ranked according to x, and not according to x_h. If the cumulative proportion of income from source h is plotted against the cumulative proportion of individuals as they are arranged in ascending order of per capita or equivalent *total* income, we get the concentration curve of source h. It is similar to the Lorenz curve (which is drawn for total income). It is important to note that unlike the Lorenz curve, the concentration curve may lie *above* the egalitarian line. This happens when income from a specific source accrues mainly to the poorer section of the society. Like the Gini coefficient, C_h is one *minus* twice the area under the egalitarian line and the concentration curve. The value of this coefficient lies between $(-1, 1)$.[3] Fei, Rais, and Kao (1978), Pyatt, Chen, and Fei (1980), Kakwani (1980), Shorrocks (1982, 1983), Lerman and Yitzhaki (1985), Silber (1989, 1993), Podder (1993b), Kakwani (1995) and several others use this yardstick to decompose the Gini coefficient into factor components.

In the decomposition of the Gini coefficient, the empirical research on China by Khan et al. (1993) and Khan and Riskin (2001) asserted that $S_h C_h/G$ is the contribution of the hth source of income to total inequality. However, Podder (1993a) and Podder and Mukhopadhaya (2002) have demonstrated that such an interpretation of the Gini decomposition is misleading. As an example, consider a component which is constant for all income recipients (such as the fixed cash benefit given to all individuals after the Global Financial Crisis, for example in Australia). The concentration coefficient of the component is then zero. This would be interpreted as the contribution of the component to overall inequality (defined by $S_h C_h/G$) is zero. However, this component, when added to total income, would reduce the total Gini (as Gini is a relative measure of income inequality). When the contribution of the new component is zero how does it then reduce the extent of inequality? Empirical research on China on this issue has not addressed this conceptual problem.

Podder and Mukhopadhaya (2002) have shown that the appropriate interpretation of the contribution should be based on the transformation of Equation (3) to:

$$\sum_{h=1}^{k} S_h (C_h - G) = 0. \qquad (5)$$

For any component h, if $(C_h - G)$ is *positive*, the component has an inequality-augmenting effect. The presence of the component makes the total inequality higher than it would otherwise be. If the above difference is *negative*, the component has an inequality-reducing effect.

It can be demonstrated that the rate of change in the Gini coefficient with respect to the mean of hth component of income would be

$$\frac{\partial G}{\partial \bar{x}_h} = \frac{1}{\bar{x}} (C_h - G). \qquad (6)$$

An equi-proportional change in the mean income of the hth component (which has no effect on the concentration coefficient) can be given by the above equation. A more useful result for the present analysis is the elasticity of the Gini coefficient with respect to the mean income from component h:

$$\varepsilon_h = \frac{\text{Percentage change in } G}{\text{Percentage change in } \bar{x}_h} = \frac{\partial G}{\partial \bar{x}_h} \frac{\bar{x}_h}{G} = \frac{1}{G}\left[\frac{\bar{x}_h}{\bar{x}}(C_h - G)\right] = \left[\frac{\bar{x}_h}{\bar{x}}\right]\left[\frac{C_h - G}{G}\right]. \quad (7)$$

The first part of the last term on the right-hand side gives us the *relative share* of that particular component and the second term gives *relative inequity*. The elasticity will be positive or negative depending on whether the component has inequality *augmenting* or *reducing* effects, respectively. From the right-hand side of Equation (7) we can say that, for any component, if the relative inequity is positive the component will have an inequality-augmenting effect. The higher the absolute value of this component the bigger will be its effect on increasing total inequality. On the other hand, if relative inequity is negative, the component will reduce total inequality. Potentially, this could be used as an instrument by policy-makers in prescribing a more equitable policy. For example, if the income share of the component is very high with an inequality-augmenting effect, a policy-maker may consider reducing the relative share of that particular component using an appropriate policy instrument. This technique provides a more succinct answer to the contribution of the component of income on total inequality.

Trend of total, urban and rural inequality

The present analysis is based on the data available from *China Statistical Yearbook*, 1981, 1983, 1988, 1991, 2001, 2004 and 2009. These publications are from the China National Bureau of Statistics (NBS). To obtain rural–urban population weights for each region, *China Population Statistics* were used for various years.[4] The Appendix provides details of the sample size, definitions of income as well as the rural and urban populations. Table 1 provides our estimates of the rural–urban income gap and inequality.

A number of things can be noticed from Table 1.

Firstly, total inequality in China increased from 1980/81 to 2008, i.e. from 0.327 to 0.508 measured by Gini coefficient. An increasing trend has also been observed by Ravallion and Chen (2007) for 1980–2001 and Bardhan (2010) for 1990–2004. Our study updates this picture.

Table 1. Gini and relative mean income: 1980–2008.

Income measure	Year	Rural	Urban	Total
Gini	1980/81	0.275	0.162	0.327
	1990	0.321	0.177	0.379
	2000	0.349	0.245	0.465
	2003	0.350	0.315	0.444
	2008	0.371	0.328	0.508
Relative mean income (with respect to total mean income), %	1980	67.95	158.62	295.53[**]
	1990	71.76	152.65	933.89[**]
	2000	59.86	164.77	3947.97[**]
	2003	55.85	162.58	5311.86[**]
	2008	56.20	146.15	11551.45[**]

Note: [**] actual (not price adjusted) Yuan.

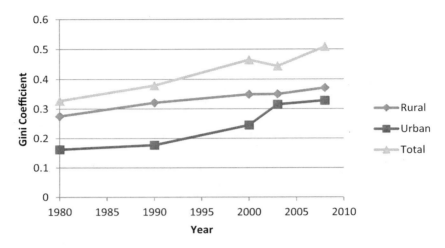

Figure 1. Total and rural–urban Gini in China: 1980–2008.

Secondly, rural inequality in China is greater than urban inequality. This is contrary to the experience of most developing countries [for example India]. This result supports Ravallion and Chen (2007).

Thirdly, rural inequality increased at an exponential rate of 1.2% while urban inequality increased at a rate of 2.7% between 1980/81 and 2008. The sharp increase in urban inequality is the main component of the increase in overall inequality in China. According to Chotikapanich, Griffiths, and Rao (2007), inequality in urban China increased so rapidly that it will exceed that of rural China in the near future. Our findings support this conjecture. In the 1980s, when full employment ('iron rice bowl') came to an end because of the restructuring of the State Owned Enterprises (SOEs), profitable firms tended to increase wages for skilled workers and a number of workers were retrenched – thus poverty and inequality became an urban issue in 1990s (Wang, Shi, and Zheng 2002; Wu 2004).[5] Figure 1 shows that rural inequality is persistently higher than urban inequality. However, the gap is decreasing. While in the 1980s and 1990s, the rural inequality was 1.7–1.8 times that of urban inequality, in the recent period there is some evidence of convergence. However, it is too early to be confident about the permanence of this development.

Within rural areas, the patterns of income distribution changed over the past quarter century. There are several causes. Zhang and Wan (2006) observed that the income inequality increased during the second half of 1990s. They argue that agriculture-led growth raised rural income and that consequently reduces income inequality in the late 1980s. In the mid-1990s, higher procurement prices were paid to the farmers for their grain deliveries. The new Chinese leadership after 2002 was looking for a more 'harmonious society'. The phasing out of agricultural land taxes (which was extremely regressive) was announced as the state started providing an increased share of funding for rural schooling. In addition, a network of cooperative medical insurance system in rural villages was re-introduced (to increase the availability of medical treatment, where higher fees were a challenge).

Two other efforts are worth mentioning: the minimum income subsidy scheme for poor rural families in various localities, and a cash payment to the old rural peasants who do not have a son to support. On the other hand, the transition to a market economy took a toll in the rural regions. Confiscation of land for encroaching cities (without adequate compensation) and wide-spread unemployment were some of the features of this transformation. People who lost their land, in several cases, did not get full urban citizenship or job opportunities in urban areas. According to Yao (2005), non-agricultural income dominates rural income inequality. Although China has the second largest land territory in the world, it has an acute shortage of land, compared to the majority of developing countries. Thus, rural income cannot depend just on land and agriculture, and the strict policy on rural to urban migration would mean that there has been increasing population pressure on land. Prosperity of a rural area depends largely on its ability to diversify out of agriculture. In the past 20 years, the prosperous regions in the east were able to develop rural industries rapidly, however, the poorer western regions were left behind implying a sharp increase in regional income inequality.

The Chinese *hukou*-based 'caste' or segregation system restricts optimal mobilisation of labour from one area to another. Knowing that several million peasants move out of agriculture, the government decided to relax migration controls cautiously. By the end of 1980s, more than 90 million peasants moved out of agriculture without going into cities. As in the 1990s, townships and village enterprises declined as people moved from rural to urban jobs. The newly booming economy had plenty of low-income job opportunities for unskilled rural labourers, but city governments remain opposed because of the lack of insufficient urban infrastructure. Initially in the 1990s, a temporary *hukou* system was introduced. With a resident permit, rural migrants could work in host city without having access to other benefits. In the second move, the quota system (that governed the conversion of agricultural *hukou* holders to non-agricultural *hukou* status) was relaxed. In 2001 it became national policy to eliminate the quota system in small cities. Non-locals who had a regular job and legal residence were qualified to become local *hukou* holders. In a medium-sized city, the requirements (to obtain local *hukou*) were higher but relatively relaxed compared to the situation a decade ago. The larger cities still strictly enforce a stringent requirement and quota system. These reforms produced a huge rural–urban labour flow on the one hand, while state housing subsidies, transportation, education and health care were denied to the migrants; existing urbanites were not affected. This change initially benefited skilled people, while the second change helped mostly investors (both foreign and domestic) and rural migrants.

The migrants are the most vulnerable group in the urban sector. Their life is characterised by low wages, wage defaults, excessive overtime, lack of jobs and social security (Zhao 2006). Knight, Song, and Jia (1999) have indicated that, on average, migrant workers earn about 80% of the wages of local workers with similar skills. Meng and Zhang (2001) showed that 82% of wage differences between migrant and urban workers arose from differences in pay for the same occupation. As reported in the 2000 Census, almost twice as many migrant workers as urban workers worked six days a week and 58% of migrant workers worked seven days a week. When state enterprises in 1990s had to lay-off large number of urban workers, the Labour Bureau often put pressure on local enterprises to dismiss migrant workers first (Zhao 2007).

Besides the presence of migrants, which is a more recent phenomenon, the rich–poor gap in the urban regions of China persists because of unemployment (which was aggravated in the period of transition from socialism to a market economy).

Fourthly, another ingredient of high Chinese income inequality, besides urban inequality and rural inequality, is the rural–urban income gap. Table 1 shows that the urban–rural per capita household income ratio has increased from 2.33 in 1980 to 2.60 in 2008. Like many other developing countries, China's rural economy is dominated by low earnings that are highly dispersed compared to the earnings of the urban economy. Estimates of the rural–urban income gap by Dwayne et al. (2008), Knight and Song (1999), Shi (1999), Yao

Table 2. Income gap between urban and rural households – a comparison (2003).

Income definition	Average urban income (Yuan)	Average rural income (Yuan)	Urban–rural income ratio
Shi and Luo (2010) and Sicular et al. (2010) estimates (PPP adjusted)			
NBS only	5487.53	2452.57	2.24
NBS + subsidies + imputed rent	9502.62	3109.93	3.06
Our estimates			
See Appendix	8636.02	2966.67	2.91

and Hao (1999) and Zhao and Tong (2000) also demonstrate that the income gap is not only high but has been increasing over time. Income inequalities between rural and urban areas within provinces differ – higher income provinces have smaller urban–rural income gaps; this difference is pronounced in poorer regions (Luo and Zhu 2008). According to Yao (2009) in 2006, urban and rural per capita income ratio for the three richest provinces (excluding Shanghai, Beijing and Tianjin) was about 2.5, while the ratio was about 4.5 in the three poorest provinces. A large part of the inequality between regions is associated with the difference between their respective rural areas and is related to the uneven degree of urbanisation across provinces. Huang and Lao (2009) indicated that acceleration of migration and urbanisation may reduce overall inequality as the proportion of the population that remains in poorer rural areas reduces over time.[6] We will return to this in the next section.

Finally, we note the comparability of our results with two other studies. Sicular et al. (2010) and Shi and Luo (2010) use data from the China Household Income Project (CHIP) Survey conducted in 1988, 1995 and 2002.[7] These are claimed to be more comprehensive and accurate data than the Income Surveys regularly reported by China's NBS. Sicular et al. (2010) have adjusted for regional variation in the cost of living which is generally higher in cities. Incomes for urban migrants are generally lower than the regular urban average income. These adjustments seem to have reduced the urban–rural income gap. Shi and Luo (2010) include estimates of the income equivalent value of subsidies in-kind received by some Chinese citizens. Table 2 provides a comparison of our results with Sicular et al. (2010) and Shi and Luo (2010) for 2003.

In Table 2, note that the difference between our result and Shi and Luo's (2010) estimate is only 5%. Furthermore, our estimates of overall and rural and urban inequality (as presented in Table 1) are comparable with the inequality values calculated by Shi and Luo (2010). The urban, rural and national Gini computed by Shi and Luo are 0.296, 0.345 and 0.438 respectively, while our estimates are 0.315, 0.350 and 0.444 respectively for 2003.[8] Note that the income figures in our estimates are based on household disposable income (for urban) and net income (for rural), while Shi and Luo's data are for individual income. This comparison establishes the robustness of our findings.

Rural and urban inequality in China: factor component decomposed

The factor income decomposition discussed earlier helps to identify the causes of inequality. As the rural and urban sectors do not have the same income sources, a decomposition for the whole population is not feasible. Decomposition of the Gini coefficients for both rural and urban population by their respective sources of income will instead be analysed. In the rural sector in the 2000s, according to the NBS classification, per capita net income consisted of wage income, family business income, property income and transfer income. The 1990s total per capita rural income was divided into income from collective united business,[9] income from the Rural New Economic Association, income from household business and others.[10] In the urban sector, the source classification of total disposable income is not available for 1990s. For this sector, the 2000s sources are classified as income from state-owned units, income from other types of ownership, income from property and income from transfers. The factor income classifications in 2003 and 2008 are also different: wage and salary income, net income from management, income from property and income from transfers.

It has already been mentioned that the decomposition of Chinese inequality into factor components is not new in the literature. Khan et al. (1993), Khan and Riskin (1998, 2001, 2005) and Yao (2005) and others have used the procedure. As mentioned, it has methodological problems. Our estimates of the elasticity values will demonstrate the percentage increase/decrease of inequality for an equi-proportional change in factor shares.

Table 3 presents the share of individual income (relative mean income), relative inequity and the elasticity estimates of various factor incomes. Note that if the relative inequity is positive the component will have an *inequality-augmenting* effect: the higher the absolute value of this component the bigger will be its effect in increasing total inequality. On the other hand, if relative inequity is negative, the component will reduce total inequality.

Table 3. Rural relative mean income, relative inequity and elasticity for various factor incomes: 1990–2008.

Measurement	1990			
	Income from collective united business	Income from rural new economic association	Income from household business	Other
Relative mean income	0.153	0.003	0.764	0.079
Relative inequity	0.656	−0.222	−0.568	0.337
Elasticity	0.408	−0.001	−0.434	0.027
Measurement	2000			
	Wage income	Family business income	Property income	Transfer income
Relative mean income	0.400	0.502	0.032	0.066
Relative inequity	0.041	−0.045	0.520	−0.157
elasticity	0.016	−0.023	0.017	−0.010
Measurement	2003			
	Wage income	Family business income	Property income	Transfer income
Relative mean income	0.371	0.566	0.026	0.037
Relative inequity	0.272	−0.208	0.407	0.171
Elasticity	0.101	−0.118	0.011	0.006
Measurement	2008			
	Income from wage and salaries	Income from household operation	Income from properties	Income from transfer
Relative mean income	0.400	0.502	0.032	0.066
Relative inequity	0.403	−0.046	0.518	−0.158
Elasticity	0.017	−0.023	0.017	−0.010

Family business or household operations are the major component of rural disposable income, while wage income share is also high (around 40%). Both the shares are relatively unchanged over the period of 2000s. Family business income and income from household operations are inequality reducing. As land resources in the rural economy are fixed, it is not easy to increase the share of household operations of agricultural production (even with advanced technology and fertiliser) for agriculture. Enhancement of rural non-farm activities could be an alternative for generating rural income. 'Non-farm' activities refer to production of non-primary agriculture or forestry or fisheries: they include trade or processing of agricultural products (even if, as in the case of micro-processing activities, they take place on the farm). In many rural areas around the world, agriculture alone cannot provide sufficient opportunities for a livelihood. Migration is not an option for everyone either. For example, Chinese policy-makers may prefer to limit the excesses of urbanisation with its associated social and environmental problems. Enhancement of rural non-farm employment can play a potentially significant role in reducing rural income inequality, as evidenced from the negative elasticity of income from household operations. However, wage employment in this type of activity is inequality augmenting (see Table 3). From this finding, we can infer that if rural non-farm activities are enhanced in the form of non-wage income (e.g. self-employment) inequality will be reduced.

Transfer income certainly has had an inequality-reducing effect in 2008, but was inequality augmenting in 2003. That would mean, in 2003 that transfer payments were not properly targeted at those on low incomes. As seen in Table 3, the share of this component is low, and there is no significant increase in it over the last decade. The 2008 results show that a 1% increase in the share of this component will reduce rural Gini by just 0.01%.

Wage income is inequality augmenting. A 1% equi-proportional increase in the wage share may increase rural inequality by 0.017% in 2008. Thus, a decrease in the wage share reduces rural inequality. One way to decrease the wage share in the rural sector is by promoting rural–urban migration. However, migration may not be considered as a long-term inequality-reducing process, as eventually the influx of low-skill workers in urban areas will increase urban inequality (this will become apparent when the urban inequality decomposition is discussed below).

The elasticity is a product of the relative share and relative inequity. The other way to increase the elasticity is by reducing the inequitable distribution of the wage component through an increase in educational opportunities and training. This will create a more equitable wage distribution both in the rural and urban sectors. Presently, the unskilled migrant workers are the most venerable to lose job and are employed at a low wage as discussed earlier. Education and training will enhance the opportunity for migrant workers to get better jobs in the urban regions.

Table 4 presents the results of the factor income decomposition for urban China. In the urban sector, wages and salaries have the maximum share in total disposable income. This factor is inequality augmenting and its elasticity is greater than that for the rural economy in the recent period. If migration is an option considered to reduce rural inequality (as asserted by Huang and Lao 2009), our findings show that it could *increase* urban inequality in at least two ways. Firstly, by increasing the wage share in total income and secondly, by increasing the factor's relative inequity. This is because low-skilled rural migrants increase the concentration at the lower part of the income distribution in the urban sector. Thus, it is clear that rural–urban migration *per se* cannot be considered as a long-term policy option for reducing total inequality. Enhancing education is an alternative option to reduce total inequality (for both rural and urban sectors). Unfortunately, available data do not allow us

Table 4. Urban relative mean income, relative inequity and elasticity for various factor incomes: 2000–2008.

Measurement	2000			
	Income from state-owned units	Income from other type of ownership	Income from property	Income from transfer
Relative mean income	0.658	0.057	0.027	0.257
Relative inequity	−0.271	4.016	0.409	−0.241
Elasticity	−0.178	0.229	0.011	−0.062
Measurement	2003			
	Wage and salary income	Net income from management	Income from property	Income from transfer
Relative mean income	0.704	0.046	0.015	0.234
Relative inequity	0.065	−0.126	0.674	−0.214
Elasticity	0.046	−0.006	0.010	−0.050
Measurement	2008			
	Wage and salary income	Net income from management	Income from property	Income from transfer
Relative mean income	0.665	0.085	0.020	0.230
Relative inequity	0.048	0.242	1.223	−0.332
Elasticity	0.032	0.020	0.024	−0.077

to explore the present relationship between personal income and the education levels of the population.[11]

Income from transfers (mainly remittances) is inequality reducing and its share is also non-trivial. In 2008, a 1% increase in transfers reduced total urban inequality by 0.08%. The property income in the urban sector is inequality augmenting. Equitability may be enhanced through property taxes. However, because of the small share of this factor in total urban income, the effect is likely to be small.

Conclusion

This paper criticises the usual factor income decomposition methodology of the Gini coefficient used for China by Khan et al. (1993) and others and employs an alternative decomposition technique advocated by Podder and Mukhopadhaya (2002). Using *China Yearbook of Statistics* data, we have addressed the following questions: What is the recent income inequality trend in China? What accounts for rural and urban income inequality? What are the implications of a Gini decomposition? Which factor incomes are inequality augmenting? What is the extent of this inequality augmentation or reduction? What else influences inequality changes in China in the rural and urban sectors? Is internal migration beneficial in reducing total income inequality in China?

The main findings in this paper are:

Finding 1: Total inequality in China increased in 2008 from 0.327 to 0.508 as measured by the Gini coefficient. In the same period, the rural Gini increased from 0.275 to 0.371, while the urban Gini increased from 0.162 to 0.328.

Finding 2: The rural–urban income gap is the third major component of high total inequality in China.

Finding 3: Family business income/household operation in the rural sectors is inequality reducing. Thus, enhancement of the non-farm sector in the form of self-employment may reduce rural income inequality in China.

Finding 4: Transfer incomes were not properly targeted at the rural poor during 2003.

Finding 5: Wage income in the rural sector is inequality augmenting. Rural–urban migration may reduce rural income inequality, particularly if the migrants are the wage earners in the rural economy. However, wage income is inequality augmenting in the urban sector as well. That means that if rural migrants are added to the pool of low wage earners in the urban community that this will increase urban inequality. As the elasticity of the Gini with respect to average income in urban areas is larger than that in rural areas, rural–urban migration cannot reduce total inequality.

Acknowledgement

An earlier version of this paper was presented in the First Annual Workshop on Economic Policy Development at East Asia, jointly organised by the Economic Growth Centre of NTU (Singapore) and the Globalisation and Development Centre of Bond University (Australia) on October 13–14, 2011 at Bond University. The author acknowledges the comments received from the participants of the workshop and from an anonymous referee of this journal. The author is grateful to Noel Gaston for his detailed comments on the draft version of the paper.

Notes

1. When total incomes are arranged in ascending order, a plot of the cumulative proportion of income against the cumulative proportion of the income earners gives the Lorenz curve of total income.
2. Gini can be written as:

$$G = \frac{2}{n\bar{x}} Cov(i, x_i),$$

where $Cov(i, x_i)$ is the covariance of income with its rank:

$$Cov(i, x_i) = \frac{1}{N} \sum_{i=1}^{N} (i - \bar{i})(x_i - \bar{x}) \text{ given } \bar{i} = \frac{1}{N} \sum_i i = \frac{N+1}{2}.$$

3. Unlike the Gini, which lies between (0, 1).
4. Like other developing countries Chinese people in the rural sector are mainly engaged in primary sector activities and in the urban sector secondary and tertiary activities are predominant. A recent phenomenon is the development of hybrid (neither predominantly rural nor urban) provinces, however, available data do not allow any classification of this nature.
5. Meng et al. (2005) using a cross-sectional household survey data from 1986 to 2000 show that urban consumption poverty (and thus urban inequality) increased in the 1990s from increasing income inequality as the price of education, housing and health care (which were previously provided free or at a highly subsidised prices by the state) increased after economic reforms were implemented.
6. For further details on studies explaining Chinese inequality see Mukhopadhaya et al. (2011).
7. Note that this data-set is not available easily, thus we have used a different data source.
8. 2003 is the latest year for which estimates are available from Shi and Luo (2010).
9. Specifically, types of rural (mainly agricultural) production in which the holdings of several farmers are run as a joint enterprise.
10. 'Others' represents the residual of all other incomes not classified elsewhere.
11. Kanbur and Zhang (2005) found that while in Chinese illiteracy rate had declined steadily between 1981 and 2000, there are large rural–urban and male–female gaps – the rural illiteracy

rate was more than double the urban rate, and female illiteracy was more than double the male rate.

References

Bardhan, P. 2010. *Awakening Giants Feet of Clay: Assessing the Economic Rise of China and India.* Princeton, Oxford: Princeton University Press.
China Statistical Yearbook. Various Years. National Bureau of Statistics, China Statistical Press, Beijing, China.
China Population Statistics. Various Years. *China Population and Employment Statistics.* National Bureau of Statistics China, China Statistics Press.
Chotikapanich, D., W. E. Griffiths, and D. S. Rao. 2007. "Estimating and Combining National Income Distributions Using Limited Data." *Journal of Business and Economic Statistics* 25: 97–109.
Dwayne, B., L. Brandt, J. Giles, and W. Sanui. 2008. "Income Inequality During China's Economic Transition." In *China's Great Economic Transformation*, edited by L. Brandt and T. G. Rawski, 729–75. New York: Cambridge University Press.
Fei, J. C., G. Ranis, and S. Kuo. 1978. "Growth and the Family Distribution of Income by Factor Components." *Quarterly Journal of Economics* 92 (1): 17–53.
Han, C., and M. K. Whyte. 2009. "Social Contours of Distributive Justice, Feeling in Contemporary China" In *Creating Wealth and Poverty in Postsocialist China*, edited by D. S. Davis and W. Feng, 193–212. Stanford: Stanford University Press.
Huang, Y., and X. Lao. 2009. "Reshaping Economic Geography: The China Experience." In *Reshaping Economic Geography in East Asia*, edited by Y. Huang and A. Magnoli Bocchi, 196–217. Washington, DC: World Banks.
Kakwani, N. C. 1980. *Income Inequality and Poverty: Methods of Estimation and Policy Application.* New York: Oxford University Press.
Kakwani, N. C. 1995. *Income Inequality, Welfare and Poverty: An Illustration using Ukranian Data.* Policy Research Working Paper no. 1411. The World Bank, Washington, DC.
Kanbur, R., and X. Zhang. 2005. "Spatial Inequality in Education and Healthcare in China." *China Economic Review* 16: 189–204.
Khan, A. R., K. Griffin, C. Riskin, and Z. Renwei. 1993. "Household Income and Its Distribution in China." In *Distribution of Income in China*, edited by K. Griffin and Z. Renwei, 25–73. New York: St Martin Place.
Khan, A. R., and C. Riskin. 1998. "Income Inequality in China: Composition Distribution and Growth of Household Income, 1988 to 1995." *China Quarterly* 154: 221–53.
Khan A. R., and C. Riskin. 2001. *Inequality and Poverty in China in the Age of Globalization.* Oxford: Oxford University Press.
Khan, A. R., and C. Riskin. 2005. "China's Household Income and its Distribution 1995 and 2002." *China Quarterly* 192: 356–84.
Knight, J, and L. Song. 1999. *The Urban-Rural Divide: Economic Disparities and Interaction in China.* New York: Oxford University Press.
Knight, J., L. Song, and H. Jia. 1999. "Chinese Rural Migrants in Urban Enterprises: Three Perspectives." *The Journal of Development Studies* 35: 73–104.
Lerman, R., and S. Yitzhaki. 1985. "Income Inequality Effects by Income Source: A New Approach and Application to the United States." *The Review of Economics and Statistics* 67 (1): 151–56.

Luo, X., and N. Zhu. 2008. *Rising Income Inequality in China: A Race to the Top*. The World Bank Policy Research Working Paper 4700. East Asia and Pacific Region, Poverty Reduction and Economic Management Department, Washington, DC.

Meng, X., R. Gregory, and Y. Wang. 2005. "Poverty, Inequality and Growth in Urban China 1986-2000." *Journal of Comparative Economics* 33: 710–29.

Meng, X., and J. Zhang. 2001. "The Two-Tier Labour Market in Urban China: Occupational Segregation and Wage Differentials Between Urban Residents and Rural Residents in Shanghai." *Journal of Comparative Economics* 29: 485–504.

Mukhopadhaya, P., G. Shantakumar, and V. V. B. Rao. 2011. *Economic Growth and Income Inequality in China, India and Singapore: Trends and Policy Implications*. London: Routledge.

Podder, N. 1993a. "A New Method of Disaggregation of the Gini by Groups." *Sankhya, Series B* 55: 262–71.

Podder, N. 1993b. "The Disaggregation of the Gini Coefficient by Factor Components and its Application to Australia." *Review of Income and Wealth* 39: 51–61.

Podder, N., and P. Mukhopadhaya. 2002. "The Changing Pattern of Sources of Income and Its Impact on Inequality: The Method and Its Application to Australia, 1975–94." *Economic Record* 77 (238): 242–51.

Pyatt, G., C. Chen, and J. Fei. 1980. "The Distribution of Income by Factor Components." *Quarterly Journal of Economics* 95(3): 451–73.

Rao, V. M. 1967. "Two Decomposition of Concentration Ratio." *Journal of Royal Statistical Society, Series A* 132: 428–35.

Ravallion, M., and S. Chen. 2007. "China's (Uneven) Progress Against Poverty." *Journal of Development Economics* 82: 1–42.

Sen, A. K. 1973. *On Economic Inequality*. Oxford: Clarendon Press.

Shi, X. 1999. "Urban-Rural Income Differentials Decomposition in China 1990s." MA thesis, China Centre for Economic Research, Peking University, Beijing.

Shi, L., and C. Luo. 2010. "Reestimating the Income Gap Between Urban and Rural Households in China." In *One Country Two Societies: Rural Urban Inequality in Contemporary China*, edited by M. K. Whyte, 105–21. Cambridge: Harvard University Press.

Shorrocks, A. F. 1982. "Inequality Decomposition by Factor Components." *Econometrica* 50: 1337–9.

Shorrocks, A. F. 1983. "Ranking Income Distribution." *Economica* 50: 3–17.

Sicular, T., Y. Ximing, B. A. Gustafsson, and L. Shi. 2010. "How Large is China's Rural-Urban Income Gap?" In *One Country Two Societies: Rural Urban Inequality in Contemporary China*, edited by M. K. Whyte, 95–104. Cambridge: Harvard University Press.

Silber, J. 1989. "Factor Components, Population Subgroups and the Computation of Gini Index on Inequality." *The Review of Economics and Statistics* 71(1): 107–15.

Silber, J. 1993. "Inequality Decomposition by Income Source: A Note." *Review of Economics and Statistics* 75: 545–7.

Wang, Q., G. Shi, and Y. Zheng. 2002. "Changes in Income Inequality and Welfare Under Economic Transition: Evidence from Urban China." *Applied Economic Letters* 9: 989–91.

Whyte, M. K. 2009. "Chinese Popular View About Inequality." *Annual Review of Sociology* 35: 4–10.

Wu, F. 2004. "Urban Poverty and Marginalization Under Market Transition: The Case of Chinese Cities." *International Journal of Urban and Regional Research* 28 (2): 401–23.

Yao, S. 2005. *Economic Growth, Income Distribution and Poverty Reduction in Contemporary China*. London, New York: RoutledgeCurzon.

Yao, Y. 2009. "The Political Economy of Government Policies Toward Regional Inequality in China." In *Reshaping Economic Geography in East Asia*, edited by Y. Huang and A. Magnoli Bocchi, 218–40. Washington, DC: World Bank.

Yao, D., and Z. Hao. 1999. "Rural Urban Disparity and Sectoral Labour Allocation in China." *Journal of Development Studies* 35 (3): 105–33.

Zhang, Y., and G. Wan. 2006. "The Impact of Growth and Inequality or Rural Poverty in China." *Journal of Comparative Economics* 34: 694–712.

Zhao, L. 2006. "Labour Market Reforms Under Hu-Wen Administration." In *China into the Hu-Wen Era*, edited by J. Wong and L. Hongyi, 351–77. Singapore: World Scientific.

Zhao, L. 2007. "Reforming Hukou to Protect Migrant Labour." In *Interpreting China's Development*, edited by W. Gungwu and J. Wong, 174–8. Singapore: World Scientific.

Zhao, X. B., and S. P. Tong. 2000. "Unequal Economic Development in China: Spatial Disparities and Regional Policy Reconsideration, 1985–1995." *Regional Studies* 34 (6): 549–61.

Appendix. Sources of data used and definition of income

Analysis in this paper is based on the data available from the *China Statistical Yearbook* for the years 1981, 1983, 1988, 1991, 2001, 2004 and 2009. These were published by the China NBS. The earliest distributional data available at present are for 1980 for rural areas and 1981 for urban areas. The reported 1980/81 figures are from these releases, while total inequality for 1980/81, the rural 1980 data are combined with the urban 1981 data. Note that, although all provinces were included in the 1980/81 data, the NSB has considered the sample size too small to estimate distributional statistics. The reported results here are obtained from the published data.

Our analysis is based on households. The total sample size of the rural population for 1980 was 15,914 while that of the urban population of 1981 was 8715; the sample sizes for the 1990 survey were 35,660 for urban and 66,478 for rural. For 2000, sample sizes were 42,220 (urban) and 68,116 (rural); for 2003, 48,028 (urban) and 68,116 (rural). The 2008 sample consists of 64,676 urban households and 68,190 rural households.

The analysis uses grouped data for per capita household disposable/net incomes. The data sources provide information of mean income for rural and urban areas by province, but there is no information about the distribution around the means. Inequality is calculated at the national, rural and urban levels assuming that each sub-population is clustered around the mean.

To obtain rural–urban population weights for each region, China *Population Statistics* (various years) are used. Rural and urban residents refer to the status registered in the household register system. This system discourages people moving from one place to another. After the success of the rural reforms when many workers were freed from agricultural activities, they moved to urban areas in search of higher incomes. Usual resident population refers to people staying at home regularly or for more than six months a year and integrated with the household economically and in terms of living. Members of households staying away from the households more than six months but keeping a close economic relation with household by sending a large portion of their income to the household are regarded as *usual* residents of households. Rural households registered in one place but whose members had moved away to make a living in another place for over one year are not included in rural households of the area where they were registered, irrespective of whether they still kept their contracted land. Therefore, some migrants are not covered in the NBS samples. This creates some bias in our calculations because migrants from rural areas may gain from higher earnings as the remittances are captured in the income figures but most possibly are poorer, on average, than registered urban residents.

Total income of urban households consists of wages and salaries, net business income, income from property and income from transfers of members of households. Thus, any subsidies provided to them or their imputed value in the form of housing, medical benefits, etc. are not considered as part of their income. We have used per capita disposable income for the urban households. This is the total income minus income tax, personal contribution to social security and subsidy for keeping diaries for a sample household.

For the rural sector, total income is defined as the income earned from various sources by the rural households and their members during the reference period; classified as incomes from wages and salaries plus income from household operations, income from property and transfer incomes. Incomes from wages and salaries refer to incomes from labour earned by the members of the rural households employed by other units or individuals. Incomes from household operations are from production and operation by rural households. Operations by rural households are classified according to their economic activity, viz. agriculture, forestry, animal husbandry, fishery, manufacturing, construction, transportation, postal and telecommunications, wholesale retail and catering, social service, culture, education, health and other household operations. Income from property is received by owners of financial assets or tangible non-productive assets to their institutional units. Income from transfers refers to the receipts of rural households and their members of goods, services, capital or rights of assets without giving or repaying accordingly, excluding capital provided to them for the formation of fixed assets. In general, it is all income received by rural households through redistribution. For our analysis of rural inequality, we have considered *net income* as the concept of income, which is total income *minus* taxes and fees paid, household operation expenses, depreciation of fixed assets of production and gifts of non-rural relatives.

The export response to exchange rates and product fragmentation: the case of Chinese manufactured exports

Nobuaki Yamashita[a] and Sisira Jayasuriya[b]

[a]School of Economics, La Trobe University, Melbourne, Australia; [b]Department of Economics, Monash University, Melbourne, Australia

This paper examines how changes in the Chinese real exchange rate affect China's exports in the context of global production networks. It highlights the misspecification inherent in conventional export models and the importance of distinguishing between the very different impacts of exchange rate changes relative to export destinations and those relative to sources of parts and components. Our empirical estimates cast further doubts on the effectiveness of Chinese exchange rate adjustments for reducing Chinese export volumes.

1. Introduction

The link between Chinese trade surpluses and its administered exchange rate regime has become a major issue of debate and a source of friction with deficit countries, in particular the United States. This has produced a large number of studies to quantify the exchange rate elasticity of Chinese exports and has focused attention on the link between the increasing importance of product fragmentation and the sensitivity of manufactured exports to exchange rate movements.[1]

One of the most salient developments in Asian manufacturing trade and investment in recent years is the growth of international production networks driven by multi-national enterprises (MNEs). In these networks, two or more vertically separated production processes are located in two or more countries and integrated by the extensive use of outsourcing and intra-firm trade (Jones and Kierkowski 2001; Athukorala and Yamashita 2006).[2] A country no longer needs to specialise in the production of an entire product, being able instead to focus on some specific segment(s) where it has a comparative cost advantage. As a consequence, there has been a rapid increase in trade in parts and components within the region linking countries specialising in different stages of production (Yamashita 2010).

In this context, China has emerged as a pivotal assembly centre, importing parts and components from other East Asian countries and exporting final products to Western industrial countries. This new pattern of production and trade has important implications for the effects of exchange rates on exports as a Chinese real exchange rate (RER) appreciation lowers the competitiveness of its exports while also lowering the cost of imported inputs.

This paper examines Chinese export response to RER changes, explicitly recognising China's role as an assembly country in the estimation procedure. The structure of the paper is as follows: We first review the literature on the Chinese currency, Renminbi (RMB) and China's trade, followed by a discussion of China's trade patterns in global supply chains in Section 3. In Section 4 we discuss the model and empirical findings and derive the policy implications of our findings. Section 5 concludes the paper.

2. Export elasticity in the context of production fragmentation

In a world of extensive production fragmentation, it is clear that export supply elasticities with respect to exchange rate changes must allow for the fact that some intermediate inputs are imported for use in export goods. In the context of significant product fragmentation, where goods are produced for export using domestic (primary) factors and imported inputs, costs are determined not only by domestic factor prices (for a given technology) but also by prices of imported intermediate goods ('parts and components'). Hence, an exchange rate appreciation relative to a country from which inputs into export production are sourced has opposite effects to a similar appreciation relative to export destination markets.

This is obviously very important in the case of China, whose exports typically incorporate a high proportion of imported parts and components. In principle, export supply and import demand elasticities in the presence of imported parts and components can be calculated (without using econometric estimation techniques) using expressions for elasticities derived from the properties of the GDP function following Kohli (1991).[3] A recent International Monetary Fund (IMF) study (Tokarick 2010) presents an empirical implementation of this approach. However, the accuracy of such calculated elasticity values is questionable. They depend on the accuracy of prior (econometric and input–output table based) estimates of a range of key parameters for many countries (such as elasticities of substitution and industry-specific factor proportions). Further, the approach also necessitates a high level of aggregation and imposition of many (often very restrictive) assumptions about the structure of the economy and market structures (such as the degree of inter-sectoral factor mobility, the extent of exchange rate pass through and so on).[4]

Most recent econometric studies examining the impact of exchange rate changes on Chinese exports acknowledge the role of imported parts and components in export supply and recognise that the traditional approach based on the imperfect substitution model to estimate the effects of the exchange rate on trade flows must be modified (see, for example, Marquez and Schindler 2007; Ahmed 2009; Cheng, Chinn, and Fujii 2010; Thorbecke and Smith 2010; Thorbecke 2011).[5] They distinguish between imports that are meant primarily for export production and 'normal' imports, and use trade data disaggregated into 'processing' and 'ordinary' trade published by the Chinese Customs Statistics (CCS).[6] Processing trade comprises imports that enter the country duty-free and are incorporated into exported goods, and exports based on processed imports. This distinction in China's exports is crucial since a driving force behind China's spectacular export growth for the past two decades has been the processing type of trade.

Marquez and Schindler (2007) argue that disaggregating China's trade into 'ordinary' and 'processing' trade yield better point estimates of China's trade elasticities. The impact of an RER appreciation for ordinary product exports is negative and significant, and ranges from 54 to 65 basis points in response to a 10% RMB appreciation. For processing exports, the effect is similarly negative but smaller and ranges from 24 to 32 basis points. Cheng, Chinn, and Fujii (2010) report some mixed results: RMB depreciation lowers China's processing exports, but increases ordinary exports. Their preferred specification implied that even a 10% appreciation of the RMB on China's overall trade surplus has only a minor impact, reducing it by less than 12%. Jongwanich (2010) based on an export-weighted RER also finds that more technology- and skill-intensive exports (that are likely to incorporate more imported parts and components) are less responsive to RER changes.

Thorbecke and Smith (2010) and Thorbecke (2011) highlight China's importance on close trade linkages with other East Asian component suppliers by constructing a so-called 'integrated exchange rate' – a combination of China's RER with RERs of nine component-supplying countries to China.[7] The basic idea underlying the integrated exchange rate is that as the bulk of value-added in China's processing exports is drawn from those component-supplying countries, their exchange rates will have an indirect influence on Chinese exports. They found that an RMB appreciation alone has a limited impact on China's trade flows: a 10% RMB application would produce only a 3% decline in processed exports (and an 11% decline in ordinary exports). A joint appreciation of the RMB and other East Asian countries' currencies would have produced a 9% reduction in processed exports. These studies highlight the fact that exports that are intensive in imported parts and components are less responsive to China's RER changes, implying that a Chinese currency appreciation will have only limited impact on China's net exports, given the large share of processing trade in total trade.

However, there are several problems with how the exchange rate variables in all these studies have been constructed. First, the use of a single real (typically a trade-weighted effective) exchange rate variable is problematic as the changes in the composite RER can be driven either by changes during the estimation period in the RERs relative to import source countries or by changes in the RERs relative to export destination countries.[8] Changes in one or the other of these two components can yield an identical change in the composite RER variable, but the estimation procedure cannot distinguish between their opposed impacts.[9] This means that the estimation model is misspecified. The two RERs that are expected to have opposite effects should be incorporated as separate variables, rather than aggregated into a single composite variable.

The approach by Thorbecke (2011), who constructed an integrated RER from effective exchange rates for China and input suppliers, is a step in the right direction in so far as it reflects a recognition that the RERs of import source countries must be treated differently from those of export destination countries.[10] However, the country-specific RER indices in his integrated RER are trade-weighted average RERs of the component supplier countries *relative to all* their important trading partners, not their RERs relative to China. This means that changes in component suppliers' RERs driven by movements relative to other (third country) trading partners, rather than movements relative to China, are assumed to significantly impact on Chinese exports. But this is difficult to justify. Different patterns of relative RER behaviour will impact quite differently on Chinese export performance. For example, an appreciation of the RER of China relative to input supplier countries, but not against the export destination countries (such as the United States), will tend to improve Chinese export performance.[11]

In the estimation procedure described below, we specify a model with separate RER variables for the countries that are primarily import source countries and those that are primarily export destination countries. This procedure, which at least partially overcomes the weaknesses and limitations of the approaches discussed above, shares similarities with the Greenaway, Kneller, and Zhang (2010) study of UK manufacturing firms' responses to exchange rate changes.

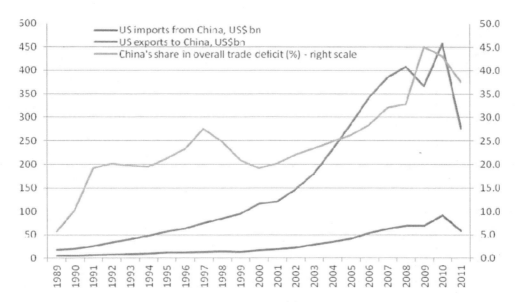

Figure 1. US trade deficit with China, 1989–2011 (US$ bn). Source: US Department of Commerce, Bureau of the Census, Foreign Trade, http://www.census.gov/foreign-trade/.

3. China's trade patterns in global production networks

Figure 1 depicts the US trade deficits with China from 1989 to 2010. China's exports to the US increased rapidly from US$120 billion in 2000 to US$400 billion in 2008, and China's share in the total US trade deficit increased from 12% in 2000 to 40% in 2008. This rapid increase in Chinese exports was accompanied by a change in the composition of Chinese trade. China's exports shifted from relatively labour-intensive products towards more capital- and technology-intensive products (Table 1A and 1B). In 1992/93, miscellaneous manufacturing (including clothing, footwear, and toys and games) accounted for around 60% in China's manufacturing exports, but steadily fell to only 34% in 2004/05. On the other hand, the share of machinery and transport equipment in exports jumped from 21% in 1992/93 to 49% in 2004/05. The export composition is particularly highly concentrated in 'information communication technology' (ICT) product categories under the Standard International Trade Classification (SITC) 75, 76 and 77. The share of office machines under SITC 75 in China's manufacturing exports increased from 2.3% in 1992/93 to 16% in 2004/05. Telecommunication sound equipment (including mobile phones) increased from 8% to 14% in 2004/05, and electrical machinery appliances (SITC 77) went up from 5.8% to 12.5%. The dominant products in China's exports are electronics-related products, but transport-related products (such as automobiles) continue to have a small share. The share of road vehicles (SITC 78) has remained at around 1% from 1992/93 to 2004/05.[12]

The share of miscellaneous manufactured products (including toys, footwear and clothing) has remained low compared with their share in exports. The share of electrical and transport equipment (SITC 7) in China's manufacturing imports increased from 49.6% in 1992/93 to nearly 60% in 2004/05. Within this category, the share of electrical machinery appliances (SITC 77) increased from 7% in 1992/93 to 27% in 2004/05.

Table 2 presents the shares of parts and components in total manufacturing trade for China and other East Asian countries during 1992–2009. These figures show that the component share in China's total manufacturing imports has increased over time, from

Table 1A. Product composition of China's manufactured exports and imports, 1992–2009

SITC	Commodity description	China export composition (%)					China export world share (%)				
		1992/93	1995/96	2000/01	2005/06	2008/09	1992/93	1995/96	2000/01	2005/06	2008/09
5	Chemicals and related products	6.3	7.0	5.5	4.9	5.7	1.4	1.9	2.2	3.6	4.7
6	Manufactured goods classified chiefly by material	22.9	23.7	18.7	18.7	18.0	3.0	4.0	5.3	10.1	12.5
7	Machinery and transport equipment	20.0	26.1	38.4	49.8	50.9	1.1	1.7	3.6	9.9	13.5
71	Power generatng.machines	1.2	1.2	1.3	1.1	1.7	0.9	1.2	1.9	3.5	6.3
72	Special.indust.machinery	1.0	0.9	0.9	1.2	1.7	0.6	0.7	1.3	3.5	5.9
73	Metalworking machinery	0.4	0.3	0.3	0.3	0.4	1.0	1.1	1.7	3.6	7.1
74	General industl.mach.nes	1.9	2.1	2.8	3.7	4.5	0.9	1.4	3.0	7.5	10.6
75	Office machines,adp mach	2.0	4.5	9.1	15.1	13.4	0.9	2.4	6.3	24.6	32.7
76	Telecomm.sound equip etc	5.9	6.8	9.4	13.4	12.5	3.4	4.7	7.6	20.8	27.0
77	Elec mch appar,parts,nes	5.1	7.2	10.7	10.9	11.6	1.5	2.2	4.4	10.3	14.5
78	Road vehicles	1.7	2.1	2.9	3.0	3.0	0.4	0.6	1.2	2.6	3.7
79	Othr.transport equipment	0.9	1.0	1.0	1.0	2.1	0.6	1.1	1.5	3.4	8.1
8	Miscellaneous manufactured articles	50.8	43.2	37.4	26.6	25.5	7.6	8.9	11.6	18.0	21.8
81	Prefab buildgs,fttng etc	0.7	0.8	1.0	0.8	0.9	3.9	5.7	11.0	18.0	23.1
82	Furniture,bedding,etc.	1.3	1.4	2.1	2.3	2.5	3.1	4.1	8.1	18.8	25.7
83	Travel goods,handbgs etc	2.3	2.2	1.7	1.0	1.1	15.8	19.3	24.5	32.4	39.1
84	Clothing and accessories	24.7	19.2	15.7	10.4	9.2	13.7	15.5	18.9	28.8	34.3
85	Footwear	6.7	5.4	4.3	2.5	2.3	13.6	15.1	22.4	31.1	35.7
87	Scientific equipment nes	0.6	0.7	1.1	2.3	2.7	0.7	1.1	2.2	8.7	12.0
88	Photo.apparat.nes;clocks	2.8	2.5	1.9	0.9	0.8	4.1	5.1	6.1	7.4	9.8
89	Misc manufctrd goods nes	11.8	11.0	9.6	6.3	6.1	5.7	7.2	9.9	14.1	16.3
	Total manufacturing	100.0	100.0	100.0	100.0	100.0	3.1	3.9	5.8	11.7	15.0

Source: UN Comtrade database: http://comtrade.un.org/db/.

Table 1B. Product composition of China's manufactured imports and imports, 1992–2009

SITC	Commodity Description	China import composition (%)					China import world share (%)				
		1992/93	1995/96	2000/01	2005/06	2008/09	1992/93	1995/96	2000/01	2005/06	2008/09
5	Chemicals and related products, n.e.s.	13.4	16.1	16.7	14.8	15.6	3.2	3.7	5.2	7.0	7.5
6	Manufactured goods classified chiefly by material	30.7	27.4	22.5	15.1	14.5	4.4	3.9	5.0	5.6	6.1
7	Machinery and transport equipment	48.3	48.9	53.4	58.2	57.5	3.0	2.9	4.0	8.0	9.2
71	Power generatng.machines	3.1	2.9	2.8	2.2	2.6	2.9	2.7	3.2	4.8	5.9
72	Special.indust.machinery	13.8	12.5	6.3	4.2	3.8	9.7	8.7	7.7	8.9	8.9
73	Metalworking machinery	2.6	3.3	1.8	1.9	1.4	8.0	9.2	8.2	16.1	14.8
74	General industl.mach.nes	5.0	6.7	4.7	4.6	5.1	2.9	3.7	4.0	6.5	7.4
75	Office machines,adp mach	1.8	2.9	6.3	6.9	6.1	0.9	1.2	3.3	7.4	8.7
76	Telecomm.sound equip etc	5.7	6.1	6.9	5.8	4.8	3.7	3.8	4.5	6.2	5.9
77	Elec mch appar,parts.nes	7.0	9.6	20.3	28.1	28.1	2.3	2.5	6.4	16.6	19.2
78	Road vehicles	5.7	2.2	2.2	2.6	3.7	1.4	0.6	0.7	1.6	2.8
79	Othr.transport equipment	3.7	2.6	2.2	1.8	1.9	3.7	3.6	3.7	5.7	5.7
8	Miscellaneous manufactured articles	7.5	7.5	7.4	11.9	12.3	1.2	1.3	1.8	5.2	6.1
81	Prefab buildgs,fttng etc	0.2	0.2	0.1	0.0	0.1	1.2	1.0	0.6	0.6	1.2
82	Furniture,bedding,etc.	0.1	0.1	0.1	0.1	0.2	0.3	0.2	0.3	0.6	1.0
83	Travel goods,handbgs etc	0.1	0.0	0.0	0.0	0.1	0.4	0.2	0.2	0.7	1.4
84	Clothing and accessories	0.6	0.9	0.7	0.3	0.3	0.4	0.6	0.6	0.6	0.6
85	Footwear	0.5	0.3	0.2	0.1	0.1	1.0	0.7	0.6	0.8	1.1
87	Scientific equipment nes	1.8	2.0	2.8	8.1	8.2	2.4	2.6	4.5	19.4	21.4
88	Photo.apparat.nes;clocks	1.9	1.7	1.7	1.5	1.6	3.1	3.0	4.5	9.4	12.4
89	Misc manufctrd goods nes	2.4	2.3	1.9	1.7	1.8	1.2	1.3	1.5	2.4	2.8
	Total manufacturing	100.0	100.0	100.0	100.0	100.0	3.5	3.4	4.6	8.0	9.0

Source: UN Comtrade database: http://comtrade.un.org/db/.

Table 2. Percentage share of parts and components (P&Cs) in total manufacturing trade, 1992–2009

	Export (%)				Import (%)			
	1992/93	2000/01	2005/06	2008/09	1992/93	2000/01	2005/06	2008/09
China	5.2	14.2	20.2	15.5	19.3	34.5	43.8	24.1
Hong Kong (China)	18.8	27.5	26.5	14.9	16.8	30	36	21
ASEAN6	27.4	38.6	40.2	18.1	34.6	48.8	43.4	24.9
Malaysia	33.4	46.1	48	20.5	42	57.4	53.1	25.4
Philippines	34.4	58.2	66.6	21.6	33.9	55.1	51.1	23.8
Singapore	33.8	43.2	43.5	18.2	38.6	50.4	46.5	25.7
Viet Nam	1.4	9.9	10.2	9.2	8.9	18.5	17.2	15.7
Thailand	21.2	27.2	27.4	18	29.1	43.6	38.2	27.5
Indonesia	3.2	12.4	19.7	15.4	24	31	32.9	26.4
Japan	26.9	34.1	32.4	24.4	18.5	26.7	25.2	19.2
South Korea	19.1	27.4	33.1	18.5	29.2	36.7	31.9	19.4
Taiwan	21.1	36.9	45.9	19.2	30.5	39.1	37.7	17.6
USA	30.3	35.6	31.2	23.8	24.5	24.1	21.5	17.7
NAFTA	29.6	32.2	29	22.8	27.4	27	23.7	19.4
EU15	18.6	20.7	19.6	18	19.1	21.7	19.7	16.6
Low-income	2.9	5.4	6.5	7.3	15.3	17.1	16.1	14.9
Low-to-middle income	8.1	17.5	21.7	15.3	21.6	31.3	34.3	22.1
High-income	22.7	26	24	19.4	21.3	24.2	22.1	17.5
World	20.8	25.1	24.1	18.2	21.7	25.6	23.9	18.2

Source: UN Comtrade database: http://comtrade.un.org/db/.

19% in 1992/93 to 44% in 2005/06, a figure similar to those of ASEAN and other East Asian countries. But the share of components in China's manufacturing exports in 2005/06 was around 20%, compared with 40% in ASEAN countries, 33% in South Korea and 46% in Taiwan. These clearly show China's emergence as an export-oriented assembly location using imported components and exporting final products.

The share of components in total manufacturing trade dropped sharply immediately after the global financial crisis (GFC) in 2008 and 2009 (see Athukorala 2011). This was largely due to a sharp decline in demand for consumer durable goods (ITC products and motor vehicles) in industrial countries. This fall in demand for exports produced a corresponding fall in component imports; the share of components in China's total manufacturing imports dropped from 44% in 2005/06 to 24% in 2008/09. A similar drop occurred in the case of ASEAN countries; on average, the share of components in manufacturing imports and imports fell to 25% and 18% respectively.

Table 3 summarises China's main export destination and import source countries and locations from 1992 to 2009, separating China's trade volumes into 'parts and components' and 'final goods'. In machinery and transport equipment (SITC 7), ASEAN countries accounted for only 2.2% of Chinese imports in 1992/93, but this increased to around 13% in 2000/01 and 17% in 2005/06 (Panel A of Table 3). The lion's share of China's component imports comes from other East Asian countries, South Korea, Taiwan and Japan: in 2005/06, South Korea and Taiwan accounted for 30% and Japan for 18% of total component imports. On the other hand, the share of the United States declined from 11% in 1992/93 to less than 6% in 2005/06, and the share of the EU15 dropped from 19% in 1992/93 to 9.4% in 2005/06.[13]

Table 3. Directions and sources of China's trade in components and final product (%), 1992–2009

(A) Imports

Year	Part and components in machinery and electrical (SITC 7)					Final products in machinery and electrical (SITC 7)				
	ASEAN	Korea + Taiwan	Japan	US	EU15	ASEAN	Korea + Taiwan	Japan	US	EU15
1992/93	2.2	15.0	33.4	10.7	19.1	1.1	15.5	28.5	14.1	25.6
2000/01	13.3	20.3	24.1	9.4	17.2	5.2	15.9	20.6	17.3	26.0
2005/06	17.2	30.1	18.2	5.7	9.4	12.1	14.1	21.5	10.2	24.3
2008/09	8.0	19.7	23.4	6.3	19.0	17.5	23.5	16.2	8.0	15.4

Year	Part and components in toys and clothing (SITC 8)					Final products in toys and clothing (SITC 8)				
	ASEAN	Korea + Taiwan	Japan	US	EU15	ASEAN	Korea + Taiwan	Japan	US	EU15
1992/93	1.0	22.1	30.5	7.2	5.2	1.4	20.5	25.0	14.9	8.6
2000/01	5.5	16.6	36.1	9.0	13.6	3.1	16.4	20.8	19.4	18.0
2005/06	4.6	31.3	30.0	7.9	8.0	4.0	44.0	16.5	7.4	8.7
2008/09	5.6	25.1	28.0	7.4	13.6	4.2	41.8	15.4	8.0	11.2

(B) Exports

Year	Part and components in machinery and electrical (SITC 7)					Final products in machinery and electrical (SITC 7)				
	ASEAN	Korea + Taiwan	Japan	US	EU15	ASEAN	Korea + Taiwan	Japan	US	EU15
1992/93	7.8	6.2	15.8	17.5	13.0	6.2	3.0	8.6	22.3	15.2
2000/01	12.8	7.8	14.9	15.4	12.8	7.0	5.2	11.1	24.4	21.3
2005/06	11.6	9.5	10.1	15.6	13.4	5.2	4.0	8.2	26.4	23.2
2008/09	8.6	7.1	8.8	14.5	16.7	8.6	5.9	5.8	19.9	17.8

Year	Part and components in toys and clothing (SITC 8)					Final products in toys and clothing (SITC 8)				
	ASEAN	Korea + Taiwan	Japan	US	EU15	ASEAN	Korea + Taiwan	Japan	US	EU15
1992/93	3.9	5.5	13.0	16.8	9.6	1.5	2.3	16.0	27.1	14.5
2000/01	4.6	5.3	19.7	27.4	9.5	2.1	3.5	20.5	27.4	14.2
2005/06	5.9	7.7	25.3	19.4	9.1	2.9	3.5	12.9	26.6	18.2
2008/09	9.1	6.7	13.4	18.4	12.1	4.8	3.2	10.6	24.0	21.4

Source: UN Comtrade database: http://comtrade.un.org/db/.

Table 3, panel B, shows China's export destinations in parts and components and final products. Similar to the import pattern, the share of ASEAN countries increased from the early 1990s, up from 7.8% in 1992/93 to 11.6% in 2005/06. The United States and EU15 countries have accounted for around 40% of China's final product exports, with little change over the past 20 years: in 1992/93, 22% of China's final good exports went to the United States and 15% to the EU15, while in 2008/09, the United States accounted for 20% and the EU15 accounted for 18%.

China's trade in the miscellaneous manufactured article category (SITC 8) – mainly toys and clothing – shows a quite different pattern. ASEAN countries account for only a small portion of China's imports and exports in this product category, which is dominated by imports from South Korea and Taiwan, which together account for around 40% of final good imports. The majority of Chinese exports in this category go to Japan, the United States and EU15 countries. Overall, the majority of China's component imports are sourced from East Asian countries, including Japan, while its final product exports go mainly to the United States and EU15 countries.

4. Export response to a Chinese RER appreciation[14]

The following empirical specification incorporates two different RER variables based on the classification of China's trading partners according to their primary role as input suppliers or export destinations. The first represents the real 'bilateral' exchange rates between China and export destination countries.[15] The second is China's RER relative to component source countries (the variable definitions are given below). We estimate the following model:

$$\ln \text{CHE}_{ijt} = \alpha + \mathbf{Z}'_{it}\beta + \phi_1 \ln \text{BER}_{it} + \phi_2 \ln \text{RER}_{jt} + \varepsilon_{ijt}, \qquad (1)$$

where subscript i denotes importing countries, and j the industry and t the year. The dependent variable (CHE) is export volume defined as final good exports from China to a set of destination countries. BER denotes the RER relative to export destination countries. The expected sign for BER is negative because it denotes a loss in price competitiveness when other factors are held constant. The variable RER is China's real effective exchange rate relative to input supplier countries. We expect its sign to be positive. $\mathbf{Z}$ is a vector of variables (other than exchange rate variables) that may influence the volume of China's exports. A dummy variable is used to differentiate the periods before and after China's entry into the World Trade Organisation (WTO). The symbol ln before a variable denotes the natural logarithm. Last, ε is a random variable that is i.i.d. normal with mean zero and variance.

We construct the RER based on China's RER movements relative to nine East Asian countries (Japan, Hong Kong - China, Taiwan, South Korea, Singapore, Malaysia, Indonesia, Thailand, the Philippines) that are the main component suppliers to China.[16] For export destination countries, we focus on China's exports to industrial countries in North America and Europe.[17] Separating countries into export destinations and component suppliers reduces correlation between BER and RER.[18] The computation of RER is based on the following formula, where each industry is indexed as j in the SITC two-digit level and East Asian exporters to China are indexed as k. The weight is determined by the share of

Table 4A. Summary statistics of variables

Variable	Definition	Obs.	Mean	Std. dev.	Min.	Max.
GDP	Export destination GDP	5104	26.79	1.25	24.56	30.08
BER	Export destination real exchange rates	6659	−1.14	1.65	−2.81	4.34
RER	Import source real exchange rates	6973	3.32	0.71	0.77	4.88
WTO	A dummy for China's entry to WTO	5104	0.49	0.50	0.00	1.00

Table 4B. Correlation matrix

		GDP	BER	RER	WTO
GDP	Export destination GDP	1.00			
BER	Export destination real exchange rates	−0.41	1.00		
RER	Import source real exchange rates	0.03	0.84	1.00	
WTO	A dummy for China's entry to WTO	0.08	−0.06	0.57	1.00

Source: Authors' calculation.

that country in China's component imports in each industry. That is,

$$\text{RER}_{jt} = \sum_k w_t^{jk} er_t^k, \quad \text{where } w_t^{jk} = \frac{M_t^{jk}}{\sum_k M_t^{jk}},$$

where M stands for China's component imports from those East Asian countries and er represents the bilateral exchange rate of each of China's component source countries against the RMB. The RERs are based on nominal exchange rates adjusted by inflation rates measured by consumer price indices (CPIs).[19] The subscript t recognises that the country trade shares (weights) vary through time. A real appreciation of RER would lower costs of imported inputs, which will enhance international competitiveness of China's final product exports.

Table 4A and 4B present summary statistics and a correlation matrix to aid in the interpretation of the results. Table 5 reports results for fixed-effects estimates. Columns (1)–(3) report the regression results, including all two-digit industries of both SITC 7 (machinery and transport equipment) and SITC 8 (miscellaneous manufacturing). As shown in Table 1A and 1B, SITC 8 includes relatively more labour-intensive goods, such as clothing and footwear. The results for industries within SITC 7 only are presented in columns (4)–(6); columns (7)–(9) show results for products in SITC 8. We run separate regressions for these two product categories because the proportions of imported parts and components in the final product exports in these categories are different: SITC 7 is more import intensive. We expect higher export elasticity with respect to RER – which takes into account the exchange rate changes relative to import suppliers – for products in the more import-intensive machinery and transport equipment industry category (SITC 7) compared with those in SITC 8. We also introduce the two RER variables in separate regressions because of the high correlation between the exchange rate indices.

Results in Table 5 show that, as expected, an appreciation of the BER – which takes into account the exchange rate changes relative to destination countries – would decrease

Table 5. China's export elasticity of change in the RMB, 1992–2008

	Electronics and transport equipments (SITC 7) and miscellaneous manufactured items (SITC 8)			Products under SITC 7			Products under SITC 8		
	(1)	(2)	(3)	(4)	(5)	(6)	(7)	(8)	(9)
Export destination GDP	0.84 [0.511]	0.98 [0.675]	1.12* [0.569]	1.05** [0.474]	1.16 [0.737]	1.39** [0.577]	0.58 [0.522]	0.69 [0.593]	0.81 [0.545]
BER	−0.96*** [0.319]	−0.76 [0.481]		−1.24*** [0.327]	−0.82 [0.545]		−0.74** [0.330]	−0.68 [0.409]	
RER	0.66*** [0.074]		0.61*** [0.084]	1.15*** [0.093]		1.06*** [0.106]	0.30*** [0.057]		0.28*** [0.066]
WTO	1.11*** [0.133]	1.62*** [0.223]	1.11*** [0.160]	0.89*** [0.131]	1.80*** [0.248]	0.91*** [0.161]	1.13*** [0.139]	1.36*** [0.196]	1.12*** [0.158]
Constant	−8.85 [13.062]	−10.33 [17.388]	−15.03 [14.926]	−16.82 [12.087]	−15.99 [18.984]	−24.09 [15.085]	0.26 [13.355]	−1.74 [15.308]	−4.94 [14.341]
Obs.	4,976	4,976	5,101	2,985	2,985	3,062	1,991	1,991	2,039
R-squared	0.643	0.587	0.635	0.689	0.589	0.677	0.658	0.632	0.648

Note: Standard errors based on White's heteroscedasticity correction cluster by importing countries for SITC two-digit industry level are given within square brackets with statistical significance (two-tailed test) denoted as: ***, 1%; **, 5%; and *, 10%.

China's final product exports (column 1): a 1% appreciation of the BER lowers final product exports by 0.96%. In contrast, an appreciation of the component import-weighted RER increases China's exports because it lowers costs of exports: a 1% appreciation of the RER increases exports by 0.66%. These effects are statistically significant at the 1% level. However, once BER and RER are included separately (columns 2 and 3 in Table 5), the statistical significance of BER is lost, although the sign remains negative (column 2). The estimated coefficient for RER in column (3) remains similar to that in column (1) and is statistically significant at 1%.[20] As expected, the export elasticity with respect to the RER is greater in machinery and transport equipment industry (SITC 7) than in the relatively more labour-intensive SITC 8: a 1% appreciation of RER increases SITC 7 exports by 1.15% (column 4), compared with only 0.3% increase of SITC 8 (column 7).[21] China's entry into the WTO is shown to have had a significant impact on export performance, consistent with other studies.

5. Conclusions

In this paper, we estimated the impact of RER changes on Chinese manufactured exports with a procedure that explicitly distinguished between movements in RERs relative to countries supplying parts and components for export production, and RER movements relative to export destination countries. We used disaggregated Chinese data on manufactured trade, constructed separate RERs for import supply and export destination countries and estimated the elasticity of export supply of two categories of Chinese manufactured exports (SITC 7 and SITC 8). As expected, export supply responds differently to the RERs of countries from which China imports parts and components and RERs of countries to which China exports processed goods. Further, the more import-intensive category of exports is more sensitive to the RER change relative to import source countries and less sensitive to exchange rates relative to destination countries. If the share of the more import-intensive exports continues to rise in the future as it has done so far, we would anticipate that the overall export supply response of Chinese manufactures will become increasingly less sensitive to exchange rate changes relative to its destination markets and even more sensitive to its exchange rate changes relative to the import source countries.

These findings have important implications for the likely impact of Chinese exchange rate changes on Chinese export volumes. While analysis of the overall impact of exchange rate changes on trade and current account balances requires a general equilibrium framework, our results suggest that a Chinese nominal exchange rate appreciation relative to exchange rates of its major export destination countries such as the US dollar and the Euro – even if it translates into a longer-term real appreciation – will have only a limited impact on Chinese manufactured exports. The impact on China's overall trade balance will be further dampened by related falls in imported parts and components, with adverse effects on the exports of component supplier countries such as Japan, Korea, Taiwan (China) and ASEAN.

This analysis highlights the methodological point that estimation procedures in analysis of trade responses to exchange rates must allow for the very different impacts that exchange rate movements relative to input and destination countries have on a country's net exports.

Acknowledgements

This paper benefitted from comments and suggestions from Noel Gaston, an anonymous reviewer, and Sandi Suardi, as well as from seminar participants at the Institute of Social and Economic Research, Osaka University, Japan, and participants of the Economic and Policy Developments in East Asia workshop held at Bond University, Gold Coast, Australia, on 13–14 October 2011. We thank the Institute of Social and Economic Research, Osaka University, Japan for providing facilities for undertaking this research.

Notes

1. Many Chinese economists, for example, assert that an appreciation of the Chinese currency will have very little impact on its net exports and the US trade deficit (see, for example, opinion pieces in *Financial Times* by Yukon Huang, Vice-president of strategic intelligence and a lead China analyst at *Stratfor*, a Texas-based private intelligence company [*Financial Times*, 5 October 2011], and Yao Yang, Director of the China Centre for Economic Research at Peking University [*Financial Times*, 6 October 2011]).
2. For example, Quanta Computer, the largest laptop original design manufacturer (ODM) originating in Taiwan, collects parts and components from around the globe – such as Intel microprocessors and Microsoft operating systems from the United States, graphic tips designed by ATI technologies from Ontario in Canada, hard disc drives from Japan, and liquid crystal display (LCD) screens and memory chips produced from companies in Taiwan and South Korea – and then assembles them at Quanta Shanghai Manufacturing City in China. Quanta Computer was listed as one of the Global Fortune 500 Enterprises in Fortune Magazine in 2006. See http://www.quantatw.com/Quanta/english/Default.aspx
3. See Dixit and Norman (1980) and Woodland (1982).
4. This study uses the GTAP database for estimates of the required parameters and presents export supply and import demand elasticities for a large number of countries, including China, under various scenarios. These calculated elasticities naturally depend on the underlying parameter values of the variables in the expression for elasticities. Many of these have been estimated using data covering varying periods of time and using different econometric approaches.
5. Jongwanich (2010) acknowledges the issue but uses an export-weighted RER in her estimation. For expositions of the traditional approach, see Goldstein and Khan (1978) and Rose (1991).
6. The CCS data contain a harmonised system (HS) eight-digit product level classification of China's trade flows administered by the Customs Office, with information on the type of trade (processing exports using imported intermediate inputs, using locally sourced inputs, normal exports and imported intermediate inputs for the purpose of exports), trading partner countries, the type of trading firms (whether MNEs, pure local firms or international joint ventures), the location of exporters and importers in the regions and cities, the values in US dollars and the quantity in eight different units. Several studies in Feenstra and Wei (2010) also use CCS trade data.
7. These countries are Germany, Japan, Malaysia, the Philippines, Singapore, South Korea, Taiwan, Thailand, and the United States.
8. In the absence of instantaneous purchasing power parity condition holding across all countries, there is no theoretical reason for these to behave in an identical manner. The empirical behaviour of bilateral RERs shows wide fluctuations.
9. To illustrate, consider the case of a country whose import source countries and export destination countries have a 50% share in total trade. Assume that the change in these shares (due to trade volume changes resulting from exchange rate changes) can be ignored, and that there is zero inflation everywhere so that nominal exchange rate changes correspond to RER changes. In this case, a 1% appreciation of the effective (trade-weighted) RER can be the result of a 2% appreciation of the exchange rate relative to import source countries or a 2% appreciation relative to the RER of the export destination countries. Obviously, these would have opposite impacts on export supply. However, the estimation procedure will yield quite different elasticity estimates in the two cases, though the underlying structural value of the export supply parameter had been unchanged.
10. Note that we use the term 'import source countries' to denote countries that are suppliers of parts and components (intermediates) for export production, rather than source countries for all imports.
11. Tokarick's (2010) approach to calculating trade elasticities ignores these exchange rate issues by assuming, in effect, a two-country model where the rest of the world is a homogeneous composite of all foreign countries.
12. The share of road vehicles (SITC 78) has remained at around 1% from 1992/93 to 2004/05.

13. During the recent crisis period in 2008/09, ASEAN's share in China's component imports declined to 8%. Similarly, the shares of South Korea and Taiwan also dropped significantly. However, in contrast to component imports, the share of ASEAN in China's final good imports actually went up from 12% in 2005/06 to 17.5% in 2008/09, while the shares of Japan, the United States and the EU15 all went down. The share of Japan in China's final product imports declined from 20% in 2000/01 to 16% in 2008/09.
14. This section is based on Yamashita (2011).
15. Note that 'bilateral' in this context refers to the real effective exchange rate between China and the relevant group of countries.
16. These are the same countries chosen by Thorbecke (2011). Australia is not included in this set of countries because, though it is a major source of imported resources, it plays no significant role as a parts and component supplier.
17. It is noted that component exports out of these countries may be by third-country firms, including firms with home bases in the export destination countries. This complex web of trade and investment linkages emphasises the need to go beyond simple measures of gross trade in measurement of bilateral trade and current account imbalances. Kierzkowski and Chen (2010), for example, show that the true China–US trade imbalance falls dramatically when trade in parts and components produced by US firms and affiliates (including those located in third countries) is taken into account.
18. Some countries, such as Japan, are both significant component suppliers and destination markets, but the basic results are robust to changes in the composition of country groupings taking account of such 'mixed' cases.
19. The use of CPI in this context is driven by data availability; other measures of price inflation were not available for all countries during the study period.
20. This loss in statistical significance of BER is probably due to the high correlation between BER and RER (see Table 4B).
21. These elasticity estimates are not strictly comparable to elasticity estimates in previous literature because our exchange rate indices, with respect to which elasticities are defined, are quite different; we treat movements of exchange rates relative to supplier countries and destination countries separately, whereas the elasticity measures in previous literature are defined relative to an aggregate index of exchange rates of both groups.

References

Ahmed, S. 2009. *Are Chinese Exports Sensitive to Changes in the Exchange Rates*. Federal Reserve Board International Finance Discussion Paper No. 987. Charlotte, NC: Federal Reserve Board.

Athukorala, P. 2011. "Production Networks and Trade Patterns in East Asia: Regionalization or Globalization?" *Asian Economic Papers* 10 (1): 66–95.

Athukorala, P., and N. Yamashita. 2006. "Production Fragmentation and Trade Integration: East Asia in Global Context." *North American Journal of Economics and Finance* 17 (3): 233–56.

Cheng, Y., M. D. Chinn, and E. Fujii. 2010. "China's Current Account and Exchange Rate." In *China's Growing Role in World Trade*, edited by R. C. Feenstra and S. Wei, 231–71. Cambridge MA: Cambridge University Press.

Dixit, A., and V. Norman. 1980. *Theory of International Trade*. Cambridge, MA: Cambridge University Press.

Feenstra, R., and Q. Wei. 2010. *China's Growing Role in World Trade*. Cambridge, MA: Cambridge University Press.

Goldberg, L. S. 2004. "Industry-Specific Exchange Rates for the United States." *FRBNY Economic Policy Review* 10 (1): 1–16.

Goldstein, M., and M. Khan. 1978. "The Supply and Demand for Exports: A Simultaneous Approach." *Review of Economics and Statistics* 60 (2): 275–86.

Greenaway, D., R. Kneller, and X. Zhang. 2010. "The Effect of Exchange Rates on Firm Exports: The Role of Imported Intermediate Inputs." *The World Economy* 33 (8): 961–86.

Jones, R. W. and H. Kierzkowski. 2001. "A Framework for Fragmentation." In *Fragmentation: New Production Patterns in the World Economy*, edited by S. W. Arndt and H. Kierzkowski. New York: Oxford University Press.

Jongwanish, J. 2010. "Determinants of Export Performance in East and Southeast Asia." *The World Economy* 33 (1): 20–41.

Kierzkowski, H. and L. Chen. 2010. "Outsourcing and Trade Imbalances: The United States and China Case." *Pacific Economic Review* 15 (1): 56–70.

Kohli, U. 1991. *Technology, Duality, and Foreign Trade: The GNP Function Approach to Modelling Imports and Exports*. Ann Arbor, MI: University of Michigan Press.

Marquez, J., and J. Schindler. 2007. "Exchange Rate Effects on China's Trade." *Review of International Economics* 15: 837–53.

Rose, A. 1991. "The Role of Exchange Rates in a Popular Model of International Trade: Does the 'Marshall-Lerner' Condition Hold?" *Journal of International Economics* 30 (3–4): 301–16.

Thorbecke, W. 2011. "Investigating the Effect of Exchange Rate Changes on China's Processed Exports." *Journal of the Japanese and International Economies* 25 (2): 33–46.

Thorbecke, W. and G. Smith. 2010. "How Would an Appreciation of the Renminbi and Other East Asian Currencies Affect China's Exports?" *Review of International Economics* 18 (1): 95–108.

Tokarick, S. 2010. *A Method for Calculating Export Supply and Import Demand Elasticities*. IMF Working Paper No. 10/180. Washington, DC: IMF.

Wang, Z., and S. Wei. 2010. "What Accounts for the Rising Sophistication of China's Exports?" In *China's Growing Role in World Trade*, edited by R. C. Feenstra and S. Wei, 63–104. Cambridge, MA: Cambridge University Press.

Woodland, A. 1982. *International Trade and Resource Allocation, Advanced Textbooks in Economics*. Vol. 19. Amsterdam: North-Holland Publishing.

Yamashita, N. 2010. *International Fragmentation of Production: The Impact of Outsourcing on the Japanese Economy*. Cheltenham: Edward Elgar.

Yamashita, N. 2011. *The Currency of the Peoples Republic of China and Production Fragmentation*. ADBI Working Paper No. 327. Tokyo: Asian Development Bank Institute.

Income volatility of Indonesian banks after the Asian Financial Crisis

Barry Williams*

Globalisation and Development Centre, School of Business, Bond University, QLD, Australia

This paper considers the factors that determine Indonesian bank risk both before and after the Asian Financial Crisis (AFC). In the pre-AFC period, bank capital holdings are positively associated with bank revenue risk, which is attributed to a combination of regulatory laxity as well as laxity of enforcement. In the post-AFC period, capital is found to reduce bank risk in a non-linear manner. Franchise value is associated with lower bank risk, but in a non-linear manner; low levels of franchise value are associated with increased bank risk, while higher levels of franchise value result in lower bank risk. It is also concluded the low-to-medium levels of bank loan growth are associated with lower bank risk; however, high levels of loan growth are risk increasing. These results point to the importance of enforcement of regulatory oversight in reducing bank risk.

1. Introduction/motivation

The recent Global Financial Crisis (GFC) has re-focused attention upon the issue of financial system risk. In particular, the issues of volatility of bank revenue and the quality of bank asset portfolios are experiencing increased scrutiny from both policy-makers and the general public. To date much of this attention has been focused upon those developed nations that have experienced large losses during the GFC, in order to provide objective evidence that will aid in the formation of better banking policies. This paper will adopt a different perspective in that it will consider the income volatility of Indonesian banks. Indonesia provides an interesting alternative perspective as its banking system was badly affected by the earlier Asian Financial Crisis (AFC). As a result (in part) of the on-going reconstruction efforts to recover from the AFC, Indonesian banks did not participate in the debt-driven housing finance boom that lead up to the GFC. Thus, study of Indonesia provides an opportunity to consider the impact of post-crisis reconstruction upon an Asian developing nation. Furthermore, many previous studies of Indonesian banking have adopted two main perspectives by either (1) considering in detail the Indonesian banking system experience of the AFC or (2) studying the input–output efficiency of Indonesian banks with a particular emphasis upon the AFC experience. By using data drawn from a longer period than previous work, as well considering income volatility, this paper will offer two contributions to the existing literature by (1) considering the evolution of determinants of bank risk in a post-crisis recovery period and (2) add a new dimension to the literature considering Indonesian banking. In addition, the Indonesian regulatory experience combined with the high rate of asset growth prior to the AFC makes Indonesia and its reconstruction process an ideal country to consider the relationship between asset growth and revenue volatility and capital holdings.

---

*Also currently a visiting researcher at KOF Swiss Economic Institute, ETH Zurich, Switzerland.

The traditional view of bank capital is that it lowers the implied value of the put options created by actual or implied deposit insurance (Merton 1977; Diamond and Dybvig 1983), and so reduces morally hazardous risk taking by management. This study finds that bank capital reduces bank risk in the Indonesian case in a non-linear manner, in that increasing bank capital generates decreasing reductions in bank risk. It is argued that the combined impacts of pre-AFC regulatory laxity combined with post-AFC regulatory forbearance generated some inconsistencies in this relationship (and associated risk seeking by bank management, consistent with Besanko and Kanatas (1996) and Calem and Rob (1999). Overall, bank capital was found to have its traditional role of acting to reduce the appetite of bank management for risk. A policy implication of this result is that if post-GFC reforms focusing upon bank capital are to impact upon bank risk, then these reforms (such as Capital Adequacy Mark III) must be accompanied by a reasonable level of enforcement.

This paper also finds that bank franchise value as represented by retail operations is associated with lower bank risk in a non-linear manner, in that lower levels of franchise value are associated with increased bank risk, while high levels of franchise values are associated with reduced bank risk. A U-shaped relationship between bank risk and bank loan growth is also found. Thus, low-to-medium levels of loan growth are beneficial to both bank risk reduction and the economy in terms of ongoing asset formation. However, high levels of loan growth are associated with increased bank risk and also with potentially hazardous economic outcomes in terms of bank failure and the resulting cessation of asset formation (bank lending). It is also found that increased non-interest income is associated with increased bank risk, particularly in the post-recovery phase of Indonesian banking.

The rest of this paper is structured as follows; the next section will discuss the evolution and structure of the Indonesian banking system. Section 3 will provide a review of the relevant literature as it deals with both the relevant aspects of the Indonesian banking system not considered in Section 2 and the broader literature that considers the relevant aspects of bank risk. During the literature review, the main hypothesis to be tested will be developed. Section 4 will detail the model to be tested as a result of the hypothesis developed in Section 3. Section 5 will detail the data and methodology that are used to test the model proposed. The results will be discussed in Section 6, while the final section provides conclusions and policy recommendations.

2. Overview of the Indonesian banking system

2.1. *Evolution of the Indonesian banking system*

The Indonesian banking system can be considered as having experienced a number of distinct phases of development since World War Two. After Indonesia achieved independence, the financial system was dominated by state-owned banks. In addition, some state banks were formed to provide finance to specified sectors of the economy. The Ministry of Finance acted as both a price setter and allocated loans, in some cases to specified borrowers (Muresan and Danila 2005). During this period, a small number of private domestic and foreign banks were permitted to operate (Margono, Sharma, and Melvin 2010). The second phase of Indonesian banking commenced with two major deregulation events in 1983 and 1985. The outcome was a rapid growth in the number of commercial banks; between 1983 and 1995 the number of banks grew from 115 to 240 (Hamada and Konishi 2010). As described by Muresan and Danila (2005, p. 4) '... *anyone with some spare cash* ... ' could apply for and receive a bank license. This post-deregulation period was characterised by regulatory laxity lacking in due diligence as well as poor enforcement of what limited regulations were in place. The outcome was increased moral hazard, with an underlying assumption that the government would bail out both private and state-owned banks. In particular, the private banks were active in lending to their own related business groups without active credit management (Muresan and Danila 2005), while the Indonesian government required the state banks to lend to both politically important projects and to state enterprises (Derina 2011). This era was also characterised by high levels of loan growth accompanied by lack of central bank supervision of bank risk (Margono, Sharma, and Melvin 2010).

The third phase of development of the Indonesian banking system was triggered by the AFC of 1997/1998. The Indonesian economy was the worst affected of those impacted by the AFC (International Monetary Fund 2007; Hadad et al. 2011). The rupiah crisis generated a severe liquidity crisis for Indonesian banks, which was exacerbated by the weak credit management and poor prudential supervision of the post-deregulation period. This crisis period also caused a re-evaluation of bank loan portfolios, resulting in a large increase in debt write-offs, particularly for related party loans and state sponsored projects. The outcome was that many state and domestic banks were re-classified as having negative capital ratios (Derina 2011). The reconstruction process thus required a period of regulatory forbearance while banks rebuilt their capital holdings (with a resulting slowdown in lending volumes), otherwise a large percentage of the banking system would have been closed down, with the state banks particularly under-capitalised and thus vulnerable to closure.[1]

In November 1997, the Indonesian government closed 16 private banks without a safety net for depositors, which prompted a further crisis in the banking system and a flight to perceived quality by depositors shifting funds to the state-owned banks (Derina 2011). Political turbulence and a second collapse of the rupiah in 1998 followed. With many banks and firms holding unhedged exposures to the US dollar, the outcome was a jump in non-performing loans to 59% of loans by March 1999 (Hamada and Konishi 2010). To restore confidence in the banking system, the government introduced a deposit guarantee in January 1998.

As a result of the AFC, the Indonesian government was forced to enter into a series of agreements with the International Monetary Fund covering a number of aspects of the economy, including the banking sector. These agreements resulted in a gradual improvement in the regulatory structure, together with a staged requirement for banks to hold more capital and to, over time, move toward the international benchmark capital adequacy framework. During this restructuring process 430 trillion rupiah, approximately 60% of Indonesian GDP, was injected as capital into the banking system. A significant proportion of this capital injection went to the state banks. Between 2000 and 2002, the reform process continued with bank lending declining, but by 2002 bank lending was starting to grow after the initial restructure period. One aspect of the AFC in Indonesia that is worth highlighting is that it was found that those (limited) regulations in place restricting lending to related parties were not being observed. Thus, in 2005 Bank Indonesia introduced new and strengthened restrictions upon bank loans to related parties and, at the same time, introduced new measures to enforce these restrictions. Thus the post-AFC recovery period can be variously dated from 2000 to 2002, or to as late as 2005.

After the reform process, the next major challenge faced by the Indonesian banking system was the impact of the GFC of 2007/2008. In contrast to the AFC period, Indonesian banking survived this global crisis relatively well. Unlike the experience of the AFC, the external shocks dominated any internal weaknesses. The main impacts were felt via losses in the demand for exports as well as a dramatic fall in capital inflows. Due to the recapitalisation efforts of the post-AFC reconstruction, Indonesian banks weathered the external storm of the GFC relatively well with increasing profits and improving levels of capital. It is also likely that the impact of the restructuring period restricted the ability of the Indonesian banks to participate in the asset boom in the United States that preceded the GFC. It has been suggested that it was the sophistication of the products that were a characteristic of the lead up to the GFC that acted as a deterrent to Indonesian bank participation. However, as discussed by authors such as Tarr (2010) and White (2009), investors in the pre-GFC period focused upon the credit ratings of the instruments rather than conducting due diligence themselves and so were not deterred by the complexity and sophistication of the underlying products. Recently Lerner and Tufano (2011) argued that the adoption of new financial products follow an 'S pattern' in which early adopters are knowledgeable while later users have a limited or inadequate grasp of the underlying product. Such an 'S pattern' characterised the investment pattern into the sophisticated products that were an important element of the housing loans growth that led up to the financial crisis of 2008.[2]

2.2. Structure of the Indonesian banking system

Banks operating in Indonesia can be categorised into several types. As discussed, the state-owned banks were initially the main source of finance in Indonesia. After the restructuring that followed the AFC, the state banks retained their place as the dominant banks and traditional safe haven for depositors (Derina 2011). Despite the difficulties experienced during the AFC and following compulsory restructuring, the private banks are the other main providers of domestic banking services. There is also a second, but less important, category of state-owned banks in Indonesia, the regional development banks owned by the provincial governments. Foreign bank participation in Indonesian banking is possible via two alternative structures. Foreign joint venture banks (Foreign JV) are the result of either an acquisition of domestic banks or a joint venture with a domestic bank. Until 1998, foreign banks were limited to a 51% ownership of a domestic bank, and subsequently foreign banks were allowed to acquire up to 99% of an Indonesian bank. Foreign banks are branch banks, which have the legal form of the ultimate parent bank, while Foreign JV banks are locally incorporated and legally separate from their ultimate foreign owner.

3. Literature review and hypothesis development

In considering the factors that determine the revenue volatility of Indonesian banks two streams of research are relevant. The first area of research endeavour are those studies that have focused on the Indonesian banking experience and the second relevant area of research endeavour are those studies considering factors determining bank revenue volatility. To date the majority of papers considering Indonesian banking have adopted various approaches to bank efficiency analysis over different periods, with an emphasis upon the impact of the AFC upon bank efficiency.[3] Other papers have considered Islamic banking in Indonesia[4] or the impact of related party lending (Hamada and Konishi 2010). Few papers have considered Indonesian bank risk. Muresan and Danila (2005) use earnings at risk to determine that Indonesian bank risk has declined in the post-AFC period up to 2003. Derina (2011) provides a valuable contribution in that she considers the evolution of Indonesian bank risk in terms of portfolio construction and capital holdings in response to the AFC. She concludes that state banks reacted differently to private and foreign banks in response to the AFC, in that the state banks did not show any change in capital holdings and risk attitude after the AFC, confirming the negative impact of moral hazard or being 'too big to fail' upon risk choices of banks considered to have implied government insurance.

Larger banks were found to have higher levels of risk aversion, which is consistent with the franchise value approach to banking that will be discussed below. It was also concluded by Derina (2011) that overall the post-AFC reconstruction period resulted in Indonesian banks holding higher than required levels of capital and adjusting their risk taking to lower levels to send signals of solvency and so avoid the severe levels of market discipline they experienced during the course of the AFC.

The international literature considering bank risk is richer with a number of papers considering a variety of issues that determine bank risk. As discussed in the previous section, Indonesian banks (and their customers) operated under the assumption of a government guarantee. This perceived guarantee extended beyond the case of 'too big to fail' and encompassed all Indonesian banks. This can be illustrated by the reaction to the closure of 16 small private Indonesian banks in November 1997, without a depositor safety net (Hamada and Konishi 2010). Despite the small total market share of these 16 banks (2.5% of total assets), a crisis of confidence in the Indonesian banking system followed (Derina 2011).

It has long been argued that the presence of deposit insurance or deposit guarantees encourages sub-optimal risk taking by banks (Merton 1977; Chan, Greenbaum, and Thakor 1992; Craine 1995). Thus, the first issue relevant to the volatility of Indonesian banks is the moral hazard caused by the actual or implied presence of deposit insurance. Deposit insurance or deposit guarantees have the benefit of protecting the financial system from the adverse liquidity effects of bank runs. However, this benefit comes at the cost of reduced depositor incentives to monitor bank risk as well as incentives for bank managers to write riskier loans (Kareken and Wallace 1978). In these circumstances it is considered to be the role of the national regulator to act as a representative agent and act on behalf of the taxpayer and offset or limit this moral hazard. As discussed by Merton (1977), one method to offset the moral hazard induced by deposit insurance or bank guarantees is to require banks to hold higher levels of capital. Increased capital holdings decrease the implicit value of the put option created by deposit insurance.

Given the importance of capital holdings to banks and the importance of the banking system, the relationship between bank risk and capital has been modelled by a number of authors. A stream of research has evolved that has considered the impacts of moral hazard and imperfect information upon the relationship between bank capital and bank portfolio risk. Koehn and Santomero (1980) show that increased capital requirements can result in increased bank risk, as does Blum (1999).[5] Of particular relevance to this study is the stream of research that considers the relationship between regulatory quality/intensity, bank risk and capital. Shrieves and Dahl (1992) show that banks will increase asset risk in the presence of capital regulations, unless regulatory intensity also increases. Besanko and Kanatas (1996) show that regulators may choose to not enforce a capital requirement if it results in lower effort by inside investors and may resist closure of an insolvent bank. Calem and Rob (1999) demonstrate that undercapitalised banks will tend to take on increased portfolio risk as any costs of default will be borne by the regulator and/or taxpayer. Both Calem and Rob (1999) and Baele, Jonghe, and Vander Vennet (2007) argue that bank risk will have a U-shaped relationship with capital holdings in that both poorly and well-capitalised banks both have incentives to increase bank risk.

An interesting feature of the Indonesian banking system prior to the reform period was the combination of regulatory laxity and laxity of enforcement. This meant that banks could choose capitals levels according to their risk aversion. Thus, this paper will argue that banks adopting higher levels of capital are in general demonstrating higher levels of risk aversion and so would be expected *ceteris paribus* to have lower risk portfolios.

Hypothesis 1: There is a U-shaped relationship between bank risk and capital.

In banking, a charter is simply the license that allows an institution to issue transactions accounts and write loans, and is often considered within the context of insured deposits (Craine 1995). A considerable literature has evolved considering the impact that a bank's franchise or charter value has in ameliorating the negative moral hazard effects caused by deposit insurance. A bank's franchise or charter value can be most simply considered at the present value of economic profits if it continues to operate as a going concern. As argued by Marcus (1984), as the bank's franchise value falls, the incentive for moral hazard increases. As discussed above, deposit insurance and the impact of the perception of being 'too big to fail' results in risk taking by banks. However, a literature has also developed that contends that a bank's market power will offset some of these socially negative outcomes. It has been argued by authors such as Keeley (1990) and Besanko and Thakor (1993) that the quasi-monopoly rents generated by increased market power act as a source of increased franchise value and also act to reduce bank competition. This charter value will be protected by banks via their choosing a lower risk portfolio of activities. One impact of the process of deregulation in Indonesia was to lower the franchise value of all banks by increasing the level of competition and by so doing reducing the quality of bank loan portfolios.

Hypothesis 2: Those banks with higher franchise value display lower levels of risk.

The issue of 'too big to fail' is one that has generated considerable attention since the failure of the Continental Illinois bank in 1984 resulted in both insured and uninsured liability holders being rescued and the term first coined. Under the concept of 'too big to fail' there is a large and important group of financial institutions in each national economy that are so central to economic well being that the national regulator will always seek to prevent their insolvency. As found by Hannan and Hanweck (1988) in the case of large (uninsured) certificates of deposits in the United States, large banks experience a systematically lower cost of funds than smaller banks, inferring the existence of risk reduction due to 'too big to fail'. Saunders, Strock, and Travlos (1990) argued that the perception of a 'too big to fail' policy will increase bank incentives to adopt higher levels of morally hazardous risk, to the detriment of the taxpayer.

Hypothesis 3: Larger banks display higher levels of risk due to the moral hazard impact of 'too big to fail'.

Over the past decades, bank income has been observed to have an increased emphasis upon non-interest revenue as well as revenue from the traditional borrowing and lending function (Lepetit et al. 2008). This observed trend can be attributed to a number of factors including changing regulatory climate, increased competition from non-traditional providers of financial services (Lepetit et al. 2008) and changes in the banking system's competitive environment (Deyoung and Rice 2004a; Van Lelyveld and Knot 2009). The traditional view of banks increasing their non-interest income is based on portfolio diversification theory. As discussed by Smith, Staikouras, and Wood (2003), this approach argues that increased non-interest income acts to stabilise the variability of interest-based revenue as well as delivering economies of scope resulting from the co-delivery of related financial services (Diamond 1984). This approach emphasised the role of interest rate risk in increasing the volatility of traditional (interest rate margin) income.

Models of intermediation developed by authors such as Diamond (1984) and Ramakrishnan and Thakor (1984) emphasise the importance of bank diversification in providing credible signals to the market-place of the bank's ability to overcome information asymmetry when screening loan applications and monitoring approved loans. However, Jensen (1986) and Berger and Ofek (1996) argue that bank focus upon specified product lines reduces the potential for agency conflict as well as allowing the bank to fully exploit its specialised managerial expertise.

The empirical evidence relating to the impact of increased bank non-interest income can be separated into two distinct groups: (1) findings using simulation approaches and (2) those using post-deregulation data in various nations to consider the actual impact of increased non-interest income upon revenue volatility. The simulation studies such as Lown et al. (2000), Santomero and Chung (1992) and Saunders and Walter (1994) generally find evidence in favour of combining banks with other financial firms, with the strongest benefits being found for the combination of banks with insurance companies. Recent empirical studies employing actual balance sheet data, such as Stiroh (2006b), Deyoung and Rice (2004b) and Stiroh and Rumble (2006) have found that higher levels of non-interest income as a percentage of total revenue is associated with higher levels of bank revenue volatility and inefficient trade-offs between risk and return. It has been suggested by Stiroh and Rumble (2006, 2158) that bank management '... *may have gotten the diversification idea wrong* ... ', and bank management were pursuing absolute return levels rather than considering the trade-off between risk and return. Stiroh and Rumble (2006) viewed the negative agency effects of 'too big to fail' and information asymmetry caused by complexity were to blame for the moral hazard. As documented by Elyasiani and Wang (2008) higher levels of non-interest income are associated with increased information asymmetry, which increase the scope for moral hazard by bank management.

Three explanations for the higher observed volatility of non-interest income has been advanced by Deyoung and Roland (2001). First, bank lending has a strong relationship component and borrowers face various costs when renegotiating loan agreements, while customers paying fees for financial services can change service providers at lower marginal costs. Second, the main input for loans is interest expense, which is a variable input while the main input for non-interest revenue is staff costs, which are relatively fixed in the short run. Thus, non-interest income has far higher operating leverage. Finally, non-interest income is less reliant upon capital as an input and so has higher financial leverage and higher risk.[6]

Hypothesis 4: Banks with higher levels of non-interest income display higher levels of risk.

The GFC has illustrated (yet again) that excessive bank loan growth will result in lower quality loan portfolios. This can be exemplified by Cocheo (1991, 48): '*If it grows fast it's probably a weed*'. As discussed by Kwan and Eisenbeis (1997), low-to-moderate levels of loan growth are important for the sustainability of bank operations. However, excessive loan growth is generally associated with deteriorating loan quality and will be viewed by bank examiners and regulators as a signal of a poor quality asset portfolio. This argument has been supported by (amongst others) Laeven (2002) and Foos, Norden, and Weber (2010). Given the behaviour of Indonesian banks in the deregulation period prior to the AFC, this negative expected relationship between bank loan growth and asset quality is particularly appropriate to this paper. This relevance is reinforced by the regulatory laxity of the deregulation period failing to act as a brake on excessive loan growth.

The high levels of loan growth prior to the AFC combined with a climate of regulatory laxity makes Indonesia an ideal country to consider the relationship with between loan growth and bank risk. It would be expected that low and medium levels of loan growth are necessary for bank survival, while higher levels of loan growth are associated with increased bank risk (Kwan and Eisenbeis 1997). Thus a non-linear relationship between loan growth and bank risk is to be expected.

Hypothesis 5: There is a U-shaped relationship between bank loan growth and levels of bank risk.

Contrary to the portfolio diversification propositions, the specialisation approach proposes that banks can best leverage the benefits from control of specialised management by having a focused portfolio. As argued by Stiroh (2004) and Goddard, Mckillop, and Wilson (2009) focus upon a bank's core competency is a lower risk strategy than diversification, which was supported by Berger, Hasan, and Zhou (2010) in the Chinese case. Further, as argued by Elyasiani and Wang (2008), increased non-interest income is associated with increased information asymmetry with the associated increased scope for moral hazard. Thus, this paper will argue that increased bank revenue focus is associated with lower bank risk.

Hypothesis 6: Banks with higher levels of income specialisation display lower risk.

4. An empirical model of bank risk

The discussion above suggests a number of variables that potentially impact upon bank risk. This paper will consider bank risk from the perspective of revenue volatility. Two aspects of revenue will be considered, return on assets (ROA) and return on equity (ROE). As banks can endogenously choose the level of equity to support their assets, some differences between the two variables would be expected.[7]

To further examine the role of franchise value in determining bank risk, we hypothesise that those banks with higher levels of retail funding have a higher franchise value by virtue of the increased infrastructure needed to raise retail deposits. The impact of franchise values due to retail operations is particularly relevant in diverse archipelago developing nation such as Indonesia. Thus, it will be argued that those banks with higher levels of short-term deposits (as a proxy for retail fund raising) have higher franchise value and so will tend to adopt lower levels of risk in their portfolios.[8]

In summary, the model that we estimate is

$$\text{Bank risk} = \alpha - \beta_1 \text{ capital holdings} + \beta_2 (\text{capital holdings})^2 + \beta_3 \text{ Size}$$
$$- \beta_4 \text{ franchise value} + \beta_5 \text{ non-interest income} - \beta_6 \text{ bank specialisation}$$
$$- \beta_7 \text{ loan growth} + \beta_8 (\text{loan growth})^2 \pm \beta_{9 \text{ to } 11} \text{bank-type dummy}.$$

5. Data and methodology

5.1. Method

The dependent variables in this model capture bank-specific risk, in this case income volatility. Measures of this type are best (in some cases can only be) calculated using multiple data points. When using annual reports as the data source (as in the case of this paper), multiple years must be used to create a single firm-specific observation. The outcome of this constraint is that the estimations will use cross sections of data drawn from different time periods. Each bank specific observation in the cross section will be constructed from a time series of observations over the relevant period or sub-period. By considering different periods and sub-periods, this paper will be able to determine if the nature of the relationship between bank revenue volatility and the explanatory variables changed as the Indonesian banking system evolved.

For the entire study period, as well as each sub-sample period, the firm-specific measure of bank risk will be calculated using range-based volatility as discussed below. Likewise, the explanatory variables are calculated for the entire sample period or the relevant sub-period as a bank level average. For each sample period or sub-period, separate cross-section regressions are estimated. As the sample (sub-sample) period changes so too do the number of bank-level observations used in each regression (due to the cyclical factors discussed in Section 2). As the decisions that underlie both ROA and ROE are determined jointly, the regressions will be estimated using Zellner's seemingly unrelated regression (Zellner 1962) to allow for correlation between the error terms of each individual equation. In each system of equations, a joint Wald test for the significant of the coefficients across all the equations will be conducted as well as a Breusch-Pagan test for independence of the residuals. In addition to control for potential nonlinearity in the relationship, the squared terms of those variables not already included in the model in a non-linear manner will be tested.[9] The outcome of these tests was the inclusion of additional non-linear transformations of capital holdings, revenue composition and franchise value.

5.2. *Data*

Data on Indonesian banks are from the Bureau van Dyke *BankScope* data base, covering from 1991 to 2009, with annual report data being collected for each bank. Given the cyclical process of banking deregulation and reform discussed previously, it is appropriate to consider a number of sub-periods of volatility over the study period. Initially, the model will be estimated over the entire data period of 1991 to 2009 to provide an overall reference result. The next sub-period will encompass the post-deregulation period as well as the AFC crisis period of 1991–1999. The final sub-period will consider the post-AFC period of 2000–2009.[10] In each case, the study will use the bank-specific measure of volatility for the reference period as the dependent variable and the bank-specific averages for each reference period (or the relevant dummy variable) as independent variables.

Revenue volatility. Traditionally in finance and economics, volatility or risk is measured using the standard deviation or variance. However, as pointed out by Parkinson (1980) and Alizadeh, Brandt, and Diebold (2002), such risk measures suffer from statistical imprecision when using relatively small samples, as this study does. Parkinson (1980) suggested using Log (high value/low value) as an efficient alternative measure of risk. While this measure is appropriate in the context of market prices, which are constrained to have positive values, in our case there will be negative as well as positive values and thus the Parkinson (1980) measure is also inappropriate. Instead, a range-based measure of risk be used, log (high value − low value), following Alizadeh, Brandt, and Diebold (2002). Range-based volatility will be calculated for each of ROA and ROE.

Capital holdings. As discussed above, Indonesia did not move to the international benchmark risk-adjusted capital adequacy system until after the AFC. Thus, the only measure of bank capital holdings that is consistently available across the entire study period is total equity holdings divided by total assets. However, the use of this variable prior to the reforms that followed the AFC has the caveat that the Indonesian banking system prior to the AFC had a high degree of regulatory laxity and this may easily have extended toward enforcement of capital holding disclosure. To control for a U-shaped relationship between bank risk and equity the model will also include (equity/total assets)^2.

Franchise value. As argued above, franchise value will be reflected by the extent to which a bank raises funds via deposits and short-term funding as opposed to international capital market raising. A number of Indonesian banks in the lead up to the AFC relied heavily upon unhedged offshore fund raisings to fund their domestic (rupiah) loan portfolio with catastrophic effects during the rupiah crisis that was an integral part of the AFC. It will be argued in this paper that banks that adopted this offshore strategy had lower franchise value.

Bank size. To control for the impact of too big to fail, we will employ both log (total assets) and $[\log(\text{total assets})]^2$ to allow for any non-linear relationships between size and bank risk. This approach will have the additional benefit of controlling for any effects of return to scale in bank risk.

Non-interest income and bank revenue specialization. To measure a bank's involvement in non-interest sources of revenue as opposed to conventional interest margin income, this paper will use total non-interest income as a percentage of total income. To measure revenue concentrations (specialisation), a revenue-based Herfindahl–Hirschman index (HHI) is used, in which revenue will be broken into two components, non-interest revenue and interest revenue. The HHI will be measured as the sum of the squared revenue shares of these two revenue components for each bank.

Bank growth. Bank growth will be measured using the annual growth rate of gross bank loans for each year for each bank. To consider the impact of a non-linear relationship between bank risk and loan growth, the model will also include loan growth squared.

Bank type. The Indonesian banking system includes a number of different organisational types of banks, which had different experiences of the AFC and different post-reconstruction outcomes. To control for these institutional-specific factors, dummy variables are included in all models estimated to represent domestic banks, foreign subsidiary banks and foreign joint venture banks, with state banks acting as the control sample.

Table 1 has the descriptive statistics and correlation matrices for the risk measures used as dependent variables, for both the total sample and each of the sub-periods analysed.

Table 2 has the descriptive statistics and correlation matrices for the explanatory variables. In general, the correlations between these variables are relatively low, reducing the risk of multicollinearity impacting upon the regression results. The highest correlation is between non-interest income as a per cent of revenue and the Herfindahl index (HHI) of revenue concentration. These variables will not be included in the same regressions. In general, the proportion of non-interest income as a percentage of revenue is far lower in the Indonesian case than has been observed in the United States (Deyoung and Roland 2001), Europe (Lepetit et al. 2008) or Australia (Williams and Prather 2010). Accordingly, Indonesian banks tend to be more specialised as traditional intermediaries as confirmed by the HHI of revenue concentration. Further, there is considerable variation in the bank's level of retail activity as measured by short-term deposits. Finally, the banking system's holdings of capital have shown strong recovery, on average after the AFC, but it is notable that even after the post-AFC reform process some banks are still benefiting from regulatory forbearance in that they have, on average over 2005–2009, negative capital, indicating that some aspects of the reform process are still underway.

6. Results

The first set of results is for the entire period. They provide a benchmark for comparison of the impact of the changes that occurred over each of the three different sub-periods. These results are shown in Table 3. Unsurprisingly, given the number of changes that have

Table 1. Descriptive statistics dependent variables. All years 1991–2009.

	Obs	Mean	Std. dev.	Min	Max
Range volatility: Return on assets	116	1.423794	1.712784	−2.125949	5.092582
Range volatility: Return on equity	110	6.231959	1.868999	2.526564	10.6088

Correlation matrix 1991–2009		
	Range volatility: Return on assets	Range volatility: Return on equity
Range volatility: Return on assets	1	
Range volatility: Return on equity	0.1326	1

1991–1999					
Variable	Obs	Mean	Std. dev.	Min	Max
Range volatility: Return on assets	93	1.3281	1.8309	−2.4834	5.0926
Range volatility: Return on equity	79	4.9083	1.3142	2.0626	9.6946

2000–2009					
	Obs	Mean	Std. dev.	Min	Max
Range volatility: Return on assets	68	0.9852	1.1718	−1.5607	4.8814
Range volatility: Return on equity	66	6.9974	1.8002	2.1329	10.5762

occurred in Indonesian banking between 1999 and 2009, few variables are significant. Of particular note is the finding that high levels of loan growth result in increased risk, while lower to medium levels of loan growth have a marginal impact on lowering bank risk. This provides some support for the arguments of Kwan and Eisenbeis (1997) that loan growth has a U-shaped relationship with bank risk, but sub-period analysis may shed further light on this issue.

The other main result is for bank capital holdings, which are mixed. For ROA the results are consistent with the risk-reducing theory discussed above, in that banks with higher levels of equity have lower volatility of ROA. The non-linear relationship, as found by Equity to Total Assets squared, shows that increases in equity holding will not continuously reduce bank risk and is consistent with Calem and Rob (1999) and Baele, Jonghe, and Vander Vennet (2007). However, for ROE the relationship found is a positive one, in that increased equity holdings are associated with higher risk of ROA. Given that the banks endogenously choose their level of equity holding, the differences between ROA and ROE will reflect a bank's ex post return to different levels of financial (gearing) risk, which may account for this difference. Further, the all years sample reflects both the pre- and post-AFC periods, thus this outcome may reflect the mixed effects of the changes caused by the AFC.[11] Thus, the morally hazardous outcomes of regulatory laxity and forbearance have resulted in some Indonesian banks choosing to adopt risk-increasing portfolio strategies to maximise the

Table 2. Descriptive statistics: Independent variables. All years: 1991–2009.

Variable	Obs	Mean	Std. dev.	Min	Max
Non-interest income as a percent of total income	116	9.0500	8.6432	−43.2771	40.4765
Herfindahl index of revenue concentration	116	0.8857	0.3423	0.54715	4.41033
Log of assets	116	7.8746	1.6270	5.0702	12.5464
(Log of assets)^2	116	64.6332	27.53102	25.7065	157.4111
Growth of loans	116	34.9319	30.9921	−48.24	185.535
(Growth of loans)^2	116	4987.366	9522.793	36.3609	53951.9
Equity to total assets *100	116	11.46816	8.5523	−7.986	49.4345
Short-term deposits	116	70.9053	17.7056	18.0526	105.4286

Correlation matrix 1991–2009

	Non-interest income as a percent of total income	Herfindahl index of revenue concentration	Log of assets	(Log of assets)^2	Growth of loans	(Growth of loans)^2	Equity to total assets *100	Short-term deposits
Non-interest income as a percent of total income	1							
Herfindahl index of revenue concentration	−0.7169	1						
Log of assets	0.1499	0.0173	1					
(Log of assets)^2	0.1411	0.0197	0.9932	1				
Growth of loans	−0.1781	0.0379	−0.0989	−0.1097	1			
(Growth of loans)^2	−0.0159	−0.0298	−0.027	−0.0428	0.7513	1		
Equity to total assets *100	0.1382	−0.0969	−0.2402	−0.2463	0.2553	0.2402	1	
Short-term deposits	−0.0925	−0.0299	0.1306	0.1426	0.0718	0.0373	−0.3781	1

1991–1999

Variable	Obs	Mean	Std. dev.	Min	Max
Non-interest income as a percent of total income	98	6.80671	8.73931	−43.2771	34.6850
Herfindahl index of revenue concentration	98	0.9287	0.3684	0.5978	4.4103
Log of assets	98	7.1020	1.3678	5.0702	12.3281
(Log of assets)^2	98	52.2905	22.0357	25.7065	151.9807
Growth of loans	93	27.0090	35.7707	−92.94	154.625
(Growth of loans)^2	93	3067.904	4417.076	36.3609	30407.17
Equity to total assets *100	98	10.0579	15.5057	−57.14	99.72
Short-term deposits	97	66.6809	21.4541	18.0526	105.4286

2000–2009

Variable	Obs	Mean	Std. dev.	Min	Max
Non-interest income as a percent of total income	73	13.65332	12.0712	0.4241	86.8079
Herfindahl index of revenue concentration	73	0.8023	0.1039	0.51569	1.0411
Log of assets	73	8.6244	1.5586	5.5413	12.5658
(Log of assets)^2	73	76.7766	27.99	30.7056	157.8988
Growth of loans	73	36.1627	37.2211	−36.47	185.535
(Growth of loans)^2	73	7087.982	16077.32	99.0025	94758.78
Equity to total assets *100	73	13.1764	10.6705	−30.71	46.71
Short-term deposits	73	76.7066	15.2545	21.7647	116.4995

Table 3. All years 1991–2009. (t-tests in parentheses).

	Range volatility: Return on equity	Range volatility: Return on assets	Range volatility: Return on equity	Range volatility: Return on assets	Wald test for collective significance of coefficients p value
Non-interest income as a percent of revenue	0.0067(−1.8613)	−0.0143(−1.5049)	−0.0064(−1.4871)	−0.02111**(−2.9228)	0.1191
Growth of gross loans	−0.0064(−1.4935)	−0.0211**(−2.9517)	−0.0064(−1.4871)	−0.02111**(−2.9228)	0.0677
(Growth of gross loans)²	0.00003**(2.6561)	0.00006**(2.9528)	0.00003**(2.6497)	0.00006** −2.9131	0.0333
Equity/total assets	0.0848**(3.2710)	−0.1916***(4.4283)	0.08459**(3.2443)	−0.1909***(4.3610)	0.0000
(Equity/total assets)²	−0.0008(1.2996)	0.0043***(4.1116)	−0.0008(1.2881)	0.0043***(4.0564)	0.0000
Log of assets	0.6828(1.5890)	−0.7675(1.0709)	0.6850(1.5857)	−0.7739(1.0673)	0.1122
Log of assets²	0.0245(0.9559)	0.0541(1.2674)	0.0244(0.9479)	0.0543(1.2586)	0.7827
Short-term deposits	0.0136(0.4825)	0.0240(0.5081)	0.0137(0.4827)	0.0239(0.5009)	0.9882
Domestic bank	0.5281(1.6352)	1.096225*(2.0202)	0.5294(1.6303)	1.0922*(1.9892)	0.3296
Foreign bank	0.7680(1.6297)	1.9222*(2.4304)	0.7714(1.6285)	1.9149*(2.3939)	0.1894
Foreign joint venture bank	1.2753*(3.5370)	2.0387***(3.3580)	1.2764***(3.5223)	2.0395***(3.3225)	0.0032
(Non-interest income as a percent of revenue)²	−0.0002*(2.0402)	0.0004(1.7951)			0.0683
(Short-term deposits)²	0.0000(.1947)	−0.0003(.8081)	0.0000(.1965)	−0.0003(.7979)	0.9485
Revenue Herfindahl index			−0.1906(1.0089)	0.3569(0.6144)	0.5993
(Revenue Herfindahl index)²			0.0006(0.0221)	0.0113(0.1162)	0.9725
Constant	−2.9061(1.5607)	4.6465(1.4961)	−2.7177(1.4449)	4.2878(1.3436)	
R^2	0.8152	0.3540	0.8147	0.3562	
Chi²	496.7717	65.2669	491.1907	63.3250	
P	0.0000	0.0000	0.0000	0.0000	
N	110				

Note: *, **, *** = significant at 5‰, 1% and 0.1% levels.
All regressions estimated as a system of equations using Zellner's Seemingly unrelated regressions (Zellner 1962). The last column shows the results of a Wald test to determine if the variable makes a significant contribution to the system of regressions.

Table 4. 1991–1999 (t-tests in parentheses).

	Range volatility: Return on equity	Range volatility: Return on assets	Range volatility: Return on equity	Range volatility: Return on assets	Wald test for significance of coefficients p value
Non-interest income as a percent of revenue	0.0132(1.5762)	−0.0099(1.1983)			0.1476
Growth of gross loans	0.01436*(1.9830)	−0.0219*(2.0938)	0.01417* − (2.0199)	−0.0218*(2.0841)	0.0208
(Growth of gross loans)^2	−0.0001(−1.1765)	0.0001(1.4720)	−0.0001(1.2052)	0.0001(1.4663)	0.2945
Equity/total assets	0.0379*(2.2836)	−0.1095***(4.5858)	0.0385*(2.3887)	−0.1097***(4.5865)	0.0000
(Equity/total assets)^2	−0.0002(0.4806)	0.0017***(3.5543)	−0.0002(.5468)	0.0017***(3.5614)	0.0044
Log of assets	−0.2349(0.2502)	−1.1097(0.8175)	−0.2333(0.2564)	−1.1079(0.8152)	0.955
Log of assets^2	0.0672(1.0618)	0.0884(0.9664)	0.0677(1.1038)	0.0880(0.9610)	0.7906
Short-term deposits	−0.0233(0.6774)	−0.0818(1.6477)	−0.0232(0.6983)	−0.0818(1.6460)	0.5938
Domestic bank	−0.3652(0.5361)	2.0325*(2.0858)	−0.3826(0.5789)	2.0393*(2.0895)	0.2197
Foreign bank	−0.4561(0.5649)	2.4815*(2.1444)	−0.4651(.5939)	2.4866*(2.1456)	0.1949
Foreign joint venture bank	0.3270(0.4523)	2.7866**(2.6946)	0.3179(0.4538)	2.7876**(2.6933)	0.1186
(Non-interest Income as a percent of revenue)^2	−0.0004(1.7663)	0.0003(1.2827)			0.1023
(Short-term deposits)^2	0.0002(0.7265)	0.0005(1.2033)	0.0002(0.7511)	0.0005(1.2009)	0.8007
Revenue Herfindahl index			0.0821(0.1554)	0.1160(0.3157)	0.9192
(Revenue Herfindahl index)^2			−0.0938(.9566)	0.03330(0.5377)	0.6216
Constant	$3.13E + 00$(.9567)	6.6478(1.4067)	$3.16E + 00$(.9871)	6.4759(1.3647)	
R^2	0.5383	0.4318	0.5415	0.4337	
Chi^2	93.6873	61.0955	100.2897	61.0674	
P	0.00001	0.00001	0.00001	0.00001	
N	79				

Note: *, ** , *** = significant at 5%, 1% and 0.1% levels.
All regressions estimated as a system of equations using Zellner's Seemingly unrelated regressions (Zellner 1962). The last column shows the results of a Wald test to determine if the variable makes a significant contribution to the system of regressions.

Table 5. 2000–2009 (*t*-tests in parentheses).

	Range volatility: Return on equity	Range volatility: Return on assets	Range volatility: Return on equity	Range volatility: Return on assets	Wald test for significance of coefficients *p* value
Non-interest income as a percent of revenue	0.0038(0.2052)	0.0174(0.8842)			0.6725
Growth of gross loans	0.0026(0.3657)	−0.0175*(2.4281)	0.0026(0.3634)	−0.0177*(2.4278)	0.0883
(Growth of gross loans)²	0.000004(0.2915)	0.00003*(2.5619)	0.000004(0.2896)	0.00004*(2.5593)	0.1224
Equity/total assets	0.0350(0.7069)	−0.1650***(3.2956)	0.0347(0.6917)	−0.1671**(3.2825)	0.0031
(Equity/total assets)²	0.0004(0.3418)	0.0040***(3.5828)	0.0004(0.3443)	0.0041***(3.5635)	0.0062
Log of assets	1.1597(1.4604)	0.4057(0.5056)	1.1612(1.4506)	0.4060(0.4997)	0.7093
Log of assets²	−0.0022(0.0518)	−0.0228(0.5228)	−0.0023(0.0530)	−0.0229(0.5177)	0.9894
Short-term deposits	0.1143(1.4037)	0.3133**(3.8067)	0.1156(1.4111)	0.3154***(3.7919)	0.0058
Domestic bank	0.3764(1.0132)	0.0330(0.0878)	0.3751(1.0012)	0.0359(0.0943)	0.8848
Foreign bank	−0.0607(0.0952)	−0.0248(0.0384)	−0.0610(0.0946)	−0.0282(0.0431)	1.0000
Foreign joint venture bank	1.0394*(2.4500)	−0.1957(0.4561)	1.0383*(2.4258)	−0.1930(0.4436)	0.0756
(Non-interest income as a percent of revenue)²	−0.0001(0.2963)	−0.0003(0.5713)			0.8245
(Short-term deposits)²	−0.0008(1.4819)	−0.0026***(4.5580)	−0.0008(1.4917)	−0.0026***(4.5496)	0.0003
Revenue Herfindahl index			0.9865(3.3209)	0.0842(0.0258)	0.9498
(Revenue Herfindahl index)²			−0.6167(0.3099)	−0.4761(0.2252)	0.934
Constant	−7.8864(1.4409)	−7.7117(1.3945)	−8.2983(1.4562)	−7.3248(1.2624)	
R^2	0.7945	0.4955	0.7942	0.4917	
Chi²	262.0856	67.3343	258.0407	65.5596	
P	0.0000	0.0000	0.0000	0.0000	
N	66				

Note: *, **, *** = significant at 5%, 1% and 0.1% levels.
All regressions estimated as a system of equations using Zellners's Seemingly unrelated regressions (Zellner 1962). The last column shows the results of a Wald test to determine if the variable makes a significant contribution to the system of regressions.

return on their equity holdings. It is notable that Bank Indonesia was permitting some banks to operate with negative or low capital holdings on average (see Table 2)[12] and consistent with Calem and Rob (1999) these banks have chosen to adopt a higher risk strategy.

The second sub-period of analysis is the post-deregulation period leading up to and including the AFC period. These results are shown in Table 4. This period encompassed a period of substantial regulatory change as well as regulatory laxity prior to the AFC, which was then immediately followed by the banking system volatility caused by the interaction between the AFC volatility effects as well as structural weaknesses caused by the pre-AFC laxity. Unsurprisingly, this volatility results in few significant variables in the model, but these results do provide a valuable starting point for comparison when considering the impact of the post-AFC reforms upon bank risk. The sub-period 1991–1999 showed some evidence of a relationship between loan growth and bank risk, in that low levels of loan growth are negatively associated with bank risk, for ROA, but higher levels of loan growth had no impact upon bank revenue risk. It is most likely that banks in the period prior to the AFC deferred recognition of any problem loans until relatively late in the downward phase of the loan quality cycle, consistent with Laeven and Majnoni (2003). Thus, those banks with higher levels of loan growth did not display higher levels of revenue volatility. This delay in recognition would have been exacerbated for some banks by their holding of related party loans (Hamada and Konishi 2010), which did not become subject to more stringent regulation until 2005.

As compared to the entire sample period, the relationship between revenue volatility and equity holdings is clearer, in that increased holdings of equity are associated with lower volatility of ROA. Furthermore, the argument that there is a non-linear relationship between bank capital and revenue (ROA) volatility is confirmed in that increasing bank equity holding will not continually reduce bank risk, as shown by the positive relations between bank equity holdings squared and ROA volatility.

The post-AFC period will be considered to encompass 2000–2009. These results are shown in Table 5. These results again highlight the role of equity capital in reducing the risk appetite of bank management, while also illustrating that this risk reduction is not monotonically linear. The other main result is that there is evidence of franchise value as measured by short-term deposits initially being associated with higher bank risk, but then as franchise value increases past a critical value, it acts in the manner discussed previously to reduce the level of bank risk.[13,14]

6.1. *Robustness tests*

The decisions that produce observed revenue volatility do not occur in isolation; but rather occurs against the backdrop of other decisions such as asset quality and capital holdings. To determine if the results are robust to inclusion of such factors in the decision matrix, the models discussed above were re-estimated with three additional risk measures included into the system of equations as dependent variables. These three additional variables are two measures of bank asset quality and one measure of bank distance to default (z-score).

6.2. *Loan quality*

As well as volatility of revenue, the quality of a bank's loan portfolio is an important measure of a bank's risk as well as its potential for future failure. Two measures of bank asset quality will be used. The first measure will be the simple average of the bank-specific ratio of impaired loans to total assets.[15] As discussed by Laeven and Majnoni (2003), there is often a delay by banks in recognising impaired loans, and as implied by Hamada and Konishi (2010), this delay would be particularly relevant to related party and directed lending.[16] As a result, range-based volatility of the ratio of impaired loans to total assets will be used to provide an additional measure of the risk of each bank's loan portfolio.[17]

6.3. *Proximity to default (z-score)*

An important issue for all stakeholders in the banking system is the bank proximity to default. Proximity to default will be measured by the z-score method applied to banking by Boyd, Graham, and Hewitt (1993). The z-score measures the distance to default in terms of the number of standard deviations below the average a bank's ROA must fall in order for that bank's capital reserves to be exhausted.

Defining $k = -E/TA$, with $E =$ firm equity and $TA =$ total assets, then applying averages the relevant sample period or sub-period:

$$z - \text{score} = \frac{\text{Average\_ROA} + \text{average\_}k}{\text{standard deviation\_ROA}}.$$

As discussed previously the small sample properties of risk measures such as standard deviation can be problematic, thus the z-score will also be calculated using the range volatility of ROA as a denominator.

Under the assumption that average ROA is always less than the absolute value of k, the z-score will always be negative as it measures the probability of loss.[18] The larger in absolute value the z-score is, the further the firm is from bankruptcy (i.e. the larger the number of standard deviations ROA must fall to eliminate the bank's equity capital base). To ensure consistent interpretation of coefficients, the z-scores will be multiplied by -1 and inverted.

The expanded model for the entire study period results in more significant coefficients, with the size measures, in particular, becoming collectively significant, and significant in the individual equations. Overall, the results of the robustness estimations do not generate any outcomes inconsistent with the previous discussions and as such are reported in the Appendix.[19]

7. Conclusions

The main result of this study was that of a U-shaped relationship between bank risk and loan growth. It is argued, following Kwan and Eisenbeis (1997), that low-to-medium levels of bank loan growth are necessary for the ongoing viability of the individual bank as well as being necessary for ongoing economic development. However, high levels of loan growth are associated with poorer quality loans and managerial agency problems, which are likely to exhibit themselves in the form of bank crises such as the AFC in Indonesia's case, as well as the recent financial crisis. This paper argues that this U-shaped relationship is due to the negative effects of information asymmetry (Elyasiani and Wang 2008) and complexity (Laeven and Levine 2007) combined with moral hazard and managerial entrenchment (Kwan and Eisenbeis 1997) to result in increased risk after bank size reaches a critical level. This study found, for the post-reform period, that increased bank non-interest income is associated with increased bank risk, consistent with the international body of knowledge in this area for both developed nations (Deyoung and Rice 2004a; Stiroh 2006a; Lepetit et al. 2008) and developing nations (Berger, Hasan, and Zhou 2010).

A second important finding was the cyclical behaviour of bank capital holding in impacting upon the bank management's observed risk appetite. Seminal work, such as Merton (1977), Diamond and Dybvig (1983) and Diamond (1984), argues that increased bank capital holdings reduce the implied value of the put option created by implied or actual deposit insurance of deposit guarantees. During the entire study period, Bank Indonesia had in place various types of capital holding regulations. Initially, these regulations were simple required leverage holdings, and this pre-AFC period was characterised by a combination of both regulatory laxity and laxity in enforcement of the limited regulations in place. This regulatory laxity can be observed by banks operating with low, and in some cases negative, capital holdings in the pre-AFC period. These factors resulted in some inconsistencies in results between sub-periods. In some cases increased bank capital was associated with increased bank risk, but in the pre-AFC period consideration of standardised coefficients produced the outcome that the risk-reducing impact of increased capital was likely to dominate. In the post-AFC periods, the observed positive relationships between bank risk and bank capital were not supported by a Wald test. Overall, these results provide empirical support for the models of Besanko and Kanatas (1996) and Calem and Rob (1999) in that in certain circumstances regulators will permit banks to operate while insolvent and this lack of regulatory effort will result in bank risk seeking activity.

In the post-AFC reform period, the need for regulatory forbearance resulted in some banks continuing to operate with negative capital holdings. This forbearance meant that the traditional role of bank capital in reducing moral hazard by bank management by lowering their appetite for risk was less apparent in each sub-period but notable for the entire post-AFC period. This outcome is instructive in a period in which regulatory authorities are endeavouring to reconstruct the global financial system in the aftermath of the GFC. The key lesson is that regulations must not only exist, but also be seen to be enforced to have any effect on bank managerial behaviour. Furthermore, the non-linear relationship found demonstrates decreasing returns in terms of risk reduction from simply increasing required bank capital holdings.

Franchise values, as represented by retail operation, are associated with lower levels of bank income volatility, particularly in the post-AFC period. It is argued, consistent with Keeley (1990) and Besanko and Thakor (1993), that the ownership of a valuable franchise is appreciated by bank management and in order to retain this value and the quasi-monopoly rents generated, we observe a lower managerial appetite for risk. It is noticeable that those banks with low levels of franchise value had higher levels of revenue volatility and it is only after franchise value increases above a critical value does it act to reduce managerial risk appetite.

Acknowledgements

The author is grateful for the comments of Tom Smith, Gulasekaran Rajaguru, Ahmed Khalid and Noel Gaston as well as the participants at the First Annual joint workshop between NTU Singapore and the Globalisation and Development Centre, Bond University and two anonymous referees. All errors remain the responsibility of the author.

Notes

1. This delay in recognition of poor asset quality following a boom lending cycle is a global phenomenon, see Laeven and Majnoni (2003).
2. The experience of the Icelandic banking system during the 2008 financial crisis demonstrates the perils of less sophisticated bankers over-reaching themselves during asset booms involving sophisticated products (see http://en.wikipedia.org/wiki/2008%E2%80%932011_

Icelandic_financial_crisis#Causes). The Icelandic experience provides a useful counterpoint to the Indonesian banking experience during the lead up to the 2008 crisis.
3. Examples of this stream of research include Sufian (2010), Omar, Majid, and Rulindo (2007), Thoraneenitiya and Avkiran (2009), Margono, Sharma, and Melvin (2010) and Hadad et al. (2011).
4. See, for example, Hutapea and Kasri (2010) as well as Shahimi, Ismail, and Ahmad (2006).
5. See also Berger, Herring, and Szego (1995), Gonzalez (2005) and Gennotte and Pyle (1991) for additional examples of this stream of research.
6. Empirical evidence examining the characteristics of banks with higher levels of non-interest income has found that they tend to be less well managed (Deyoung and Rice 2004b) and have higher risk loan portfolios (Lepetit et al. 2008).
7. As a bank holds less equity, it would be expected to be ceteris paribus, riskier and thus have more ex post volatility. However, in some short-run periods this choice to adopt a riskier portfolio of funding decisions can have the potential to yield higher ex post returns. This issue is particularly germane to the pre-AFC period in Indonesia.
8. As an alternative source of funds, many Indonesian banks were active in raising offshore wholesale funding (largely unhedged in foreign currencies). This exposure contributed to the banking crisis after the large rupiah devaluation during the AFC, thus franchise value also provides a control for foreign currency risk.
9. We are indebted to an anonymous referee for comments in this area.
10. Additional post-AFC sub-period analysis suffered from difficulties of reduced degrees of freedom.
11. Calculation of standardised coefficients for equity to total assets finds that a one-standard deviation increase in equity holding across the study period results in a 33% increase in ROA range volatility but also a 95% reduction in ROE volatility. However, given that the all years sample includes several sub-periods incorporating different regulatory and economic regimes the sub-period analysis may be more illuminating.
12. Consistent with Besanko and Kanatas (1996). BI choose not to enforce the limited regulations in place with respect to capital holdings.
13. Put another way, low levels of franchise value are associated with increased bank risk but as franchise value increases it acts to reduce risk in the manner posited by Marcus (1984) and Besanko and Thakor (1993).
14. Additional sub-period analysis broke the post-AFC period into two further sub-periods; 2000–2004 and 2005–2009. Both of these sets of additional analysis suffered from reduced degrees of freedom and as such are not reported in this paper. Tentative results indicated that post-AFC regulatory forbearance during the reconstruction period of 2000 to 2004 reduced the effectiveness of capital in mitigating bank risk. Bank non-interest income was found to be risk increasing in the sub-period 2005–2009. Further analysis to confirm these results would be a valuable follow-up to this study when more data are available.
15. This variable is used as it is reported in BankScope in the most consistent manner.
16. Derina (2011) also considered that the political implications of directed lending resulted in delays in recognition of impaired loans.
17. This paper will argue that those banks displaying higher variation in loan losses are inherently riskier.
18. It is possible that a firm with a positive ex post ROA has a low level of capital to assets, and so a positive z-score, reflecting higher returns to a risky leveraged position. This can create some noise when using z-scores as an ex post risk measure.
19. It should be noted that the data requirements of the robustness tests resulted in a considerable reduction in degrees of freedom (especially for the sub-period of 1991–1999).
20. Omitted in some regressions due to multicollinearity resulting from the small sample.

References

Alizadeh, S., M. Brandt, and F. Diebold. 2002. "Range-based Estimation of Stochastic Volatility Models." *Journal of Finance* LVII: 1047–91.

Baele, L., O. D. Jonghe, and R. Vander Vennet. 2007. "Does the Stock Market Value Bank Diversification?" *Journal of Banking and Finance* 31: 1999–2023.

Berger, A. N., I. Hasan, and M. Zhou. 2010. "The Effects of Focus Versus Diversification on Bank Performance: Evidence From Chinese Banks." *Journal of Banking and Finance* 34: 1417–35.

Berger, A. N., R. Herring, and G. Szego. 1995. "The Role of Capital in Financial Institutions." *Journal of Banking and Finance* 19: 393–430.

Berger, P., and E. Ofek. 1996. "Bustup Takeovers of Value-Destroying Diversified Firms." *The Journal of Finance* 51: 1175–200.

Besanko, D., and G. Kanatas. 1996. "The Regulation of Bank Capital: Do Capital Standards Promote Bank Safety?" *Journal of Financial Intermediation* 5: 160–83.

Besanko, D., and A. Thakor. 1993. "Relationship Banking, Deposit Insurance and Bank Portfolio Choice." In *Capital Markets and Financial Intermediation*, edited by C. Mayer and X. Vives, 292–319. Cambridge University Press.

Blum, J. 1999. "Do Capital Adequacy Requirements Reduce Risks in Banking?" *Journal of Banking and Finance* 23: 755–71.

Boyd, J., S. Graham, and R. S. Hewitt. 1993. "Bank Holding Company Mergers With Non-bank Financial Firms: Effects on the Risk of Failure." *Journal of Banking and Finance* 17: 43–63.

Calem, P., and R. Rob. 1999. "The Impact of Capital-Based Regulation on Bank Risk-Taking." *Journal of Financial Intermediation* 8: 317–52.

Chan, Y.-S., S. Greenbaum, and A. Thakor. 1992. "Is Fairly Priced Deposit Insurance Possible?" *The Journal of Finance* 47: 227–45.

Cocheo, S. 1991. "It Grows Fast, It's Probably a Weed." *ABA Banking Journal* 83: 48–51.

Craine, R. 1995. "Fairly Priced Deposit Insurance and Bank Charter Policy." *The Journal of Finance* 50: 1735–46.

Derina, R. 2011. *The Impact of Changes of Capital Regulations on Bank Capital and Portfolio Risk Decisions: A Case Study of Indonesian Banks*. Adelaide: The University of Adelaide.

Deyoung, R., and T. Rice. 2004a. "How do Banks Make Money? The Fallacies of Fee Income." *Economic Perspectives, Federal Reserve Bank of Chicago* 2004: 34–51.

Deyoung, R., and T. Rice. 2004b. "Non-interest Income and Financial Performance at U.S. commercial banks." *The Financial Review* 39: 101–27.

Deyoung, R., and K. Roland. 2001. "Product Mix and Earnings Volatility of Commercial Banks: Evidence From a Degree of Total Leverage Model." *Journal of Financial Intermediation* 10: 54–84.

Diamond, D. 1984. "Financial Intermediation and Delegated Monitoring." *Review of Economic Studies* 59: 393–414.

Diamond, D., and P. Dybvig. 1983. "Bank Runs, Deposit Insurance and Liquidity." *Journal of Political Economy* 91: 401–19.

Elyasiani, E., and Y. Wang. 2008. "Non-Interest Income Diversification and Information Asymmetry of Bank Holding Companies." *Financial Management Association Annual Meeting*. Grapevine, TX, October 2008.

Foos, D., L. Norden, and M. Weber. 2010. "Loan Growth and Riskiness of Banks." *Journal of Banking and Finance* 24: 2929–40.

Gennotte, G., and D. Pyle. 1991. "Capital Controls and Bank Risk." *Journal of Banking and Finance* 15: 805–24.

Goddard, J., D. Mckillop, and J. O. S. Wilson. 2009. "The Diversification and Financial Performance of US Credit Unions." *Journal of Banking and Finance* 32: 1836–49.

Gonzalez, F. 2005. "Bank Regulation and Risk Taking Incentives: An International Comparison of Bank Risk." *Journal of Banking and Finance* 29: 1153–84.

Hadad, M., M. Hall, K. Kenjegalieva, W. Santoso, and R. Simper. 2011. "Productivity Changes and Risk Management in Indonesian Banking: A Malmquist Analysis." *Applied Financial Economics* 21: 847–61.

Hamada, M., and M. Konishi. 2010. "Related Lending and Bank Performance: Evidence From Indonesia." *Institute of Developing Economies Discussion Paper* 229, Institute of Developing Economies (IDE) JETRO, Chiba, Japan.

Hannan, T., and G. Hanweck. 1988. "Bank Insolvency Risk and the Market for Large Certificates of Deposit." *Journal of Money, Credit and Banking* 20: 203–11.

Hutapea, E., and R. Kasri. 2010. "Bank Margin Determination: A Comparison Between Islamic and Conventional Banks in Indonesia." *International Journal of Islamic and Middle Eastern Finance and Management* 3: 65–82.

International Monetary Fund. 2007. *Indonesia: Selected Issues*. IMF Country Report No. 07/273, Washington DC. http://www.imf.org/external/pubs/ft/scr/2007/cr07273.pdf.

Jensen, M. 1986. "Agency Costs of Free Cash Flow, Corporate Finance, and Takeovers." *American Economic Review* 76: 323–9.

Kareken, J., and N. Wallace. 1978. "Deposit Insurance and Bank Deregulation: A Partial Equilibrium Exposition." *The Journal of Business* 51: 413–38.

Keeley, M. 1990. "Deposit Insurance, Risk and Market Power in Banking." *American Economic Review* 80: 1183–200.

Koehn, M., and A. Santomero. 1980. "Regulation of Bank Capital and Risk." *Journal of Finance* 35: 1235–44.

Kwan, S., and R. Eisenbeis. 1997. "Bank Risk, Capitalization, and Operating Efficiency." *Journal of Financial Services Research* 12: 117–31.

Laeven, L. 2002. "Bank Risk and Deposit Insurance." *The World Bank Economic Review* 16: 109–37.

Laeven, L., and R. Levine. 2007. "Is There a Diversification Discount in Financial Conglomerates?" *Journal of Financial Economics* 85: 331–67.

Laeven, L., and G. Majnoni. 2003. "Loan Loss Provisioning and Economic Slowdowns: Too Much Too Late?" *Journal of Financial Intermediation* 12: 178–97.

Lepetit, L., E. Nys, P. Rous, and A. Tarazi. 2008. "The Expansion of Services in European Banking: Implications for Loan Pricing and Interest Margins." *Journal of Banking and Finance* 32: 2325–35.

Lerner, J., and P. Tufano. 2011. "The Consequences of Financial Innovation: A Counterfactual Research Agenda." NBER Working Paper No. w16780. http://ssrn.com/abstract=1759852.

Lown, C. S., C. S. Osler, P. Strahan, and A. Sufi. 2000. "The Changing Landscape of the Financial Service Industry: What Lies Ahead?" *Economic Policy Review, Federal Reserve Bank of New York* 6: 39–54.

Marcus, A. 1984. "Deregulation and Bank Financial Policy." *Journal of Banking and Finance* 8: 559–65.

Margono, H., S. Sharma, and Melvin, P. D. 2010. "Cost Efficiency, Economies of Scale, Technological Progress and Productivity in Indonesian Banks." *Journal of Asian Economics* 21: 53–65.

Merton, R. C. 1977. "An Analytic Derivation of the Cost of Deposit Insurance and Loan Guarantees: An Application of Modern Option Pricing Theory." *Journal of Banking and Finance* 1: 3–11.

Muresan, E. R., and N. Danila. 2005. "Using Earnings-at-Risk to Asses the Risk of Indonesian Banks." *19th Annual Conference on Pacific Basin Finance, Economics, Accounting, and Management*. Taipei, Taiwan.

Omar, M. A., M. S. A. Majid, and R. Rulindo. 2007. "Efficiency and Productivity Performance of the National Private Banks in Indonesia." *Gadjah Mada International Journal of Business* 9: 1–18.

Parkinson, M. 1980. "The Extreme Value Method for Estimating the Variance of the Rate of Return." *Journal of Business* 53: 61–5.

Ramakrishnan, R., and A. Thakor. 1984. "Information Reliability and a Theory of Financial Intermediation." *Review of Economic Studies* 51: 415–32.

Santomero, A., and E.-J. Chung. 1992. "Evidence in Support of Broader Banking Powers." *Financial Markets, Institutions, and Instruments* 1: 1–69.

Saunders, A., E. Strock, and N. Travlos. 1990. "Ownership Control, Regulation and Bank Risk-Taking." *The Journal of Finance* 45: 643–54.

Saunders, A., and I. Walter. 1994. *Universal Banking in the United States: What Could We Gain? What Could We Lose?* New York: Oxford University Press.

Shahimi, S. B., A. G. B. Ismail, and S. Ahmad. 2006. "A Panel Data Analysis of Fee Income Activities in Islamic Banks." *Journal of King Abdulaziz University, Islamic Economics* 19: 23–35.

Shrieves, R., and D. Dahl. 1992. "The Relationship Between Risk and Capital in Commercial Banks." *Journal of Banking and Finance* 16: 439–57.

Smith, R., C. Staikouras, and G. Wood. 2003. "Non-Interest Income and Total Income Stability." *Bank of England Working Paper*. No. 198. Cass Business School Research Paper, London. http://ssrn.com/abstract=530687.

Stiroh, K. 2004. "Do Community Banks Benefit From Diversification?" *Journal of Financial Services Research* 25: 135–60.

Stiroh, K. 2006a. "New Evidence on the Determinants of Bank Risk." *Journal of Financial Services Research* 30: 237–63.

Stiroh, K. 2006b. "A Portfolio View of Banking With Interest and Non Interest Income." *Journal of Money, Credit, and Banking* 28: 1351–61.

Stiroh, K., and A. Rumble. 2006. "The Dark Side of Diversification: The Case of US Financial Holding Companies." *Journal of Banking and Finance* 30: 2131–61.

Sufian, F. 2010. "Evolution in the Efficiency of the Indonesian Banking Sector: A DEA Approach." *International Journal of Applied Management Science* 2: 388–414.

Tarr, D. G. 2010. "The Political, Regulatory and Market Failures that Caused the US Financial Crisis: What are the Lessons." *Journal of Financial Economic Policy* 2(2): 163–86.

Thoraneenitiya, N., and N. Avkiran. 2009. "Measuring the Impact of Restructuring and Country-Specific Factors on the Efficiency of Post Crisis East Asian Banking Systems: Integrating DEA With SFA." *Socio-Economic Planning Sciences* 43: 240–52.

Van Lelyveld, I., and K. Knot. 2009. "Do Financial Conglomerates Create or Destroy Value? Evidence for the EU." *Journal of Banking and Finance* 33: 2312–21.

White, L. J. 2009. "The Credit Rating Agencies: Understanding Their Central Role in the Subprime Debacle of 2007–2008." http://ssrn.com/abstract=1434483.

Williams, B., and L. Prather. 2010. "Bank Risk and Return: The Impact of Bank Non-Interest Income." *International Journal of Managerial Finance* 6: 220–44.

Zellner, A. 1962. "An Efficient Method of Estimating Seemingly Unrelated Regressions and Tests for Aggregation Bias." *Journal of the American Statistical Association* 57: 348–68.

Appendix

Table A1. Robustness tests including additional risk measures. All years 1991–2009.

	Range volatility: Return on equity	Range volatility: Return on assets	Impaired assets/total assets *100	Range volatility: (Impaired assets/total assets)*100	Z-score	Chi-squared test for collective significance of coefficients p value
Non-interest income as a percent of revenue	0.0033(0.1851)	0.0352(1.3915)	0.1615(0.5965)	−0.0119(0.3775)	0.0243(0.7618)	0.2993
Growth of gross loans	−0.0162*(2.4849)	−0.0188*(2.0579)	0.1580(1.6166)	−0.0207(1.8088)	−0.0089(0.7704)	0.0300
(Growth of gross loans)^2	0.00005**(3.2339)	0.00005*(2.2520)	−0.0004(1.5109)	0.00003(0.9498)	0.00002(0.6099)	0.0155
Equity/total assets	0.0718**(2.7540)	−0.2288***(6.2643)	−2.4488**(6.2728)	−0.1264*(2.7704)	0.2670***(5.7961)	0.00001
(Equity/total assets)^2	−0.0009(1.3951)	0.0040**(4.5379)	0.0458**(4.8192)	0.0025*(2.2093)	−0.0053**(4.7297)	0.0000
Log of assets	1.1995*(2.1358)	−0.8553(1.0866)	−17.4084*(2.0691)	1.9919*(2.0259)	−0.5979(0.6021)	0.00001
Log of assets^2	−0.0102(0.3194)	0.0423(0.9486)	0.8517(1.7876)	−0.1133*(2.0352)	0.0461(0.8200)	0.0001
Short-term deposits	0.1179*(2.3807)	0.2082*(2.9996)	1.1284(1.5211)	0.3013***(3.4754)	−0.2172*(2.4807)	0.00001
Domestic bank	0.1037(0.2771)	0.2772(0.5285)	11.6001*(2.0686)	0.9887(1.5088)	0.9236(1.3955)	0.2968
Foreign bank	−0.0442(0.0801)	−0.2912(0.3770)	21.1074*(2.5525)	2.0005*(2.0734)	0.7523(0.7720)	0.0958
Foreign joint venture bank	0.3772(0.8595)	−0.2863(0.4656)	17.6484**(2.6847)	1.1092(1.4439)	0.6244(0.8049)	0.0547
(Short-term deposits)^2	−0.0009*(2.3991)	−0.0020***(3.6628)	−0.0108(1.8810)	−0.0026***(3.8277)	0.0018**(2.5924)	0.0000
Constant	−6.3708*(2.1331)	3.6059(0.8615)	71.9674(1.6085)	−13.7024**(2.6207)	4.8674(0.9218)	
R^2	0.8242	0.5596	0.5126	0.4115	0.4457	
Chi^2	323.5026	87.6911	72.5761	48.2487	55.4848	
P	0.00001	0.00001	0.00001	0.00001	0.00001	
N	69					

Note: *, **, *** = significant at 5%, 1% and 0.1% levels.
All regressions estimated as a system of equations using Zellner's Seemingly unrelated regressions (Zellner 1962). The last column shows the results of a Wald test to determine if the variable makes a significant contribution to the system of regressions.

Table A2. Robustness tests including additional risk measures. 1991–1999.

	Range volatility: Return on equity	Range volatility: Return on assets	Impaired assets/total assets *100	Range volatility: (Impaired assets/total assets)*100	Z-score	Chi-squared test for collective significance of coefficients p value
Non-interest income as a percent of revenue	−0.0180(−1.1230)	−0.0491*(2.2329)	−0.0780(0.2585)	−0.0926*(1.978553)	−0.0063(0.3585)	0.00001
Growth of gross loans	0.0888***(5.1740)	0.0082(0.3467)	−0.3174(0.9840)	0.0521(1.0424)	0.0276(1.4771)	0.00001
(Growth of gross loans)²	−0.0002(1.4596)	−0.00001(0.0736)	0.0049(1.7691)	−0.0004(0.8601)	−0.0005**(3.1325)	0.00001
Equity/total assets	−0.1327(1.6272)	−0.7766***(6.9496)	−3.1490*(2.0535)	−0.5161*(2.1708)	−0.0077(0.0871)	0.00001
(Equity/total assets)²	0.0136**(3.0858)	0.0347***(5.7612)	0.0011(0.0131)	0.0186(1.4497)	0.0035(0.7227)	0.00001
Log of assets	5.9561*(2.6813)	13.2112***(4.3410)	64.8975(1.5540)	13.9682*(2.1574)	0.5889(0.2438)	0.00001
Log of assets²	−0.3550(2.3576)	−0.8837***(4.2831)	−6.3661*(2.2487)	−0.9896*(2.2548)	0.0146(0.0890)	0.00001
Short-term deposits	−0.2915***(8.0479)	−0.0570(1.1481)	−0.4208(−0.6179)	−0.0487(−0.4612)	−0.0279(−0.7094)	0.00001
Domestic bank[20]	−17.3949*(2.1851)	0.0000	0.0000	−43.2439(1.8638)	−3.8763(0.4479)	0.0002
Foreign bank	−15.2197*(1.9828)	1.1524(1.6986)	−22.0599(2.3697)	−41.7931(1.8680)	−3.0686(0.3677)	0.0004
Foreign joint venture bank	−14.9476(1.9199)	0.5131(0.9967)	−6.3805(0.9033)	−42.4101(1.8690)	−3.9539(0.4671)	0.0041
(Short-term deposits)²	0.0029***(8.0312)	0.0004(−0.7210)	0.0041(−0.6131)	0.0005(−0.5162)	0.0001(−0.3400)	0.00001
Constant	0.0000	−42.1677***(−3.8663)	−65.4739(0.4375)	0.0000	0.0000	
R^2	0.9304	0.9180	0.9283	0.6415	0.8019	
Chi²	4408.7520	190.4364	220.2060	199.0374	69.4257	
P	0.00001	0.00001	0.00001	0.00001	0.00001	
N	17					

Note: *, **, *** = significant at 5%, 1% and 0.1% levels.
All regressions estimated as a system of equations using Zellner's Seemingly unrelated regressions (Zellner 1962). The last column shows the results of a Wald test to determine if the variable makes a significant contribution to the system of regressions.

Table A3. Robustness tests including additional risk measures. 2000–2009.

	Range volatility: Return on equity	Range volatility: Return on assets	Impaired assets/total assets *100	Range volatility: (Impaired assets/total assets)*100	Z-score	Chi-squared test for collective significance of coefficients p value
Non-interest income as a percent of revenue	−0.0083(0.4232)	.05125*(2.4858)	0.1853(1.4712)	0.0408(1.4918)	0.0028(1.2300)	0.0158
Growth of gross loans	−0.0029(0.3663)	−0.0133(1.5852)	−0.0434(0.8482)	−0.0065(0.5857)	−0.0017(1.8452)	0.5523
(Growth of gross loans)^2	0.00003(1.7498)	0.00004(1.9423)	0.000007(0.0648)	0.00001(0.4884)	0.000005**(2.6890)	0.0785
Equity/total assets	0.0529(1.0763)	−0.2231***(4.3269)	−0.8899*(2.8250)	−0.1307(1.9087)	−0.0153**(2.6906)	0.0000
(Equity/total assets)^2	−0.0001(0.0899)	0.0049***(4.4570)	0.02421***(3.5812)	0.0028(1.9310)	0.0002(1.8316)	0.0000
Log of assets	1.5125*(2.0058)	0.7278(0.9198)	−7.4549(1.5422)	0.9520(0.9062)	0.0807(0.9264)	0.2839
Log of assets^2	−0.0222(0.5441)	−0.0441(1.0295)	0.3592(1.3720)	−0.0591(1.0388)	−0.0044(0.9419)	0.5366
Short-term deposits	0.0883(1.1402)	0.3070***(3.7769)	1.1843**(2.3855)	0.2263*(2.0978)	0.0251**(2.8065)	0.0012
Domestic bank	0.1773(0.4846)	−0.1778(0.4630)	0.7649(0.3261)	−0.0730(0.1431)	−0.1157**(2.7387)	0.0002
Foreign bank	−0.3737(0.6158)	−0.4874(0.7654)	8.5288*(2.1922)	0.1743(0.2061)	−0.1592*(2.2715)	0.0052
Foreign joint venture bank	0.7528(1.7784)	−0.6520(1.4677)	3.9581(1.4586)	0.3156(0.5352)	−0.1512*(3.0934)	0.0002
(Short-term deposits)^2	−0.0006(1.1477)	−0.0025***(4.5630)	−0.0082*(2.4158)	−0.0019**(2.5841)	−0.0002**(3.4592)	0.0001
Constant	−8.4134(1.5976)	−8.2258(1.4884)	3.5080(0.1039)	−7.5121(1.0239)	−0.6436(1.0584)	
R^2	0.8362	0.5635	0.4654	0.4111	0.5045	
Chi^2	316.5119	80.0268	53.9684	43.2821	63.1211	
p	0.00001	0.00001	0.00001	0.00001	0.00001	
N	62					

Note: *, **, *** = significant at 5%, 1% and 0.1% levels.
All regressions estimated as a system of equations using Zellner's Seemingly unrelated regressions (Zellner 1962). The last column shows the results of a Wald test to determine if the variable makes a significant contribution to the system of regressions.

Index

Note:
Page numbers in **bold** type refer to figures
Page numbers in *italic* type refer to tables
Page numbers followed by 'n' refer to notes

ageing: demographic 79
Aksoy, A. 38
alienation: China 113
anti-corruption measures: popularity 108n
Asia Pacific (AP) region 11; government expenditure ratio versus GDP growth rate 17; government-growth 12
Asia-Pacific Economic Cooperation (APEC) 61
Asian Bond Market Initiative 61
Asian financial crisis (1997–8) 3, 63, 101; bank efficiency 144; income volatility of Indonesian banks 141–66
Asian immigrants: profile 91
Asian Miracle 11
Association of South East Asian Nations (ASEAN) 63, 65, 139n
Au, J.: and Gemmell, N. 1, 11–37
Australia 11, 79; corruption 107; migrants 94n; population increase 80
authoritarian regimes: shift to democracy 98–9

Bangladesh 108n
Bank of International Settlement 69
bank risk: bank loan growth 142; capital 142; capital holdings 145; franchise value 148; Indonesia 2, 141–66; model 148
banks: foreign joint venture 144; franchise value 146; lending 142; too big to fail 144–6, *see also* Indonesian banks
BankScope (Bureau van Dyke) 149
Barro, R. 17, 19, 23; long-run growth effects model *18*, 35n
Baxter, M. 23
bilateral trade 61, 67
black market premium channel: trade liberalization and growth *45*, 54n
Bleaney, M. 23, 26
Borjas, G.J. 80, 83
brain drain 79
Breusch-Pagan test 149
bribery: willingness to pay 99
Bureau van Dyke: *BankScope* 149

business cycle synchronization 61–2; bilateral financial integration 67; bilateral trade intensity 67; comparison of estimation methods 72–6; control for policy and exchange rate coordination 72, *75*; correlations 65–7; direct and indirect channels 62; econometric issues 64–5; estimated density plots 66; exogenous variables 68; normal probability plot of residuals (transformed) **73**; normal probability plot of residuals (untransformed) **73**; policy coordination 64; results 69–76; robustness check 72, *74*; scatter plot **71**; similarity in industry specialization 67; simultaneous equations (1984–96) *75*; simultaneous equations (1999–2007) *76*; specialization 64; system of simultaneous equations 63–4; three-stage least-square regression results *70*; three-stage least-square results 70–2; trade 63–4; unconditional correlations 69
business cycles: financial integration 62

Campbell, N.: and Saha, S. 1, 98–111
Canada 79; consumption (private) 4, 9
capital: bank 142
Capital Adequacy Mark III 142
capital formation 1; trade liberalization and growth 43–4
capital holdings: bank risk 145; Indonesian banking system 149, 159
caste system: China 117
centralized corruption 99
Cheng, T.: Chia, W-M. and Xie, S. 1, 61–78
Chiang Mai Initiative Multilateralization (CMIM) 61
China 12; alienation 113; caste system 117; Census (2000) 117; directions and sources of trade in components and final product *133*; disaggregating trade 127; economic growth 112; electronics-related products 129; exchange rates 2; export elasticity of change in RMB (1992–2008) *136*; export elasticity

INDEX

and product fragmentation 127–9; export response to RER appreciation 134–7; exports and RER correlation matrix *135*; exports and RER summary statistics *135*; full employment 116; harmonious society 116; *hukou* system 117; illiteracy 122–3n; integrated exchange rate 128; land shortage 117; manufactured products 129; measures 69, 77n; migrants 117; migration and urbanization 118; percentage share of parts and components in total manufacturing trade *132*; product composition of manufactured exports and imports *130–1*; real exchange rate (RER) 126; renminbi (RMB) 127, 128; rural sector 122n; rural taxes and subsidies 116; State Owned Enterprises (SOEs) 116; strikes 113; trade patterns in global production networks 129–34; trade surpluses 126; urban consumption poverty 122n; US trade deficit (1980–2011) 129; USA 126; WTO 134
China Household Income Project (CHIP) 118
China National Board of Statistics (NBS) 115, 118, 125
China Population Statistics (NBS) 115, 125
China Statistical Yearbook 115, 125
Chinese Customs Statistics (CCS) 127, 138n
Chinese income inequality 2, 112–25; coastal-inland development gap 112; elasticity 120; factor component decomposed 118–21; findings 121–2; Gini coefficient 113–15; Gini and relative mean income (1980–2008) *115*; inequality-augmenting effect 119; rural 116; rural relative inequity and elasticity *119*; rural-urban divide 112; rural-urban income gap 117–18, *118*; sources of data and income definition 125; total inequality 115; total and rural-urban Gini 115; transfer income 120; trend 115–18; urban relative inequity and elasticity *121*; wage income 120
Cho, K. 101
Chun Doo-Hwan 101, 102
Chung Jo-Yung 102
Cocheo, S. 147
compensation hypothesis: trade liberalization and growth 45
compositional amenities 82
compulsory donations 101
consumption (private) 4; Canada 4, 9; determinants: GDP growth 5; determinants: household income growth 5; determinants for growth 8–9; employment 8; France 4, 9; G7 countries 4; Germany 4, 9; household savings rates 6–7, *6*; Japan 4, 9–10; trends in growth 4–5; United Kingdom 4, 9
Continental Illinois Bank 146
cooperative initiatives 61

corporate tax 26
corruption 10; centralized 99; GDP growth 109n
corruption and democracy 1, 98–111; countries analysed *111*; data 103–4; data sources *111*; descriptive statistics *111*; empirical model 102–3; impact (all countries) *105*; impact (Asia-Pacific) *106*; relationship *104*; results 104–7
corruption perception index (CPI): Transparency International (TI) 102–3
crisis *see* Asian financial crisis (1997–8); global financial crisis (GFC, 2007–8)
cronyism 100
currency: exchange rate 69; global foreign exchange market turnover 77n
currency union 62

decentralized corruption 99
democracy: authoritarian regimes shift to 98–9; electoral 98–9, 108n; mature 98–9, *see also* corruption and democracy
Democratic Republican Party (DRP, South Korea) 100
demographic ageing 79
deposit guarantee: Indonesian banking system 143, 145
distortionary taxes 17, 22, 26
dividend collecting 101
dollar, US 137
donations: compulsory 101; political 99
drain gain 79

economic growth: China 112
Economic Intelligence Unit database 69
economic prosperity: government size 11–37
efficiency hypothesis: trade liberalization and growth 45
Eisenbeis, R.: and Kwan, S. 147, 148, 151, 158
electoral democracy 98–9; definition 108n
electronics-related products 129
emigration 93
employment: private consumption 8
endogenous growth: model 34n; theory 23
Euro 137
exchange rates: China 2, 126–40; cooperation 1; currency 69; variability 64
export elasticity: product fragmentation 127–9
exposure effect 85; unemployment 82
External Wealth of Nations Mark II database 67

Falvey, R.: Foster-McGregor, N and Khalid, A. 1, 38–60
fertility 79

INDEX

financial crisis: global (GFC, 2007–8) 4, 93, 141–4, *see also* Asian financial crisis (1997–8)
financial integration 61, 67; business cycles 62
financial system risk 141
fiscal leakages 31
fiscal policy: growth 22
foreign joint venture banks: Indonesia 144
Foster-McGregor, N: Khalid, A. and Falvey, R. 1, 38–60
France: consumption (private) 4, 9
franchise value: bank risk 148; banks 146; Indonesian banking system 150, 159
Freedom House: political rights and civil liberties 103, 107

G7 countries: private consumption trends 3–10
Gaston, N.: and Rajaguru, G. 1, 79–97
GDP growth: consumption (private) 5; rates 4
Gemmell, N.: and Au, J. 1, 11–37
Germany: consumption (private) 4, 9
Gini coefficient 81; Chinese income inequality 113–15; decomposition 113–15; Lorenz curve 113
global financial crisis (GFC, 2007–8) 4, 93, 141–4
globalization 97; effects and welfare state spending 90
government budget constraint (GBC) 18, 23
government expenditure ratio: versus average real GDP growth rate 16; versus average real per capita GDP growth rate 14, 15; versus GDP growth rate in Asia Pacific region 17; versus GDP per capita 13
government share channel: trade liberalization and growth 46
government size: economic prosperity 11–37; trade liberalization and growth 45–6
government-growth relationship 1, 11; Asia Pacific region 12; evidence from recent studies 22–30; expected 17–22; GDP level effects of 1distortionary tax changes 28; government size and output growth 22; government size and output levels 21; limitations 30–2; long-run evidence from panel studies 24–6; recent panel estimate of growth effects of taxation 27; recent panel studies 25; scepticism 13–17; short-run evidence from vector auto regression studies 23–4; simple model 18–22; tax change measures 29
Greece: emigration 93
growth: fiscal policy 22; trade liberalization 38–60
growth equation *42*
growth model: endogenous 34n
growth rates: GDP *4*

growth theory: endogenous 23

Herfindahl-Hirschman index (HHI) 150
high income Asia and Oceania (HIAO) 91
Hodrick-Prescott filter 65, 73, 77n
Horioka, C. 1, 3–10
household income *4*; growth and consumption (private) 5; ratios 7
household savings rates: consumption (private) 6–7, *6*
household wealth 7
Huang, Y.: and Lao, X. 112, 118, 120
hukou system (China) 117
Hyundai 102

Iceland: banking system 159n
illiteracy: China 122–3n
Imbs, J. 62–4, 67–8, 70–1, 76
immigration: Asian perspective 79–97; citizen attitudes 83; effects model 83; far right politics 82; fiscal effects 82; inequality 81; labour market 84; points systems 80; political economy of 82–5; reasons for attracting migrants 79; share of OECD immigrants by sending region *81*; social effects 82; surplus 83; use of welfare state 94n; wages 83
income: household 5, 7
income inequality *see* Chinese income inequality
income volatility: Indonesian banks 141–66
India 12, 109n; rural-urban inequality 116
Indonesian banking system: bank growth 150; bank size 150; bank type 150; capital holdings 149, 159; deposit guarantee 143, 145; descriptive statistics dependent variables (1991–2009) *151*; descriptive statistics independent variables (1991–2009) *152–3*; evolution 142–3; franchise values 150, 159; IMF 143; liquidity crisis 143; literature review and hypothesis development 144–8; loan quality 157–8; model data 149–50; model method 148–9; non-interest income 147; non-interest income and bank revenue specialization 150; proximity to default (z-score) 158; results 150–7; revenue volatility 149; robustness tests 157; robustness tests (1991–7) *165*; robustness tests (1991–2009) *164*; robustness tests (2000–9) *165*; structure 144; t-tests (1991–2009) *154*; t-tests (2000–9) *156*
Indonesian banks: foreign joint venture 144; income volatility 141–66; Islamic 144; risk 2, 141–66
industry specialization 67
inequality 81
inequality index: decomposition 113–15

INDEX

inequality-augmenting effect: Chinese income 119
insurance effect 85
integrated exchange rate: China 128
integration 61
International Financial Statistics online (IMF) 67
International Migration Database (1980–2007) (OECD) 97
International Monetary Fund (IMF) 38, 54n, 127; and Indonesian banking system 143; International Financial Statistics online 67
international production networks 126
interventionism 11
investment channel: trade liberalization and growth *44*
Ireland: emigration 93
iron rice bowl 116
Islamic banking: Indonesia 144
Italy: consumption (private) 4

Japan: Chinese imports 139n; consumption (private) 4, 9–10; *Lost Decades* 3; stagnation 1, 3, 9
joint venture banks: foreign 144
Jonwanich, J. 128, 138n

Kang, D.C. 100–2
Khalid, A.: Falvey, R. and Foster-McGregor, N. 1, 38–60
Khan, A.R. 114, 119, 121; and Rishkin, C. 114, 119
Khu, H.Y.: and Salwen, M.B. 101
Kim Dae-Jung 102
Kim Young-Sam 101, 102
King, R.G. 23
Kneller, R. 23, 24, 26, 28–31
Kohli, U. 127
Korea 11; Criminal Code Procedure 101; Republic of *see* South Korea
Kwan, S.: and Eisenbeis, R. 147, 148, 151, 158

labour market: flexibility 81; immigration 84
laissez-faire 11
law: rule of 99
lending: bank 142
liberalizing countries: trade liberalization and growth 56
liquidity 62
liquidity crisis: Indonesian banking system 143
loan growth: bank risk 142
lobbying models: policy 84
lobbying models policy 84
long-run growth effects model (Barro) *18*
long-run growth regressions 31
Lorenz curve: Gini coefficient 113
Lost Decades (Japan) 3

Luo, C.: and Shi, L 118

macroeconomic policy: trade liberalization and growth 44
Marquez, J.: and Schindler, J. 127
mature democracy 98–9
migrants 94n; estimated number (1990–2010) 80
migration 1; effects model 83; policy 79–80; political economy of 82–5, *see also* immigration
money politics 100
moral hazard: too big to fail 144–6
Moran, J. 101
Mukhopadhaya, P. 2, 112–25; and Podder, N. 114, 121
multi-national enterprises (MNEs) 126

nationalism 79
nepotism 99, 100
New Village Movement 100
New Zealand 11; corruption 107

Organization for Economic Development and Cooperation (OECD): *International Migration Database (1980–2007)* 97; *Social Expenditure Database (1980–2007)* 97
outsourcing 126

Park Chung-Hee 100, 101
Podder, N. 114; and Mukhopadhaya, P. 114, 121
points systems: immigration 80
political donations 99
political economy modelling 83
politics: money 100
population growth 79
press freedom 101
private consumption *see* consumption (private)
product fragmentation: export elasticity 127–9
public services: tax 1

Quanta Computer 138n
quasi-taxes 100

race to the bottom 90
Rajaguru, G.: and Gaston, N. 1, 79–97
real exchange rate (RER): China 126, 128, 134–7
Rebolo, S. 23
redistribution 84; effect 82, 85
regulation 62
renminbi (RMB) 127, 128
revenue volatility: Indonesian banking system 149
Rishkin, C.: and Khan, A.R. 114, 119
risk: financial system 141, *see also* bank risk

INDEX

Rodriguez, F. 38, 54n
Rodrik, D. 38, 54n
Roh Tae-Woo 101, 102
Romer, C.D.: and Romer, D.H. 29, 31–3
rule of law 99, 109n

Saha, S.: and Campbell, N. 1, 98–111
Salinas, G. 38
Salwen, M.B.: and Khu, H.Y. 101
Sanz, I. 26, 28–31
Sassen, S. 79
Scandinavia 11
Schindler, J.: and Marquez, J. 127
security 79
Sen, A. 98
Shi, L: and Luo, C. 118
Shleifer, A: and Vishny, R.W. 99
shocks: industry-specific 62
simultaneous equations model 63
Singapore 109n
single equation estimates: trade liberalization and growth 42–7
skill shortages 79
skilled workers 81
Slemrod, J. 12–14, 16, 18, 32, 35n
Slovak Republic 16
Smith, G.: and Thorbecke, W. 128
social effects: immigration 82
Social Expenditure Database (1980–2007) (OECD) 97
social integration 79
South Korea 100–2; constitution 101; corruption and democracy 98–111; press freedom 101
spatial voting models 84
specialization 62; business cycle synchronization 64; trade integration 71
stagnation: Japan 1, 3, 9
strikes: China 113
Sung, H-E. 107
synchronization: bilateral trade 61; business cycle 64

tax 17, 34n; change 29, 31–3; corporate 26; distortionary 17, 22, 26; effect 85; output 28; public services 1; quasi- 100; ratio change versus average real per capita GDP growth rate 15
tax-budget effects: welfare state spending 88–90
tax-growth effects: endogeneity 28–9
temporary workers 81
Thorbecke, W. 128; and Smith, G. 128
tolerance 83
too big to fail: moral hazard 144–6
trade 63–4; agreements 61; bilateral 61, 67; business cycle synchronization 63–4; components 126; disaggregating 127; integration specialization 71; openness 46; share channel 47; surpluses (China) 126
trade liberalization and growth 1, 38–60; black market premium channel 45, 54n; capital formation 43–4; compensation hypothesis 45; data description 41; data and empirical methodology 41; effects 49, 51–2; efficiency hypothesis 45; estimated effects 50; government share channel 46; government size 45–6; growth equation 42; investment channel 44; liberalising countries 56; macroeconomic policy 44; openness 46; share channel 47; single equation estimates 42–7; SUR results excluding liberalization 58–60; SUR results including liberalization 48; system results 47–53; threshold regressions 57
trade policy openness index 40
Transparency International (TI): CPI 102–3

unemployment 79; exposure effect 82; rates (2002–7) 8; risk 85
United Kingdom (UK): consumption (private) 4, 9
United Nations (UN): Commodity Trade Statistics Database (Comtrade) 67; Population Division (POP) 79
United States of America (USA) 79; and China 126; consumption (private) 4; trade deficit (1980–2011) with China 129
US dollar 137

Vishny, R.W.: and Shleifer, A. 99

Wacziarg, R. 38–40, 43, 47, 49, 52–3, 54n
wages: immigration 83
Wedeman, A. 101
Welch, K. 38, 40, 54n
welfare state spending: autarchy 85; challenges following GFC 93–4; descriptive statistics for 25 OECD countries 87; econometric evidence 88–93; globalization effects 90; immigration effects 91; immigration link 79–97; immigration and social expenditures 87; international migration 79–97; model 85–6; political/institutional effects 90; sensitivity analysis 91–3, 92; tax/budget effects 88–90; variable description and data sources 97; visual evidence 86–7
Williams, B. 2, 141–66
workers: skilled 81; temporary 81
World Bank 38; database 65
World Development Indicators (WDI) 65, 69
World Trade Organization (WTO) 134

Xie, S.: Cheng, T. and Chia, W-M. 1, 61–78

INDEX

Yamashita, N.: and Jayasuriya 2, 126–40
You, J.S. 101, 102

Zellner, A. 149